D0197171

Winning Ugly

Mental Warfare in Tennis— Lessons From a Master

BY
BRAD GILBERT
AND
STEVE JAMISON

A FIRESIDE BOOK
Published by Simon & Schuster
New York London Toronto Sydney

To a gentleman and great champion,
Arthur Ashe, who fought for human dignity
and the worth of the individual

FIRESIDE
Rockefeller Center
1230 Avenue of the Americas
New York, New York 10020

Copyright © 1993 by Brad Gilbert and Steve Jamison

All rights reserved
including the right of reproduction
in whole or in part in any form.

First Fireside Edition 1994
Published by arrangement with Carol Publishing Group

FIRESIDE and colophon are registered trademarks
of Simon & Schuster Inc.

Manufactured in the United States of America

37 39 40 38

Library of Congress Cataloging-in-Publication Data
Gilbert, Brad.
    Winning ugly : mental warfare in tennis—lessons from a master / by
Brad Gilbert and Steve Jamison.
        p.   cm.
    Originally published: Secaucus, N.J. : Carol Pub. Group, 1993.
    "A Fireside book."
    1. Tennis—Psychological aspects.   I. Jamison, Steve.
[GV1002.9.P75G54   1992]
796.342'01'9—dc20   93-37993
                                                               CIP

ISBN-13: 978-0-671-88400-0
ISBN-10:   0-671-88400-X

Preface

Winning Ugly?

"How in the hell does this guy win? He hits like a caveman who found a tennis racket!" That's the incredulous opinion I overheard during the finals of a Volvo Tennis/San Francisco Classic while Brad Gilbert was battling and beating Anders Jarryd to win the championship and $32,000. The prize was part of $1.5 million he would win during the year. My reaction surprised me. As one of thousands of fans there to see our hometown hero (Brad lives just outside of San Francisco in San Rafael, California) I didn't like hearing him criticized. However, I had to admit the caveman reference wasn't altogether inappropriate. Brad does have a unique style.

It got me thinking. Why does he win? How does he beat players like Boris Becker who are supposedly better than him? Looks are deceiving, and with Brad (whose style has been described as "ugly") looks are *very* deceiving. He has won over $5 million in tournament prize money. He was in the Top 10 internationally for five years and rose as high as number four in the world in 1990. He is an Olympic medalist and has successfully representd the United States in Davis Cup competition many times. Brad Gilbert has been one of the top players in tennis for almost ten years. All because he was able to beat players the experts said he shouldn't have been able to beat. How does he do it?

Brad's success comes from the fact that he is a thinking person's tennis player. In tennis, he is the best in the world at the mental side of the game. What spectators see are his strokes, and those strokes aren't always pretty. What people don't see are the mental machinations that lead him to victory, what goes on in his head before, during, and after a match. Most tennis players are mentally lazy on the court. Brad uses this to his advantage and believes you can do the same. He utilizes every second of a match to try and figure out a way to gain an advantage. Without overwhelming physical gifts or astonishing shots, Brad wins because he outthinks and outplans opponents.

Tim Gallwey's book, *The Inner Game of Tennis,* focused on the right-brain, or intuitive process. Brad's focus is on the left-brain, or analytical process. Gallwey pursued the joys of playing. Brad pursues the joys of winning. Gallwey was concerned with the "inner game." Brad is concerned with knowing what's going on right in front of him and taking advantage of it.

Winning Ugly tells how to do the same thing with your own tennis game. Brad describes his formula for making the most out of what you've got. And it works. In writing this book with him I learned about a part of the game I had never focused on before: the mental aspect of tennis. My game improved, and so will yours.

After you've put Brad's formula to the test, if anyone ever accuses you of "winning ugly" just say, "Thank you. I've been working on it."

Steve Jamison

Acknowledgments

Brad Gilbert
    My wife, Kim; my son, Zach; my daughter, Julie
    My parents, Barry, Sr., and Elaine Gilbert
    My brother, Barry, Jr., and my sister, Dana
    My coach, Tom Chivington, and Georgie Chivington
    All the kids at the Brad Gilbert Tennis Camps

Steve Jamison Edstrom:
    My dad, Ev, who is the world's best coach
    My mother, Mary, who is the world's best
    Pat, Krs, Kate, and Kim, my sisters
    The Edstroms, Cronens, McKegneys, Brands, and Starks,
        our family
    Dr. George Sheehan—a runner who inspired a lot of us to become
        athletes

Contents

I
THE EARLY EDGE:
The Match Begins Before the Match Begins

II
PLAYING SMART:
Finding a Way to Win

III
MIND GAMES, PSYCHING, AND GAMESMANSHIP:
Tales From the Tour

McEnroe: A Master Loses Ugly

John McEnroe was having his worst nightmare. Except it wasn't a nightmare. It was the Masters at Madison Square Garden in front of thousands of his loyal, screaming, stomping New York City fans. Tonight McEnroe, defending champion and ranked number two in the world, was slowly realizing that he was going to lose to a guy he didn't like and whose game he despised. That guy was me. It was humiliating for him and he was seething.

His eyes gave him away first. They had the look of a kid who had just set fire to the neighbor's cat: scared and mean. His face had that hateful McEnroe scowl. On a changeover he snarled over in my direction, "Gilbert, you don't deserve to be on the same court with me!" He was heading over the edge. We crossed within a few feet of each other. In case I'd missed his point he added, "You are the worst. *The* ———— worst!"

McEnroe continued to go downhill, complaining about the electronic line-calling machine, arguing heatedly with a spectator during the second set, receiving a code of conduct warning later for a "visible obscenity." He was completely nuts. Screaming at himself, slamming his racket, storming around and taunting the crowd (his own fans!). At times it looked like he was having a public nervous breakdown.

It was one of his better performances. But, in the end, the guy who didn't "deserve to be on the same court" with him won in three tough sets. Well, actually, two tough sets. The third was a breeze: 5–7, 6–4, 6–1. By match point John was a pussycat. But that wasn't the end.

Afterwards he dropped a bombshell. McEnroe announced his "retirement" from tennis at the age of twenty-seven. And he blamed part of it on me! Mac explained that he needed a sabbatical because,

"When I start losing to players like him ["him" being yours truly] I've got to reconsider what I'm doing even playing this game." If he thought I'd be insulted he was wrong. In fact, I loved it. In seven previous matches I had won only one set. That victory in the Masters was a great win. *Too* great as it turned out, but more on that later.

The Bank Doesn't Think I'm Ugly

John McEnroe and I have never exactly been what you'd call best friends. I guess that can happen when two people don't like each other. He thinks I've got bad strokes. I think he's got a bad attitude. But the truth of the matter is that McEnroe is right. On paper he shouldn't lose to me. And neither should Becker, Agassi, Connors, Chang, Edberg, Courier, Forget, Sampras, Stich, Wheaton, and a lot of other guys with better strokes and more so-called natural ability.

Fortunately for me, tennis matches aren't played on paper. They're played on tennis courts. And because they are I've been able to beat those players and others to the tune of $5,000,000. By 1991 I was eighth on the all-time prize money list. When you add in the endorsements and exhibitions that resulted from those victories my total income from tennis by 1993 is close to $8,000,000. Winning ugly? All the way to the bank.

It happened because I've used whatever talent and skills I do have in a calculated way that maximizes their potential; that gives me my best chance to win. It's why I've been able to beat players who are supposedly "better" than me. You can do the same. Make the most of what you've got. Play better tennis without better strokes.

The New, Improved You: 20 Percent Better

First, I want to tell you one thing about your game. The way to make the biggest improvement in the shortest time is to better understand and use the *opportunities for gaining an advantage* that exist in every match you play. The big opportunities and the small opportunities. Especially the small opportunities, the ones players neglect because of ignorance or laziness. If you want to call that winning ugly, go ahead and get ugly. Develop your powers of observation and analysis and then *use* the information, and your chances of winning will go up by 20 percent or more.

Brain-Dead Tennis: The Unaware Player

Most weekend players, most club players, most recreational players are brain-dead on the tennis court. They go out and run around with no plan, no thought, no nothing. They give it as much study and consideration as jumping rope. And that's why they can be had. With two players of roughly equal ability the one who's aware of and takes advantage of the dynamics, opportunities, and openings before, during, and after the match will win.

The person driving the fancy little sports car may look like he (or she) should come in first. I'll put my money on the grease monkey in the modified stock car who knows how to get around the track. It's the same for tennis. Pretty strokes are okay. But there's a lot more to the game than that.

Smart Tennis Is a Three-Step Process

1. Recognize your opportunity.
2. Analyze your options.
3. Capitalize on the opportunity
   by using the best option.

Recognize. Analyze. Capitalize. That applies before, during, and after a match to all aspects of the game: mental, physical, and emotional. It even involves your equipment. Example? Opportunity exists early with the spin of the racket. You should recognize it. Depending on your opponent and the conditions, you should choose and capitalize on the right option.

At tennis clubs and public courts the wrong choice is made about 85 percent of the time. Coming up I'll tell you how to get the most benefit out of that situation. It's a very small element of your total match, but it is an element that contains opportunity. You just have to know what to do with it.

And there are scores of other openings a smart player uses to gain an edge. I believe if you recognize and take advantage of those opportunities in enough ways and enough times you'll probably win.

Mental Management

> "I don't think his game is so good. But he makes up
> for it with his mental ability."
> —David Wheaton, following a loss
> to Brad Gilbert

Unlike jumping rope, a tennis match doesn't begin when it starts and end when it stops. Tennis begins off the court, continues through your pre-match regimen and into the match, and goes on after you've won (or lost) the final point. Smart players know how to prepare correctly for a match and once the contest is under way how to control their emotions. They know how to think their way through a match, avoiding low percentage shots that carry unnecessary risk at inappropriate times. Smart players observe what's going on in a match and analyze the information. They know how to capitalize on what they know.

Obviously, it takes some discipline, commitment, and effort. I mention this because most players will bust their buns to improve a particular stroke. They'll take lessons, hit on the ball machine, bang against the backboard, practice in the hot sun. Blood, sweat, and tears, the whole bit. Then having improved whatever stroke they're trying to perfect, they won't spend a minute figuring out how to use it to maximum effect during a match. Brain-dead. Hard workers, but brain-dead.

Ahead in this book are the opportunities that you should be aware of, the options you have, and the ways to capitalize on them from pre-match through post-match. How to mentally and physically prepare for battle on the court. How to play against all types of tennis styles. How to recognize important dynamics within a match. How to handle pressure and psyching. And more.

It's the nuts and bolts of what I've learned at all levels from junior tennis to a Top 5 ranking and a bank account I never dreamed possible. And you can apply it to your game. Some of the ideas are obvious. Others aren't so obvious. Some of it will apply to your game and some of it won't. But all of it is directed to the most neglected aspect of tennis: the mental part of your game. Let's start before the beginning.

I

The Early Edge

The Match Begins Before the Match Begins

> "I don't think much of Brad Gilbert."
> —John McEnroe

1

Mental Preparation: The Pre-Match Advantage

Turning Pro: Young and Innocent

One of the first lessons I learned when I turned pro in 1982 was how much of an edge could be gained before the match even got started. It became obvious to me that for the best players in the world their match had begun a long time before the first serve. They *came* ready to play and wanted to grab me by the throat as soon as they could.

As a member of the tennis teams at Foothill Junior College and Pepperdine, I liked to just show up and play. I'd settle into the match mentally and physically during the first set. A lot of times I could get away with it because my opponent was doing it too. Do you approach your matches the same way?

On tour this wasn't such a good idea. The slow start didn't work against McEnroe, Lendl, Connors, and some of the veterans. By the time I got settled into some of those matches, the match was already over. One time I started out by losing the first sixteen points of the match. It was over so fast I almost didn't need to take a shower afterwards. Brutal—I was learning the hard way.

The top players came expecting to have me for lunch, and they'd been thinking about taking that first bite since they found out I was on the menu. Four or five games to work up an appetite? They arrived ready to eat. The main course? Glazed Gilbert.

Being down a couple of breaks early, with no rhythm, no plan, no continuity, put me at too great a disadvantage. I was clobbered regularly by the smart guys on tour. They knew something I didn't.

Start Your Match Before It Begins

What I discovered by looking, listening, and losing was simple. The guys making money out there started honing in on their target (me, for example) before the target was even in sight. The smart ones were consciously and subconsciously reviewing information about the opponent ahead of them as soon as they knew who that player was. The process began hours before the match. The smart players wanted to seek and seize advantage as early as possible. And they wanted to do it in as many *ways* as possible. For them, one of the big opportunies was good mental preparation. And that means *early* mental preparation.

When Does Your Warm-up Begin?

Let me tell you when the warm-up doesn't begin. It doesn't begin when you arrive on the court. It may for your opponent, but it shouldn't for you. A smart player starts to prepare for the match *on the way to the match*, or even before. The warm-up should continue on into the locker room and out onto the court.

The warm-up begins with your *brain*. Your mind is usually the last part of you to get activated (if it gets activated at all). Players stretch incorrectly for a minute, hit a couple of forehands, and three serves, and it's "Let's start." They barely warm up the body, but that's more attention than they give to their mental preparation. The mind is a terrible thing to waste, and tennis players waste it all the time.

Get into the habit of evaluating your opponent and thinking about the match before you arrive at the court. If you drive to the match your car is the place where your warm-up begins. If you walk to the courts, then the sidewalk is where it happens. No matter what, *your warm-up starts on the way to the match*.

For me it can begin even earlier than that. The night before a match I'll be in my hotel room thinking about the next day's competition. I'll actually play points out in my mind. I can see myself making shots and winning points. I visualize points we've played in the past. I'll see myself making specific shots against that player. It's almost like watching a videotape of segments of a match. In the morning I'll continue the process.

That little five-minute warm-up you see before a match begins for the players on tour is probably misleading. It looks like we just trot out to the court with that big bag over our shoulder, hit for a couple of minutes, and start the match. For most of us the process has been going on throughout the day—hitting, stretching, loosening up, a massage, and most of all, that mental review.

The Pre-Match Mental Checklist

Whether I won or lost to a player in our last match, I want to think about the reasons. How did I beat him? What does he do with his shot selection and pattern? Does he attack? Is he a retriever? Does he serve big? What's his return of serve like? Did I make mistakes against him last time? What kind and why? What shots are his best? His worst? Was he forcing me to do something that bothered me? Does he start strong and get too cautious on pressure points? Was it a close match? Were the points long? I review everything that pertains to my opponent's game (as far as strokes and shot tendencies are concerned).

It is also important to consider the "personality" of the game your opponent produces. What does he do to affect the atmosphere, mood, or tempo of the match? Is she very slow between points? Does he get emotional? Does she protest a lot of calls? Is he great when he gets a lead, but not so great when he's losing? Do your opponents give you a lot of small talk on changeovers, taking your mind off the match like McEnroe tried to do to me? Do they always show up ten minutes late? Do they rush through the warm-up and want to start the match as soon as possible?

Prepare yourself mentally for the "stuff" certain players bring with them into the match. I want to be mentally and emotionally set for the fast play of Andre Agassi or the deliberate methodical match tempo of Ivan Lendl. I want to be ready for the temperamental outbursts of Connors and McEnroe or the stonefaces of Michael Chang or Jim Courier. It makes a big difference to me because I'm better able to control my own game plan, tempo, and composure if I know what's likely to be happening on the other side of the net. Believe me, it can make a huge difference, as you'll see later.

The Game Plan

This process of review will lead me right into the equally important process of planning my strategy:

1. What do I want to *make* happen?
2. What do I want to *prevent* from happening?

By evaluating my opponent I start solidifying my own approach to the match. As I review their game style and strokes I'm preparing my basic game plan. If they broke down my backhand last time I'll be thinking about how to prevent the same thing from happening this time. If their serve is weak I'm alerting myself and going over how to take advantage of that. I'm planning a specific approach for that specific player. All of this *before I even see them at the court*.

Set Your Compass

Your body will try to do what your mind tells it to do. In this pre-match review you're programming your mind to give the body correct information once the match begins and things start happening quickly under fire. You're setting the course you want to take to arrive at your destination. That destination is victory.

In its most basic form your plan evolves as you answer these questions:

1. What is my opponent's best weapon?
2. Where is my opponent weak?
3. What is my best shot and how can I direct it at my opponent's weakness?
4. What can I do to keep my opponent away from my own weakness?

Your pre-match effort creates a mental compass. You know where you want to go and how you're going to get there. There may be detours along the way, your opponent may present some surprises, you may get lost, but the basic route is laid out in your head in advance and your mental compass keeps you on course. (Coming up I'll show you how following this procedure helped me beat both Boris Becker and Jimmy Connors, in totally different ways.)

Even if you tend to play the same people over and over (your tennis buddies) it is still important to zero in on the specific player for a particular day. Get your mind on that one player. If you're playing each other regularly it can be even more advantageous to review and refine your tactics because you've got a backlog of information. That's when it really starts to get interesting.

Watch the tour players. The great ones are very intent on getting off to a good start because they know that it can often set the tone for the entire match. Getting the other player under your thumb right out of the chute puts them in a "catch up" position. Sometimes they'll recover. A lot of times they won't. And that's what you want to do to *your* opponent. As early as possible you want to force them to be considering the idea that "maybe it's just not gonna be my day today." It can happen very early, believe me. Your pre-match preparation and visualization can make you the one somebody else is trying to catch up to.

You're thinking, "Hey, Brad. Gimme a break! *I've got a life.* I can't be thinking about tennis all the time." That's right. But what I'm talking about takes less than ten minutes of attention on the way to your match and then the effort of following a plan once you get there. Maybe you can squeeze that in for opponents you really want to beat. By giving yourself a good chance to start right you're giving yourself a good chance to finish right. That's worth the extra attention.

Let me take you through my own mental preparation exactly as I've used it before important matches.

Preparation on Tour: Becker and Connors (Different Strokes for Different Folks)

When I started seriously using my pre-match opportunities in this way I started winning more often. Let's say my opponent in the round of 16 at the U.S. Open was Boris Becker (because it was). My own mental review before I got to the locker room at Flushing Meadow would go like this:

Becker can attack my weak second serve. He knows how to exploit it for maximum effect. This is a polite way of saying he creams it. Therefore, I don't want to let him see many seconds. That means I want to get my first serve in more consistently, to put a premium on reducing first serve faults. Obviously, I'll have to hit with less abandon and take fewer risks on my first serve, but the reward will be that he doesn't get the opportunity to make me eat my second serve.

Also, I want to serve to his forehand, try and get him missing some forehand groundstrokes. Why? I know that Boris has a great forehand. It anchors the rest of his game. But if he starts screwing up with it, everything else can suffer. He gets frustrated when the forehand doesn't meet his expectations.

I've learned (and tell myself again in the pre-match review) that when he starts to miss on the forehand side, the rest of his game can start to wobble. That's when he'll start screaming at himself in German. So I want to be sharp serving to his forehand without getting too ambitious, get a high percentage in.

Also, I should give him no pace. Boris will win any battle over who can hit the ball hardest. Without pace he still wants to hit the ball hard and often overhits as a result. Especially on the forehand side.

Before I get to the court I go over all of that in my mental review. I also remind myself to try and open up the court on Boris by hitting intelligently to his forehand. This means that I know from past matches with him that when I hit wide to the forehand (either with my serve or a groundstroke) his tendency, or shot pattern, is to hit it crosscourt right back to *my* forehand. If it's even a little short I'll look to hit a forehand approach (my best weapon) down the line to his backhand. Then I'll follow it in and camp near the alley.

So, my game plan when I serve should regularly follow this pattern: Serve wide to the Becker forehand. Look for an opportunity to hit a forehand approach shot to his backhand. Then follow it in and camp near the alley. That's my 1–2–3 punch.

Two elements come into play with that combination that I've experienced in past matches. First of all, Boris is going to have to move from his forehand grip (under the racket) to his backhand grip (somewhat over the racket) while moving from the deuce court to the ad court on the full gallop. In the past I've seen that he doesn't always do that well. It's just a little glitch that shows up from time to time. And, if he *does* make the grip change and take a good cut at the ball his tendency is to go *down the line*—not all the time, but that's his *first choice*.

Watch him on the tube. You'll see he favors that shot. What happens when he does? There I am camping near the alley. Bingo. Forehand volley to an open court. I've run that combination of shots successfully on Boris many, many, many times.

And, on *his* serve I tell myself, "Boris has a huge serve. Don't try to do too much with it. Get the ball back in play. Make him play an extra ball or two each point. Keep the ball *in play*. That's the key for me against Boris, making him run down an extra ball over and over again. Becker can get frustrated and I want to frustrate him. Obviously, if he's swarming winners I'm in trouble, but I tell myself that in the match ahead I've got to stay in every point possible. Keep cool. Be patient. Don't try to make things happen too quickly.

Busting My Butt for Boris

I also think about the "personality" of the competition and the competitor ahead. Boris Becker is like a thoroughbred. His physicality, power, and movement are so pure that it can be intimidating. He's big *and* he plays big. I get myself ready for any Becker match by reminding myself, "Don't be impressed. Don't let his presence be overwhelming. Keep your eye on your game plan and not on his game." I have to do that or I'd take one look at what Becker brings onto the court and retire. (And that's important in your own tennis. Don't be impressed until *after* the match. Never before.)

I want him to see me busting my buns for everything, throwing everything back. I want to show him that I'm going to compete on every single point of every single game if the match goes on for a week. I want him to believe that I will *never* give up. I want him to get the feeling that I'm not going away. That I'm permanent. I know that Boris can get frustrated out on the court. Against someone like Michael Chang this wouldn't matter. With Becker it can be very important. He doesn't have great patience if points, games, and the match drag on.

I know that if he gets impatient he'll start missing shots because he's trying to end it quick. As I mentally program myself for Becker's game I'm getting ready to try to exploit both his physical and emotional tendencies and weaknesses.

My Mental Review and Game Plan for Becker

1. Increase my first serve percentage. Don't try to hit aces or service winners. Don't let him see many second serves.
2. Serve to his forehand regularly. Look for short crosscourt return. Approach down the line. Camp near the alley.
3. Try to create mistakes on his forehand. Don't give him any pace. Repeat: No Pace.
4. Don't try to do too much with my service return. Get it back. Make him hit another shot.
5. Work hard on every point. Show Boris some hustle. He gets impatient.
6. Don't be impressed with anything he does. Let him pound the ball as hard as he wants. But, make him pound it *over and over!* Always try and make him hit one more shot.
7. Boris can get frustrated if things don't go his way. Try and make him stay around longer than he wants to. If he starts screaming at himself in German he's getting wobbly.

Does it work? Yes. Does it work all the time? Yes. You won't *win* every time, obviously. But my procedure will improve your chance of winning every time. And that's all I'm trying to do when I play, improve my chance of winning.

U.S. Open 1987—Grandstand Court
Becker vs. Gilbert
Round of 16

I've used this plan very effectively against Becker. Most notably in the round of sixteen in the 1987 U.S. Open. At the time he was ranked number four in the world. I was still trying to crack into the Top 10.

Boris had rolled over me in the first set 6–2 and then won a tiebreaker for the second set. Now he was leading 3–0 in the third. I was very close to the point of no return and Boris knew it. He could end this match very soon.

Boris exudes so much confidence when he's ahead that it can break down your belief in yourself. His hair gets redder. His eyelashes get so white they almost disappear against his pale skin. He's physically bigger than me *and* he carries himself even bigger. A pure athletic aura surrounds him when he's rolling, and you can feel it across the net. He has tremendous presence. When he's running with a lead the confidence he displays goes beyond arrogance. He tells you with his body language that he knows he is better than the rest. Except I didn't believe it.

The third set continues with me serving. I hold to stay in the match at 3–1, but I knew if Boris holds to go up 4–1 I'm history. Then he makes a serious mental mistake. Boris seems to have a lapse in concentration. He plays a very casual service game, almost lethargic. He donates a couple of points with double faults and suddenly I'm back on serve at 2–3. There's hope in my mind because of what I know (and have reviewed) about Becker. Suddenly I can see a way to win. Here's how.

Our scheduled afternoon match had been delayed because of rain. As a result we started very late and in extreme heat and humidity. The temperature that Monday in New York was pushing 90°. On the grandstand court it felt like 190°. It was like playing on a muggy day in the jungle, a jungle that had jets flying low overhead every fifteen minutes. Concentration was difficult.

Even though I don't like hot weather I felt this could work in my favor. I knew that a few weeks earlier I had beaten Boris in Washington, D.C., in this same kind of weather when he fell apart in the last set. I felt that if I could somehow claw out of this third set it might have a very negative effect on Boris. It might get him thinking about our last match in hot humid weather and what had happened.

I believed he had already made the assumption that he was going to win in straight sets. If I could steal this set after he was so close to winning the match (up two sets with a 3–0 lead) he might get upset with himself. If I could make him play more tennis in these conditions he might get *very* upset with himself.

And I knew what that could mean. This became a great motivator. I honestly felt that I was nearing an opportunity to get into Becker's mind, to upset his composure in a big way. And this opportunity existed because I was way behind. Or, more to the point, it existed because Boris was so close to winning the match that he could taste it.

If I could get him feeling that things *were* dragging on in this grandstand heat and humidity, the quality of his game would drop because the quality of his thinking would drop. I had seen it happen before. I told myself if I could win the third set I could win the match. Sound too optimistic? Here's what happened.

At 2–3 I held serve to even the set at three games apiece. We're now two hours and thirty minutes into the match. I've won three games in a row and it's gotten his attention . Now, we each hold serve, but Boris is becoming increasingly unhappy and irritable. Twice he starts screaming something in German. I make a little joke and tell myself the translation is "My feet are burning up. I want to stick them in ice." Boris picks up the pace and is playing more quickly. As though he wanted to end it as soon as possible.

His composure is changing. We each hold again. And again. Suddenly it's 6–all and we're in another tiebreak.

Boris seems to get himself together and grabs an early mini-break. He's serving at 2–1. It's exactly where I don't want to be, down a mini-break in a tiebreaker that could send me back home. But Boris now plays two points that became crucial in the outcome of the match, both for what they did to the score and what they did to his composure.

Serving at 2–1 in the tiebreak Boris double-faults. He puts me back on serve and I don't even have to swing my racket. It's a major error on his part. I believe it was brought on because he was getting impatient, rushing things just a little bit. He wanted to get the job done too quickly. Perfect.

Then immediately another critical exchange at 2–2. Boris serves and attacks the net. As he moves to his right (just inches from the net), his feet slip out from under him and he crashes to the ground. I see him fall, and as he frantically struggles to get back up, I hit a backhand crosscourt lob that sends him racing toward the baseline. He doesn't get there. At the service line his feet go out from under him again. And again his body slams into the court. This time he doesn't get up.

Becker is lying face down on the court screaming uncontrollably at himself in German. He's fallen so hard that his gold watch has slid down from his wrist to around his fingers. He's furious with himself and about what's happening. He raises up to one knee and lets out a terrible scream. Nobody in tennis has a scream as fearful as Becker's when he loses control. It's the sound of pure and total anguish. It is beautiful to hear. Boris is coming apart.

At 3–2 in the breaker I serve again to his forehand. Boris nets it and immediately unleashes another bloodcurdling screech. This time I can't hear him. Another huge jet is directly overhead and obliterates all other sound. It's a very strange sensation. The court is actually vibrating from the jet's noise. I can see Boris screaming, but I hear nothing except the huge noise of the jet. Boris takes a vicious swipe at the court with his racket. I know he feels like he's drowning and can't swim. No matter how hard he tries, he feels things are only getting worse.

It's interesting how distractions affect you when you've got some momemtum and are winning points. The heat, the humidity, the incredible white noise of the jets flying overhead, none of it bothered me. But when you're struggling like Boris was struggling it is almost impossible to stay focused. The distractions become crippling. Your mind gets totally berserk. You just want to get out of there.

We continue to 5–4 in the tiebreak on my serve. I remember my game plan is to go selectively to his forehand. And that's what I do. Boris nets it, 6–4. Set point now, and again I decide to go to his forehand with my serve. Again he nets it! The tactic works beautifully.

I've cracked through to win the breaker and with it the set 7–6 (7–4). Boris's march to victory has been slowed. I'm still alive. More than alive. I know I can win the match.

The fourth set is tough, but my game remains steady. Nothing flashy, but exactly what I had planned on doing. I got a break and gave it back. Boris was unhappy, but he still understands that he isn't far from sending me back to California. I'm hanging in there, hitting to his forehand when possible and approaching to his backhand with success. He's seeing no pace unless he supplies it himself. I'm not letting him see many second serves. I'm patient.

Then something happened I hadn't expected. Word began to spread through the tennis complex that Boris Becker was in trouble. The grandstand seats started to fill up with fans from the stadium court where John McEnroe was beating on Andres Gomez. And those fans wanted to see some more tennis. They knew for that to happen I had to win the fourth set. The crowd packing into the grandstand seats was totally on my side! Cheering for me on every shot. Yelping and hooting as I ran down everything and worked my butt off in what was a real steam bath. They loved it. And I loved it too.

Becker was affected. The long wailing shrieks in German continued: "My feet are burning. I want to stick them in ice!" It was like a shot of adrenalin into my system. I knew that when he loses control I have beaten him. Boris was becoming very frustrated. He had gone from being two points away from the match (when I was serving in the third set at 4–5, 30–30) and a trip to the quarterfinals, to having a lot of work in front of him. And in conditions that a camel would hate.

At 5–all Boris threatened to break my serve. Twice he tries and fails. It's not a pretty hold, but I hold. Boris will serve next at 5–6. We head to our chairs for the changeover. I decide to change shirts to give myself a little mental boost, to put on something fresh and dry. And I really start working on my thinking. I review my game plan: "Stay alert. Don't give up any stupid points. Make him play some balls and keep hitting to his forehand. Let him make some mistakes!"

In the background I can hear something, some noise in the crowd. It breaks my concentration. I look up and see two teenagers running through the aisles. They're waving American flags and the crowd is picking up on it: "U.S.A.! U.S.A.! U.S.A.!" It gets louder and louder. The fans have really gotten into it. "U.S.A.! U.S.A.!" I look over at the section where my family is sitting with my coach, Tom Chivington. They're standing and cheering. The emotion running through the grandstand was electric. I actually got goose bumps in 90° heat; really pumped up and confident.

We go out onto the court with Boris serving at 5–6. The crowd is buzzing. Boris serves four times. He doesn't win a point. I break him *at love* and win the set 7–5! It's electric. The crowd is roaring and gives me a standing ovation: "U.S.A., U.S.A." More flags are waving. Suddenly we're at two sets each. The match is all even, right? Wrong.

I've won. The match isn't over, but I've won. I glance at Boris and I can see that he's finished. His energy is gone. The eyes are dead with no fight or spark in them. His body language told me he was through battling for that day.

It wasn't physical either. It was mental. Boris is a super athlete in fantastic shape. What had weakened was his resolve. Boris had gotten frustrated with the match. He just wanted out of there. Just as I thought might happen.

Beginning of the fifth set. My serve. And again Becker doesn't threaten. I hold easily. Boris has gotten only two points in two games. The rout is on. I break, hold, break, and hold. I'm up 5–0 and it took ten minutes. At least it felt that fast. Boris managed to get a game out of it, but lost 6–1.

The match had taken four hours and seventeen minutes in oppressive heat and humidity—a sweatbox. Even though it was scheduled to be an afternoon match it was now almost 10 P.M.. I had lost seven pounds. But I was so exhilarated I felt like I could run a marathon. Jimmy Connors "de-exhilarated" me two days later in the quarters. But it took nothing away from the pride I took in battling back from two sets down to beat him in five. Never before had Boris Becker lost after leading by two sets.

Pre-Match Preparation Pays Off

A lot of things went right for me that day, but I was only able to take advantage of them because I'd prepared myself before the match for the game and temperament of Boris Becker. When he had me on the ropes I still saw a way to win because I understood his game and his temperament. I had gone into the match with *strong mental preparation*. I knew what I wanted to make happen and what I wanted to prevent from happening. Part of it had to do with strokes and strategy. Part of it had to do with personality, both mine and my opponent's. That preparation served me well when I needed it.

When things were getting desperate I had a mental compass that kept me on course and gave me a way to get back in the match. Instead of rolling over and accepting defeat I believed there was a way to win.

Boris Becker is a gentleman. Later that night I was at a disco called the Heartbreak on Varick Street in Manhattan. At about midnight I feel a tap on my shoulder. It's Boris. He congratulates me and we talk about the match over a beer. He says he hates that kind of heat and humidity. I tell him I love it. He says they've got to do something about the planes flying overhead during a match. I tell him I love those planes. He kids me a little and says I won't be so lucky next time around. Five months later I beat him in the Masters at Madison Square Garden—no planes, no heat, no humidity.

Every Player Is Unique, But Connors Is the Most Unique!

Against Jimmy Connors my "auto"-visualization or pre-match analysis and conclusions are completely different because his game and personality differ so much from Becker's. First and foremost I remind myself to block out the elements—not the sun or wind, but the chaos he can create with the fans and the officials. Jimmy treats the crowd like he's a conductor and they're the band. He gets them to do what he wants.

At an important point Jimmy could suddenly get 14,000 people going crazy, cheering for him and against his opponent (namely, me) in an uproar. I'll tell myself to expect it and ignore it. It's part of his game plan. As you'll see, against Connors this is easier said than done.

(If it had been Jimmy instead of Boris in the U.S. Open match I just described, Connors would have done something disruptive with the crowd when I started to make my move in the third set. And, when I pulled ahead in the tiebreak, I guarantee there would have been some "stuff" going on to shake up my momentum—an argument about a line call, an obscenity, or something else. He would *never* just let you cruise to victory.)

Also, with Jimmy I'll plan to hit slice shots into his forehand (I call it slicing the roast beef). Nothing hard. Just a ball that stays lower on the bounce. I know that when it hits on the service line Connors will tend to chip his forehand back. If he does, that's the one I'm waiting for. I want to be ready to step up, bust it, and move in behind it.

The Connors service return also needs special pre-match consideration. He has one of the best service returns ever. His specialty is making a play off a great serve. He manages to get the racket on the ball and keep it in play. What should be a winner or an ace comes back at you and Jimmy stays in the point. He doesn't necessarily kill the ball. He makes fantastic gets and then is able to hit the ball with direction (to put it where you can't make your best shot).

He immediately takes your advantage and turns it into a disadvantage. And he does it because he guesses a lot. When he guesses right even the best serve can come back.

But the important thing is *he doesn't kill that service return*. What this allows me to do is go for a winner or one that produces a weaker return off my first serve. If he guesses right it'll come back. If he guesses wrong I win the point. And, if I fault I know he won't stick the second serve back down my throat like Becker.

It changes my entire strategy in serving. By taking the pressure off my second serve Jimmy allows me more leeway with my first serve. I know going in that a serve that would ace anybody else might come back. I'm not going to let myself be surprised. That's what Connors brings to the party. If you let it bother you he'll get you letting up on that first serve or trying to hit bigger and bigger. My approach is to go for great serves and *expect* them back. I don't worry about having to serve up seconds if I fault on the first.

In fact, the truth is that my second serve bothers him (as you'll soon see). Jimbo loves pace. He feeds on it. My second serve is a lollipop. I honestly think it bothers him a little because it has no pace. So, I don't worry about having to hit second serves because Connors (unlike Becker) doesn't make you pay the big penalty.

My Review and Game Plan for Connors

1. Expect Jimmy to manipulate the crowd at key moments. Be prepared for disruption and stay focused.
2. Serve big on the first serve. If I miss he won't come in on my second.
3. Hit slice to his forehand.
4. He doesn't like junk. Massage the ball.

The Masters 1987—Madison Square Garden
Connors vs. Gilbert

Connors and I faced each other in the 1987 Masters several months after he had beaten me in the U.S. Open quarterfinals following my five-set comeback against Becker. Neither of us was in great shape. I had just played four tournaments on four different continents in four weeks. Jimmy had been fighting a bad cold.

Nevertheless, I went into our match with great focus and motivation. Part of it came from a desire to avenge that loss at the Open. He had kept me out of the semis and given me one of my toughest losses. I felt strongly that if I stuck to my game plan and kept my concentration I could beat him. It looked like I was right.

I began thumping on him immediately and went up 6–4, 4–1. I felt like I could just grind it out and win the match. And to add to my confidence it looked like Jimmy agreed. His attitude during the second set became completely different from what it usually was. He almost looked like he was clowning around. He got pulled wide on a shot and kept running until he was nearly in the stands. Then he stopped and started kidding with a couple of fans (he took somebody's napkin and blew his nose). The crowd loved it. A little later he got upset with himself and starting grabbing his crotch (a move Michael Jackson stole from him). The crowd was thoroughly entertained. Also, it was apparent he was feeling the effects of the cold. He appeared winded at times.

Now, at 3–5 in the second set (and down a set) Jimmy is getting ready to serve. He turns to a fan behind him and says loud enough for me to hear, "I've got Gilbert right where I want him." Jimmy's got this big grin on his face. The crowd is laughing and applauding: "Jimbo. Jimbo." And I like it, too. I figure Connors knows he's tired and out of the match and just wants to have a little fun with the audience before it's over. Big mistake.

The next time I look up at the scoreboard Connors and Gilbert are tied 5–5. Just like that he had held and broken. He had worked on the crowd and gotten to me; not by creating turmoil, but by going for some laughs and changing the tenor of the match. I couldn't believe he had broken my concentration. He had gotten me watching his antics and believing that he was through for the day, that he was going to lay down. I had lost my focus. It was a shock to realize what had happened. Such a shock that I woke up. I hold and so does Jimmy. Six–all. Tiebreaker.

I knew I was in trouble if we went to a third set. The crowd was beginning to be a factor, and if Jimmy took it to three they would definitely become a major asset for him. I reviewed my game plan: "Keep some balls in play. No pace. Make him try to hit winners. Nothing fancy. Let's win it right here."

And I did. Connors let it get away from him even though he led 5–3 at one point during the breaker. Then he made a couple of errors on backhand volleys to even it up at five apiece. My serve. I go for a big serve. Fault. My next serve is a lollipop and Jimmy nets it. He hates junk (remember my service strategy?).

On match point we get into a long rally. He hits a deep approach shot to my backhand. I'm ready and just crush it for a winner and the match. The comeback was over, Gilbert 6–4, 7–6 (7–5). Jimbo had almost worked his magic of crowd control to take back the match. This time he failed. As you'll see later, I'm not always so fortunate.

Connors is superb at turning things around when he's behind. He stops your momentum in a variety of ways and makes you come out of your game by taking you out of your concentration. He tries to make you play on his terms, not yours. He can do it by joking around with the crowd as he did here. Or, he can use intimidation and rage to take control.

At the '87 Masters I recognized what had happened before it was too late. I had gotten ahead by following my pre-game plan and staying focused. When Jimmy successfully got me "unfocused" I was able to get back on course because I had a strong understanding of his tactics. They had been mentally locked in place during the pre-match mental review and planning. I realized it wasn't my strokes that were responsible for his comeback, it was my mind and the fact that it had weakened.

Totally Great, Totally Different

So, two great players, Becker and Connors, with totally different games, styles, and temperaments. Both require special attention, specific game plans and attitudes that I try to cement in place before I even see them on the day of a match.

One capitalizes on my weak second serve. The other doesn't. One orchestrates the crowd. The other doesn't. Becker gets frustrated if the match drags on. Connors loves being out there so much he actually hates to see it end. Boris has a huge first serve and a great second serve. Jimmy has neither.

Before I ever see an opponent on the day we play I've completely reviewed our match history, his game, and my plan for the match. I've mentally reviewed exactly what I want to *make* happen. And I know exactly what I want to *prevent* from happening. I know where I want to go and how I'm going to get there. Olympic swimmer Nelson Diebold said right after he had won the gold medal in 1992, "Good mental preparation is as important as good physical preparation." It's true in all sports, especially tennis.

The process I go through in getting ready for Becker and Connors (or Lendl, Chang, Courier, or any other player) is *exactly* how you should mentally prepare for your own Beckers and Lendls. If you're smart. Don't think because you play A, B, or C tennis that the advantages don't add up. I believe they add up even more. Here's why.

The guys I play are generally sizing me up just like I'm trying to figure them out. They're also masters at not letting me do what I'm trying to do. You don't have that problem. Most of your opponents are mentally lazy before and during the match.

Depending on your level of play you may not meet one player a month who seriously considers your game and knows how to exploit it. Plus, their relatively modest level of tennis skill makes *them* vulnerable to a player who's good at exploiting opportunities. Good early mental preparation is an opportunity waiting to be exploited by you.

Be *Ready to Play* When It's Time to Play

In early visualization and planning, your sub-conscious starts to pull in information from other encounters. The brain starts throwing switches and turning dials that program you for that particular player. It's tough to do once the action begins because too much else is going on. You need that mental compass you establish before the match starts as a reliable reference point, one that can get you back on a winning course.

Make it a new habit. *Your* match begins before the match begins, in your car or at your home when you calmly review what you know about the opponent and how you plan to use the information. It takes very little time, but get it done before you arrive. By the time that first point is under way you'll have already "played" your opponent and be into the match.

The Importance of Pre-Match Preparation
(And a Little Bit of a Hustle)

Here's a terrific example (although an extreme one) of the tremendous advantage the average player can get with good pre-match preparation. And of what a disadvantage "just showing up" can be. This particular player at the San Francisco Tennis Club used good mental preparation, good physical preparation, and some gamesmanship against a guy who just showed up and wanted to start playing. Here's what happened.

For a big match (and he liked to bet $100 per set with certain players) this fellow (a bit of a hustler) would get to the court one hour early. He had already spent time looking over his notes (yes, he kept notes of past matches). He had given some attention to his game plan. Next would be the stretching exercises to get completely loosened up.

Now would come the warm-up, *before* his opponent even arrived at the court. The "hustler" would hit with the club pro for thirty minutes, going through the strokes and touching up anything that was giving him trouble that day. Nothing intense. Just a real good warm-up. Then he would leave the court, go to the locker room, and change clothes.

So, now that he's reviewed his game plan, checked his notes, done his stretching exercises, had a great warm-up, and changed into dry clothes, would he head back out to the court? Of course not. It was time for the final stage of the hustle. He'd make sure he got there ten minutes *late*, apologize for the delay, and suggest that they cut the warm-up short.

Obviously, his opponent would be a little upset by the late arrival and want to get started to save time. They'd move right into the match with only a "quickie" warm-up. The "pigeon" would be handing over the money in straight sets. He would have saved himself $200 if he'd anticipated the behavior and prepared properly himself. He got taken instead. He had no plan, no system, no nothing. He let the other player control events because he *wasn't prepared*. He'd have been a lousy Boy Scout.

The interesting thing about what this "hustler" did was that everything (except arriving intentionally late) was excellent preparation.

It's how a conscientious player should get ready to play a match. Throwing in that last twist by arriving late was probably unnecessary (not to mention unsportsmanlike). He was way ahead by doing everything else. You can give yourself that same advantage.

Having the "Want" to Win

Most recreational players really don't care enough about winning to do much more than show up for the match and chase down some balls during it. Recreational players are usually long on running and short on thinking. That description probably fits many of the people you play. If it does, you're lucky because you can take advantage of their mental laziness to win more often. But only if you care about winning and are willing to push yourself mentally to do it, only if you activate your brain from the "git go."

Do it and the early edge is yours, and with it often goes match point.

Next: Your mind is ready. Make sure your equipment is.

2

Tools of the Trade: How Equipment Can Help You Win

Hey, What's in That Big Bag the Pros Carry?

> When Bradley was a child he wasn't very good
> at the basic skills around the house, like
> cleaning his room or washing the dishes. He
> just couldn't seem to figure out how to do it.
> —Mrs. Elaine Gilbert, Brad's mother

The player who understands the significance of gaining a small advantage (and of doing so repeatedly) might still underestimate the role that tennis equipment can play in helping you win. Most players figure they're ready for the match if they bring along tennis shoes, socks, shorts, shirt, racket, and a jockstrap or sports bra. They're all set right there—they're hoping the opponent will bring the tennis balls. A player who's serious about winning goes beyond the bare minimum, and that list *is* a bare minimum.

The serious player wants to insure not only that the equipment they bring to a match helps them, but that it doesn't *hurt* them. They make sure every possible piece of equipment they might need during a match is with them when they show up. Because of the stakes involved, tour players are *very* sure they've got what they need with them. It's no joke at that level. If losing is no joke to you, do the same.

My wife, Kim, thinks I go overboard when it comes to packing my equipment before a match. She says I'm a fanatic about it. I pack the same way for a practice session. I am meticulous about what I bring to the court and take great pains to make sure everything I might need is in order. In a sense, it's my office. My needs are specific and probably somewhat different from yours, but here's the list of equipment I make sure is with me when I arrive on court. You may agree with my wife when you read it.

My Tools of the Trade

The Secret Energy Drink: Water

Water is the best energy drink of all. But since it's usually free, people don't appreciate it. I bring water. I drink water. And I drink it throughout the match. I've lost because I didn't do it. Now I make sure I've got water when I practice or play and I make sure that I *drink it*. Not just when I'm thirsty, but continually through a practice session or match. I want to avoid even *getting* thirsty. By then the toll is already being inflicted on my body because of dehydration. So I bring it and I drink it. I avoid the loss of muscle strength and coordination that happens when you start to dehydrate.

So I can "hydrate," I make sure water is always available. I bring my own even though most of the places I play supply water and other liquids. By having your own container next to your chair you're more likely to make a habit of sipping on it. In the two hours *before* a match I make sure to drink two or three glasses of water—more in hot weather.

Dehydration hurts your game, even before you know it's happening. That's why drinking water throughout the match is vital. It's one of those "obvious" things that club players are careless about. The next time you see a tournament, watch the pros. They take a drink *on the first changeover*. Because they're thirsty? No. It's insurance. You don't wait to fill up your gas tank until you run out of gas do you? Don't wait to drink water until your tongue's hanging out.

I also stay away from carbonated drinks. Plain water is the best. And, here's a good rule of thumb: Drink water before the match to protect yourself in the first set. Drink water during the first set to protect yourself in the second set. In other words, drink water *before* you need it.

Energy Food

You've heard about the "sugar shakes"? It happens when your blood-sugar level drops and suddenly your knees get weak. It can happen at the worst times and hit without warning. The solution is simple. Eat something. Before you can eat something you've got to bring something. I never assume that there'll be food available at the court. I've been surprised too many times. Now I bring my own stuff.

For me it's fruit. At least a couple of bananas. Easy to digest. Good energy right away. Candy bars? Nutritionists don't like the idea. They say the quick sugar rush is always followed by the big energy letdown. I don't know. It seems like if that's true, just be sure to bring enough candy bars along. When the energy from one wears off, eat another one. In any case, bring *something* along. I can tell you this: if you get caught needing a quick boost, a candy bar is better than nothing. And don't assume there's a snack machine at the court with anything in it. Because when you need it most, the machine will be empty.

Extra Rackets

Other than breaking your leg during a match, nothing can put you out of it quicker than breaking your racket or a string. The pros bring plenty, eight or nine. You're thinking, "Who's gonna break eight or nine rackets?" Other than McEnroe, nobody. But there's something else involved.

Obviously, extras are important in case one breaks. But I also bring rackets along with different string tensions. Some are strung looser and some tighter. The reason is that on a day when control is a problem, I might go to a tighter string tension for better control. On a day when I'm getting overpowered by the other guy's strokes, I might choose to go with a racket strung looser. It gives me more power off the same stroke.

For you? Obviously you should bring two rackets, minimum. It's a sloppy player (or one who's pretty cheap) who doesn't care enough to make sure he plays with the same kind of racket for the entire match. Some players bring a second racket, but it's like a spare tire, beat up, worn out, and just good enough to let you limp along. You don't want to be limping along in a tennis match because your good racket just lost a string. So, two is the minimum. If you can afford the luxury of having a third strung slightly looser or tighter, do it. You'll find in certain situations having that option will save a match.

Tape/Band-Aids

I take enough tape and Band-Aids along to wrap a mummy. I want to make sure that if for some reason a blister develops it won't take me out of a match or make winning that match even more difficult. I've got tender feet, and a sore toe makes starting and stopping four or five hundred times no fun. I'm ready to tape it up in a second.

Extra Shoes

"Turf Toe" sounds like a horse that ran eighth in the Kentucky Derby. It's not. "Turf Toe" happens when a toenail starts to disintegrate from constantly slamming into the front of your tennis shoe. First it disintegrates, and then it gets infected. I'll spare you further details, but the pain is incredible. It's like trying to eat popcorn when you've got an abscessed tooth—excruciating. I've had Turf Toe and eventually solved the problem by having the toenail on my big toe taken off surgically. I just decided I didn't want to be bothered by it anymore. But during the days when it was a problem, I'd switch shoes if it started to bother me. I'd put on a shoe that was a size or size-and-a-half too big just so I wouldn't slam into the front of it.

New shoes can also cause blisters and other aches and pains. You never know when a pair of shoes will rub you the wrong way. If you really do some running during a match, a new pair of shoes that doesn't quite match up with your feet can become a painful problem. It happened to me in the finals of the '87 Volvo/Stratton Mountain Tournament against Jim Pugh. For whatever reason, the little toe on my right foot began throbbing whenever I stopped suddenly. It was like a toothache. And it was getting worse. He was up a break at 5–2 in the first set.

At that point I realized if this kept up I was in trouble (in fact, I was *already* in trouble). Even if I could play through the pain, it was becoming a major distraction. I grabbed an old standby right shoe out of my bag and put it on during the changeover. It helped. I didn't lose another game during the rest of the match, and won 7–5, 6–0. I picked up a check for $114,000 wearing a brand-new left shoe and a battered old right shoe. After that I started thinking of that old right shoe as my "rally" shoe, kind of a good luck charm that would get me going when I needed a mental boost. I've still got it at home, my $114,000 old right shoe.

I'll usually break in a new pair of shoes by wearing them around the house for a couple of weeks before they ever see a tennis court. When you've had the kind of foot problems I've had, you are very cautious about what you put them in. I had forgotten to do that at Stratton Mountain. Fortunately I had a well-stocked equipment bag.

Extra Socks

I bring dry socks to prevent blisters. When your feet get wet from perspiration, you start sliding around inside your shoes, and that can cause a problem. It happens because a tennis shoe is generally a little bigger than you'd normally wear to give you a little room in the toe. When you start sliding into the front of that shoe, problems come up.

On a hot day I change socks during a match to prevent blisters. It also gives me a little psychological lift to put something dry on. When it's late in a match and I want to get into a "charge" state of mind, I'll change socks. Just a little thing like that helps get your focus back and tells your body to really get going.

Flex-All 454

Are you over thirty-five? Are you under thirty-five and playing a *lot* of tennis? Either way you're going to get sore, especially after a tournament. There are a bunch of products on the market that you rub on for aches and pains. Some smell worse than others. Some work better than others. Find one that doesn't smell too bad that works for you. I put Flex-All 454 on before I play and during a match or practice when something starts hurting.

I notice the older I get the more of it I use. First I was buying it by the tube. Then by the jar. Do they sell it by the bucket? It's a great

quick fix for a sore muscle or an aching back. I put it on before and
after playing. It works.

I.B.'s

Ibuprofen is the long name. Advil, Nuprin, they're all basically
ibuprofen. It's what takes out the aches and pains. I take two just
before I go out on the court and two more when I finish. It really
helps reduce the stiffness in the joints and muscles.

Electrolyte Pills

In hot weather I worry about cramping up. Water helps reduce the
chance of that happening, but if I start to feel any cramps I take
electrolyte pills to stop them. It's effective and works fast. Chang
could have used them in the quarterfinals of the 1989 French Open
against Lendl. He cramped up and could hardly walk. Fortunately for
Michael it completely psyched Lendl out. In fact, here's an interesting question. Would Chang have beaten Lendl if he (Chang) *hadn't*
cramped up and changed his strategy? Maybe. Maybe not.

Grips

Grips get soaked or occasionally unravel during a match. I don't
like to have to change rackets because of that, so I carry spares. I use a
type that was made by the Rocky Mountain Sports Company. It's a
fabric like a towel, only it's in strips that you can wrap on. In addition
to its effectiveness it became kind of a good luck thing. I'd been using
it for years and winning a lot of money. When I heard that the
company was stopping production of it I got concerned. I arranged to
buy the five-hundred they had remaining in stock. I figure they
should last until the year 2001.

If you play intensely and use a grip, carry extras.

Shoe Laces

You're right. Now I'm getting paranoid. You're thinking, "Geez,
does he carry extra jockstraps, too?" No, but now that you mention
it . . .

String a Lings

These prolong the life of the racket strings a little. In case one starts to fray I'll stick these on so I don't have to switch rackets. I hate to change if it's working well for me. Once I'm comfortable with something I tend to stick with it until it falls apart. And that happens with rackets, shoes, socks, shoelaces, *and* strings.

A Cap With a Visor

I keep one in the bag on a permanent basis. Sometimes I'm hitting outside and sometimes inside. I always have one stashed in there. Mine happens to be a beat up old Oakland A's cap that I've had for years. Before that I had a Raiders cap.

Towels

Sweating is your body's cooling mechanism, but it also can cause problems. Sweaty hands can slip on the grip when you hit hard. Perspiration in your eyes means you can't see. Wiping off the face, neck, arms, hands, and legs can help a lot in the cooling-off process. Towels are great for other things as well. I split my pants during an exhibition in Asia and the officials stood around me with towels while I changed.

Also, I use the towel for something completely unrelated to sweat. On changeovers I'll put it over my head to block everything out—that helps me focus on what is happening in the match. It's like a mini-office. You see a lot of the pros doing it as a self-made seclusion during a match. It blots out the crowd, the officials, the other player, everything. When you really want to sit down and have a little serious talk with yourself, the towel is important.

Ice

Not real ice. I bring the artificial ice that comes in a bag you can carry with you all the time. When you need it, just activate it. This means if you sprain an ankle or pull a muscle you can ice it down immediately. But be careful with this stuff. It is very cold. Leave it on too long and you can actually get frostbite.

Sweatbands

They're really just mini-towels, but very important because you take them out on the court with you. You can use them *right now*.

Dry Shirts

I keep extra shirts in my bag for a couple of reasons. Obviously, when one gets soaked I want to change. But also when things aren't going right (or if I want to give myself a little boost) I'll change shirts just to change things around a little bit. Putting on a fresh shirt gets my attention and helps to shake things up a little. It's a small fresh start.

Jolly Ranchers

These are not happy farmers. They're candy. Again, just something I've gotten used to and like to tuck in my cheek for a little boost. Something familiar that relaxes me. Dentists and nutritionists won't like it, but I always have them in my bag.

Paper and Pencil

During a practice session I will get some ideas on a stroke or on how to play somebody more effectively. I write it down immediately. Some of the ideas are valuable and get forgotten if you don't record them right away.

Sunglasses

I carry a pair of RayBan sunglasses for outdoor matches where glare is a problem. Some surfaces under bright conditions outside just seem to kick up a lot of glare. The sunglasses reduce the effect considerably.

So that's what at least one player on tour has stuffed in the bag you see being carried out on the court before a match: eight or ten rackets, food, candy, grips, socks, shirts, towels, water or juice, shoelaces, everything that could be needed during a match. My wife thinks I'm like a kid wanting his security blanket all the time. But I do know every single thing I carry gets used at one time or another.

Pre-Flight Checklist

Before takeoff a pilot goes through a checklist to make sure the plane is ready to fly, since once those wheels leave the ground it may be too late. But in going through the checklist the pilot is also mentally settling into the job ahead. His or her mind is focusing on the specifics on the list, but it is also locking into the upcoming flight itself. Packing my equipment bag is my "checklist"—it starts bringing me into the match ahead.

I recommend that you pack yours too if you want to win. Make it a very deliberate process. It's part of my "D.R.M." approach: Don't Rush Me. You gain in two ways. You'll have the equipment you need for any circumstances that come up during the match. You'll also have started off in the right frame of mind, totally focused on tennis.

It may seem like I'm going overboard, but I'm not. *I want to win!* When $2 million is at stake, like it was during a tournament in Germany, I don't want to take even the slightest chance that a blister, a cramp, dehydration, hunger, broken rackets, strings, sweaty socks or grips, shoelaces, or anything else could affect my take-home pay. I don't leave anything to chance.

You're thinking, "Listen, if I was playing for $2,000,000 I'd take an extra pair of socks along, too. But I'm just playing for fun." That's right. And *it's a lot more fun to win.*

I tell players I work with if they don't *really* care about winning or losing, then don't keep score. It must be a sorry son-of-gun who doesn't feel any different with a victory than with a defeat. *That* person should see a doctor and have his or her pulse checked.

Your Equipment Checklist
The Basic Daily Requirement

For yourself, shorten the list. Here's what you should take to the tennis court with you for every match.

1. **Water.** Bring it. Sip it throughout the match. Don't wait until
    you get thirsty. And drink water *before* your match.
2. **Two Rackets.** Two is the minimum. And remember to alter-
    nate them from match to match. They'll last longer. Bring a
    third that is strung a little looser, and a fourth strung tighter if
    you play a lot.
3. **Energy Food.** Fruit. A candy bar. Something for a quick sugar
    boost.
4. **Flex-All 454.** If you're over thirty-five, stop kidding yourself.
    Why suffer? Take anything that'll help you play with less pain.
5. **I.B.'s.** Ditto.
6. **Chemical Ice.** For emergency muscle pulls, twisted ankles,
    and assorted other problems. The quicker you get ice on it, the
    quicker your recovery.
7. **Towels.** Only if you sweat. And use it for your own isolation
    booth when you want to concentrate. Put it over your head
    during a changeover and think.
8. **Sweatbands.** Again, only if you sweat. If you don't sweat,
    maybe you should be trying harder during your matches or
    playing tougher opponents.
9. **Cap With Visor.** The team insignia is up to you. However, I
    do recommend the A's or Golden State Warriors.
10. **Dry Shirts.** Keep several in your bag so you don't have to pack
    one each time.
11. **Additional Equipment.** How much do you play? How many
    tournaments do you enter? Do you really want to have the
    equipment necessary to win available? Then decide for your-
    self what additional emergency supplies would be good insur-
    ance. It's hard to bring too much. It's easy to be undersup-
    plied.

The Completely Equipped Player

It's *hard* to bring too much to the court, but it's not impossible. I
found that out when I met Peter Pammer. (That's not his real name.
He says he never realized he had overdone things until I asked if I
could mention his name in this book. "No. *Please* don't use my

name.") He's a recreational player dedicated to finding, buying, bringing, and wearing *everything* when it comes to tennis. Like what?

Peter brings water, two kinds. One with carbonation, one without. Three rackets. A visor. Neoprene sleeves for both elbows and both knees. A canvas strap that he wears over the neoprene on the elbow that hurts worst that day. Gum. Candy bars. Fruit juice. Ben-Gay. Eyedrops. Breath mints.

He has a rosin bag which he takes out on the court with him. Before each of his serves he runs the rosin bag on the grip for better traction or something. (After a match he's spread so much white rosin dust around, it looks like it's been snowing on the baselines.) He brings towels and ice, pills, and a golf glove to prevent blisters on his hand. Sweatlets. Headbands. (Have you ever seen anybody wearing a visor *and* a headband?) He wears high tops to protect his ankles.

When Peter got into his full battle gear, he looked like the Pillsbury Doughboy. But do you know what? He never lost a match because he had too much equipment. And he probably won a few because he was prepared. The Boy Scouts should give him an honorary merit badge for "Tennis Emergency Preparedness."

So for yourself, carry my "basic minimums." It will ensure that you're ready for any emergencies, big or little. And while you're packing it and getting ready, your brain will know it's time to start thinking tennis.

Next: You've packed your bag. Now stretch for success.

3

Stretching for Success

In 1988 I thought my tennis career was over. My left ankle was exploding with intermittent jolts of pain. At times when I'd push off on that side it felt like someone had stuck a screwdriver in and was twisting it around. It became so swollen and painful any time I played for an extended period that I'd hobble around for days after a match. Bone chips and tendon damage threatened to kill my tennis life. Ten or fifteen years ago surgery might not have been able to solve my problem, but I was lucky. Doctors were able to get me back on my feet again and playing without pain.

Now, I faced another problem. Coming back is always tough, but in my case it was made especially difficult by the fact that conditioning had never been high on my list of priorities. When I was nineteen or twenty I didn't see much sense in it and as I got older that attitude just stayed with me. It hurt my game. My coach, Tom Chivington, had been noticing that my effectiveness seemed to drop significantly in matches that went three sets or beyond. I was stubborn and did nothing to change it.

After the ankle surgery I knew I was going to have to really work at it if I wanted to get back to the physical level I was at before (which Tom claimed wasn't that good). If I wanted to be better than before, I was going to have to work at conditioning with great discipline and intelligence.

I approached the job seriously. When you drop off the tour and sit home watching the guys on TV battle it out on courts around the world, you seem a long way from the action, a long way from being competitive. It was scary. I realized how much I loved competing during those months of rehab.

That's when I started working conscientiously with Mark Grabow, one of the top conditioning and strength experts in the the United States. He is a former soccer player who represented the United States in the Pan-American games. He has worked with the Stanford University men's and women's tennis teams and is currently the strength and conditioning coach for the Golden State Warriors in the NBA. Chris Mullin, a member of the 1992 Olympic Dream Team, is one of his star pupils. He has also worked with Aaron Krickstein and Jennifer Capriati. And, more important, he has worked with thousands of recreational tennis players on preparing for a tennis match correctly.

Not only did Mark get me into the best shape I'd ever been in physically, he also developed a pre-match routine for warming up and stretching that has become extremely important to me in *starting the match* at peak performance level.

Together we have refined a pre-game program that you should go through *automatically* before a match. It's short, painless, and effective. It will help your tennis *and* prevent injuries. It's another opportunity waiting to be taken advantage of.

Mark's Magical Four (or Five) Minutes

Your goal during this brief pre-game warm-up program is twofold: to enhance your tennis abilities early in the match (which will affect how you play later in the match) and to prevent injury. Ideally, you should spend twenty to twenty-five minutes preparing your body for the stress of playing a match (at any level) before you even touch a racket. However, it's a rare recreational tennis player who will do that. Don't worry, because you can do a tremendous amount of good for yourself and your game if you incorporate four (or five) minutes of Mark's recommendations into your routine.

The first 3 minutes are for literally warming up your muscles. These stretches are called dynamic flexibility movements. The next minute is for stretching muscle groups. These stretches are called static flexibility movements. The dynamic (or moving) warm-ups should be done first. Static (or stretching) movements should really be done after a muscle is warm.

Dynamic Flexibility Warm-Up

Tennis is a skill sport that starts from the ground up. Everything is initiated with the legs. This is the part of the body that should get the first and the most attention, the large muscle groups of the legs. Recreational tennis players almost always automatically warm up mainly the arms and hands. They go onto the court, do a couple of bend-overs or calf raises (which I call pretending to stretch) and immediately start slapping groundstrokes at each other. Watch your friends warming up. You see mostly arms and hands moving around.

What you want to do first is a very sport-specific (i.e., specifically for tennis), low intensity warm-up that will raise the core temperature of the primary muscle groups between the hips and the feet—this means the legs. These movements actually raise the temperature of the muscles being used because of increased blood flow. The muscles will subsequently be able to contract more forcefully and quickly with less risk of injury. It means when you *start your match* you will move better. The results will show up in your game.

Your warm-up will mimic the leg movements used during a match, but at a much lower intensity. The following fundamental movements will get your largest muscle groups ready for action. Do them while your opponent is pretending to stretch or fiddling around with equipment. The time involved is brief (between four and five minutes) and the results are valuable. Incidentally, you'll know you've done the job right if you get a little bit of a sweat going during the first movements—even a little moisture on your forehead indicates you've gotten the blood moving. *After* that you stretch.

CIRCLE THE SQUARE

This is the first movement of your warm-up and should be done very gently and at a low intensity. Basically you're going to jog around your half of the tennis court (the "square") while always facing the net.

Start back at the point where the doubles sideline intersects the baseline. Then slowly jog forward along the doubles sideline towards the net. When you get one yard from the net change direction and glide parallel to the net at the same pace. Your body will still be facing the net as you jog sideways along it. When you reach the other doubles alley, change direction (while continuing to face the net) and begin jogging slowly backwards toward the baseline. Keep at a very easy pace. When you get to the baseline again change direction (while still facing the net) and jog sideways along the baseline to the opposite alley.

Repeat the pattern two to four times, gradually increasing your pace. You are jogging around one half of the court (always facing the net) and putting your leg muscles through a great all around warm-up.

If you do nothing more than what I've just outlined you'll have done your legs a great service by using forward, backward, and lateral movement. You've gotten the blood moving into the big muscle groups and the results will show up in your game (not to mention lower the risk of injury). However, Mark and I also recommend you add something to the Circle the Square routine to increase its effectiveness.

Kick Your Butt

After you've circled the square twice, add this to what you're doing. As you run forward to the net (and then backwards away from it) begin increasing the height of your heel kick. On each step raise your heel up toward your butt as if you were trying to kick yourself in the behind.

Don't overdo it. The key to a good warm-up is a *gradual* increase of movement. This will continue the warming up of your legs, especially the quads (the fronts of your thighs). Do this for a minimum of one time around the circle.

The High Stepper

Finally, add this to your Circle the Square procedure *after* you've done Kick Your Butt. When you are moving forward and backward (toward and away from the net) bring your knees up higher and closer to your waistline—step high. Imagine bringing your knees up to your chest.

One time around the circle with this and you're ready to run hard from the first point. If you have time to continue this routine, take advantage of it.

Static Flexibility Warm-Up

When the large muscle groups have been activated and warmed up it's time to very briefly do some static (non-moving) exercises. Once you've *warmed* the muscles, a better stretch is possible. Better stretching will allow for a greater range of motion when you start playing, with less chance for injury.

THE STORK

This stretching exercise is easy to remember. You end up looking like a stork. Start out by standing near the net so you can hold it if you need balance. Raise one foot up behind you (bring your heel toward your butt) and grasp the top of your foot with your hand. Very gradually and gently pull your foot closer toward your butt. Don't overdo it. This will continue to stretch out your quads, or thigh muscles.

Do this for fifteen seconds on each leg, gradually stretching and releasing, stretching and releasing.

BOW TO THE EMPEROR

Standing with your feet slightly apart, bend over at the waist as if you were bowing to royalty. Keep your knees slightly flexed and your back relatively straight. Let your arms extend down toward the ground. Do this for ten seconds and repeat.

You'll feel it in the back of your legs (the hamstrings) and lower back as you bend farther over. *Don't force* this or any movement. And *don't bounce* as you attempt to get a full stretch. Never strain while stretching. The movements are gradual, gentle, and smooth.

PULL YOUR OWN GROIN

Groin injuries are very common, and this simple little exercise is great preventive medicine.

Stand with your feet about twenty-four inches apart. Gradually transfer your weight over to your right foot (without moving either foot). As you do this flex your right knee (it will move slightly forward) so you can accommodate the weight transfer. Keep your left foot solidly on the ground and your leg straight.

You'll start to feel a pull in your left groin. Gradually move into it and stretch. Hold it for ten seconds.

Then do the same movement for the other leg.

This series of exercises will prepare your body for the job ahead. Just as most players don't start thinking about the match until it is underway, they also don't warm up their bodies until the match is four or five games old. Those four or five games count.

Give your body a chance to help you get off to the best start. Warm it up and stretch it for success. Your results early in the match will be better, and this can dramatically affect what follows. You'll also have reduced your chance for injury.

It only takes about five minutes, so make it a habit.

And finally, if you want to prevent stiffness and keep yourself limber, do the static flexibility exercises *after* your match. This is very important, especially as you get older. You'll be a lot less stiff the next day if you have a good stretch right after you play and before you cool off.

Next: Your body is warmed up. Now warm up your strokes.

4

The Microwave Warm-up: Defrost Your Strokes Quick

As you move through the pre-match preparation to the beginning of play, you come to the last important element before the match starts: warming up your strokes. Most recreational tennis players waste or minimize this part of the pre-match routine because they don't understand how much it can contribute to winning.

Here's a fundamental rule for me: *Have a plan.* Each stage of the match should be recognized as having some potential for helping you achieve victory. Having a plan helps ensure that you accomplish it. Knowing what you want to accomplish during the warm-up will get it done.

Two Extremes: Both Wrong

There are two kinds of warm-ups I see with club players: too much or not enough. Some players come out and warm up for a month. Are they hoping they'll suddenly get better? It's not going to happen in the warm-up. Are they afraid to start the match? Are they trying to lose weight? Whichever it is, you know the type (and I hope you aren't one of them). They go out on the court and for twenty minutes they work on *all* their strokes . . . with your help!

Don't let your opponent use you as a human ball machine. When you're ready to go, get started. Tell your opponent you have to leave a little early. Tell them you want to make sure you can get the match finished. Or agree in advance on how long the warm-up will last. Don't let them drag you through *their* practice session. They can practice on their own time. This is a warm-up. Besides, putting you through all of that doesn't help your game.

Most players, however, hate the warm-up. In fact, generally the worse the player is the less they warm up. It's like phys. ed. in high school, something you do to graduate. Their warm-up is wasted and the opportunity is thrown away. They rush through it and hit their favorite shot a few times, ignore their weaker ones, and move into the match. If you're sloppy, rushed, and careless during this valuable period immediately preceding the match it's guaranteed to carry over into the match itself. The player who's prepared can take advantage of one who doesn't fully utilize the warm-up period.

The warm-up is your final opportunity to set the stage for getting off to a good start, to get a jump on your opponent that can affect the entire match and get you ready to play your best. Have a plan for this period and execute it. Here's how to do it.

The Plan: Short and Simple

The warm-up doesn't have to be long, but there are three things you want to accomplish with it:

1. Continue the physical warming up of your body and mind that began with stretching and pre-match planning and visualization.
2. Get your eyes and body working together for successful stroke production, *which includes managing nerves*.
3. Learn as much as you can about your opponent.

The tour players come out on court *already* warmed-up. What happens in front of the crowd just before the match is the very last bit of preparation. It helps with the butterflies and loosens everyone up a little. But for you the warm-up on court is probably the *entire* preparation. So make it count. It's why the sandbagger who warmed up with his club pro before the match had such a tremendous advantage. He was up to speed and off to the races four or five games before the pigeon woke up.

How to Defrost Your Strokes
in Seven Minutes and Forty-Five Seconds

Here is a very specific warm-up procedure guaranteed to set you up correctly for the match, both physically and mentally. When you go on the court, use it. Your opponent will probably go along with anything you say if you're nice about it. You may choose to use your own variation. That's fine as long as you remember to cover all these strokes and to have a regular routine you follow in doing it. The pattern you establish adds to the process of telling your mind and body that tennis is on the agenda.

Ninety Seconds: Volley to Volley

You want to get the eyes and hands working together. Don't run out on the court and start banging groundstrokes. Especially if you're a B or C player and especially if you haven't played for several days.

It's dumb to start hitting the shot that requires the most movement and uses the biggest muscle groups first when you haven't played in a week. If you're playing all the time it's different. Then you may want to start with the groundies and later move on to volleys. Most players aren't so lucky, however.

Tell your opponent you want to hit easy volleys back and forth, both of you inside your service boxes four or five feet from the net. It's just a little wake-up call for the old eye–hand motor function.

Believe me, it works. It gets your eyes watching the ball and your racket hitting the ball with the least effort and best chance for good contact. Your opponent is going to make a face when you start it. Forget the face. They have no plan and are only proceeding by habit of laziness. This is a real help in establishing a good rhythm for yourself (and, unfortunately, for your opponent, too).

Pop the ball back and forth to the backhand and forehand. Stay on the balls of your feet. Just make good contact. It gets your eyes successfully tracking the ball so that the sweet spot of your racket gets a little use.

Four Minutes: Groundstrokes the Correct Way

First thing to remember: Try and hit your initial groundstrokes deep, just inside the baseline. In fact, if the ball is a little long, great.

Aim for just inside the baseline. Try to hit your first six or seven shots with plenty of depth. Don't let a ball fall short. Pay attention to what you're doing. If a ball lands in or near the service box, correct it and go for that baseline.

Why? Nerves tend to shorten strokes and shots. Get the stroke extended by hitting deep. It sets an early pattern of hitting to the back of the court, which is one of the single most important habits you can have. In your match it's better to hit one out of five shots long than four out of five short. So start hitting deep early.

Remember, you're not trying to impress your opponent with power in those groundies. Start out nice and easy. Work your way up to speed (which won't happen until the fourth or fifth game). It's very important to establish a comfortable and effective rhythm initially. Club players love to start the warm-up by flailing away immediately. *Avoid it.* Go easy. Let your body come up to speed in a comfortable way.

Don't Cheat

During most warm-ups the average player will run around their weakest side on groundstrokes (the backhand) about 70 percent of the time. I've seen players warming up who actually caught the ball instead of taking a swing at it on their weak side. They love to hit what's comfortable and avoid what isn't so comfortable. If you count the times you actually avoid hitting from that side it would surprise you.

In fact, you should be doing just the opposite: run around the stronger side when possible. Hit your backhand as much as you can. Get it fired up. Get used to hitting it. Believe me, if your opponent is smart you'll be hitting it plenty once the match begins. So don't ignore it. Give it at least equal time. It'll pay off short term and long term.

One of the reasons you see a big difference in a player's weaker side and stronger side as they keep playing over the years is this: they are constantly looking to hit the shot they like and avoid the shot they don't like. It feeds on itself. Over the months and years a player lets the weaker side kind of wither on the vine. Lack of attention equals lack of effectiveness.

In a match it might make sense to run around it. In the warm-up give the weaker side a little real attention. Among other things it will build up your confidence. You'll get used to hitting it. And the warm-up is a regular, no penalty opportunity to work on it.

Thirty Seconds: Overheads

Overheads get ignored in the warm-up, especially by B and C level players. Here's why. It may be the shot you hit worst and hate most. Nobody likes to look bad in front of their opponent. Nobody likes to look bad in front of themselves. That overhead can make you look *real* bad. It's the most difficult shot to time right, especially when you've just started. So a lot of players just don't want to mess with it. What do they do? They wait until it *counts* to hit their first overhead. This is not intelligent. They figure it's just easier to skip it entirely. Don't.

The overhead warm-up does two things. Obviously, it warms up the overhead. But it also starts warming up your serve. It gets you doing all the things you need to be doing during the serve: looking up, following through, transferring your weight. It gives you just a little more time to bring the serve up to speed. Your objective is modest. Just make solid contact on the swing. Don't worry about power. Don't worry about great angles. Just take a relaxed cut at the ball and don't get fancy.

Fifteen Seconds: The Toss

As the toss goes so goes your serve. When was the last time you actually practiced your toss? Before you serve, practice your toss four or five times. Just focus on doing it smoothly and putting the ball where you want it. Toss it up. Then catch it without moving your feet. It's a great way to improve your serve with very little effort. (And during the match if your serve starts to give you trouble, slow things down and take a couple of practice tosses. I've found it helps to get things back on track. If your toss is all over the place it's impossible to have a reliable serve.)

Finally, on this much overlooked but crucial part of the game, don't be afraid to stop your service motion if the toss is terrible. Catch it! Toss it again. Club players will chase a bad toss into the locker room trying to salvage it.

One Minute: The Serve

I want you to hit four serves to *both* courts, both wide and down the center. Most club players tend to hit just to the deuce court. I want you to hit to both courts for this reason. The service warm-up is aimed primarily at setting up a good comfortable motion for yourself early in the match so you don't needlessly double-fault.

Hit your initial serves with an easy, relaxed motion. Keep your wrist very loose—almost floppy. Hit your first three or four serves with almost a lazy motion. Aim for the service line *or beyond*. Then gradually increase velocity.

You want to help yourself as much as you can for that first service game. You want to be comfortable with the stroke and you don't want to be serving to the ad court for the first time during the match, so serve to it in the warm-up.

Thirty Seconds: Service Return

When your opponent is hitting serves during the warm-up, don't catch them, *hit them back*. Practice hitting their serve with a good service return. I believe it can be one of your most important weapons and it is seldom worked on. *Work on it*. And work on it in the warm-up. Hit some focused, rhythmic, and connected returns. Remember, this is probably the shot you'll hit first (especially if you follow my later advice). The time to get it going is in the warm-up.

That's the "quick-and-slick-it'll-do-the-trick" 7-minute-and-45-second Microwave Warm-up. Yes, it may take a couple of minutes longer if your opponent wants to hit some overheads or anything else. But *your* game, at least, will be ready to roll. Do this and you come out hot (or at least warm).

Learn About Your Opponent: The Quick Study

Another objective during this final stage of the pre-match opportunity is to see if your opponent is showing you anything about their game that you can use against them. This is important with someone you haven't played before. Here's how to do it.

Hit a ball down the middle. Which way do they step? Do they run around the backhand? If you've never seen your opponent before, they've just told you something; namely, they favor one side over the other.

When they're at the net volleying, throw a surprise lob up. Do they cover smoothly? Are they quick or clumsy with their footwork?

Also, when they're at the net, hit a ball low to their feet. Do they bend their knees or do they drop the racket head (the lazy man's volley).

During the rally pay attention to how they move and how they strike the ball when they're moving. Are they sharp on one side and inconsistent on the other? Do they hit one shot more than another— slice, topspin, or flat? Do they take big, looping strokes or short, compact strokes? Remember the following Gilbert Golden Rule: *The strokes that are prettiest in the warm-up are the ugliest under pressure.* Never be *too* impressed by what you see in the warm-up. But do remember any little problems or glitches in their strokes or movement that you might want to exploit in the match.

5

Four "Nervebusters": Overcoming Pre-Match Nervousness

Finally, we deal with the issue of nervousness at the beginning of a match. You know what nerves are, don't you? Nerves mean you're afraid, you fear something. Do you know what fear is? It's a defense mechanism. It's your body's way of gearing up for trouble. When your mind or body senses danger, fear is the natural way to get ready to deal with it—the "fight or flight" mechanism. The adrenalin starts pumping. The senses are heightened. All systems are go! Only sometimes they don't.

It's natural to feel nerves before a big match, whether the cause is a certain player you really want to beat or a tournament you've entered. In those situations, if you *don't* feel nerves you'll lose. The quality players are helped by nerves because they use the good part and control the bad part. They know that the energy from nerves can work for you, making you try harder, focus sharper, and do more. That's the good part. The bad part can cause damage.

The damage is major, too. Uncontrolled nervousness makes your legs heavy and your feet stick to the ground. Nerves take the oil out of your strokes. They freeze you up. Ever hear about "The Elbow"? Nerves. And it happens at all levels of tennis. Maybe most of all among the pros, because of the stakes involved.

Nerves can make you stop thinking on the court and try stupid shots. A nervous player will kick himself afterwards and say, *"Why did I try that drop shot from behind the baseline?"* Nerves, that's why. Nerves can make you *really* brain dead. What was easy to do suddenly isn't so easy.

Maybe the worst case I ever saw happened to Miloslav Mecir. He got "The Elbow" big time. During a World Team Cup match he was serving to Connors 5–3 in the third set to win the match and the title for Czechoslovakia. All he had to do was *hold serve*. Nerves got him. He started double-faulting. By the end of his service game he had double-faulted four times! During his next service game (at 5–all) he started faulting again. It got so bad he started serving underhand on second serves just to get the ball in. There was no other way he could get it in the box. It was painful to watch because you felt so sorry for the guy. He was a great player, but nerves took their toll on him and he lost the match because he couldn't control them.

I've had my own experience with nerves. I played Davis Cup for the United States in '86 when we lost three to two to Australia. And I lost both of my matches. It was a horrible feeling. I was depressed and embarrassed. Inside I felt like I'd let my country down, and nerves were a big part of it. I had wanted to win for the U.S.A. so much that I was tight, nervous, anxious, wanting to end points too soon. Nerves will do that.

That experience was my worst in tennis, because the losses laid on me for three years. That's a long time to wait to redeem yourself. When I finally got invited back I had learned a lot. I won because I had a ferocious desire to prove myself and I was much better at handling nerves. Let me tell you what I do.

During the warm-up nerves will start affecting you immediately. Your feet don't want to move. You can't catch your breath. Your movement is stiff. And so are your strokes. I have four very simple and mechanical things I do to loosen the grip of nerves before a match.

Gilbert's Nerve Busters

1. Breathe Like You've Got Asthma

When you get nervous your breathing pattern changes. It's the first thing you should check. Your breathing tells you about the level of your anxiety. And, more important, your breathing can help you control your anxiety. When you're nervous you take short, shallow, quick breaths. And that's exactly how you feel. Everything is jumpy, racy, and out of sync when you get nervous.

When that happens, control your breathing. Take smooth, rhythmic, deep breaths. You can start even before you're on the court. Before a match that really has me tight I make sure that I'm breathing correctly—deep, smooth, rhythmic. I sound like I've got asthma, but it helps reduce my nervousness.

2. Get Happy Feet

Let me tell you about footwork. It is the most important part of the game. It's everything. And nerves can destroy it. Good footwork gets you to the right position in time. If you're there in time you have options. If you have options you have a better chance of winning the point. You can slice the ball. You can hit over the ball. You can hit it early. But mainly you can hit it squarely. Options. The more options you have the less likely you are to be attacked effectively and the more likely you are to control the point. That's what good footwork can do *for* you. Here's what *bad* footwork can do *to* you.

If you have bad footwork and get to the ball late, or wait for the ball to come to you (or don't have yourself in the best position to hit the shot you want), you have fewer options. The ball is playing you. If it's tight to your body all you can do is fight it off. Bad footwork hurts your timing, your balance, your power, and your consistency.

Pre-match tension can absolutely kill footwork. Nerves make your feet stick to the court like you've got Velcro on the bottom of your shoes. Nerves make you stop moving. Your legs get sluggish. Short, quick, light steps become lunging, slow, big steps. And it goes right through your body. The strokes are bad. The timing is bad. The contact is bad. And your confidence evaporates because you can sense that "I'm just not hitting the ball today." Bad footwork.

How do you get good footwork? Simple. Think "toes." If you stay on your toes (the balls of your feet) you *have* to be taking light, quick, short steps. Heels are for digging in, for carrying the load, for holding your ground. Being on your heels is how you get passed in tennis. And nerves put you back on your heels quicker than anything else. So when it comes to good footwork, think like a ballet star—get up on your toes.

I consciously tell myself to move my feet. It's an order I give to myself when I'm nervous. "Bounce. Get up on your toes, Brad. Stay light on your feet! Bounce." I keep telling myself to bounce, to stay light, to keep moving. It helps me work *into* good footwork and *out* of nervousness. I want happy feet, not heavy feet.

Movement reduces nerves. Lack of movement increases nerves. You've heard people say, "He got nervous and *froze up.*" They're not talking about body temperature. They're talking about movement, or lack of it.

You'll notice in your own game that when you're feeling good, when you're confident and ahead, you move naturally and smoothly. But mainly *you move.* Same with the pros. When they're relaxed they don't just stand there leaning back on their heels. They're up and bouncing, moving.

It's the player who's tight, afraid, and tied up by tension (or just exhausted) who stands there flatfooted. And you can fight the tendency to freeze up when you're nervous by reminding yourself (ordering yourself) to get up on your toes and be light on your feet.

Remember this not only during the warm-up, but in the pressure points of the match. Watch Courier before a big point. Watch him shift from foot to foot, knees bent, bouncing on his toes. Is he nervous? You bet. But he knows how to deal with it. The good ones never just *stand* there. They fight nerves and stay loose by moving. And so should you. Talk to yourself. Tell yourself, "Toes not heels."

There is another benefit to doing this. It is good body language. It tells your opponent that you're loose (even if you're not). It tells them you're not tired (even if you are). It tells them you're confident and positive (even if you aren't).

In addition to the good it does your own game it works on your opponent's mind. Especially late in the match. You've been in a battle for three sets. Your opponent is looking for some sign of fatigue, or nerves, or resignation in you. They look across the net and see the opposite. You're up (on your toes)! You're energized (or at least look like you are)! You're bouncing lightly from foot to foot. Your body language is telling them that you're ready and eager to fight to the end. Believe me, it does have an effect not only in the beginning of a match, but during it.

3. Read the Label

During the initial part of the warm-up, when I'm anxious and trying to settle down, there's another little trick I use to fight nerves. I read the print on the ball. I try to see "Wilson" or "Penn" or "Slazenger" as the ball is coming at me. You'll find that trying to see the writing not only helps get your eyes tracking the ball, but it gets your mind off nerves and onto something else. At first, you probably won't see anything. Your eyes will improve and you'll start seeing a blur. If that's as far as you get, fine. What matters is that you've taken your mind off a problem by distracting it. Nerves aren't what you're thinking about. The label is what you're thinking about.

4. Sing a Song

This one sounds a little strange. I distract myself from nerves by singing under my breath early in the warm-up. I'll get a Tom Petty song going through my head and sing the lyrics to myself. I'm just trying to keep everything calm and easy to start with. And believe it or not, this little trick works for me.

So when you go out on the court and you feel that pre-match tightness, remember my four Nerve Busters:

1. Breath like you've got asthma
2. Get happy feet
3. Read the label
4. Sing a song

You may think it's amazing that I can even hit the ball with all that breathing, bouncing, reading, and singing going on. I use it selectively. Mainly, I'm checking myself out to see how I'm moving and whether nerves are a problem that day. If I need to help myself get through nerves during a warm-up or during a match, I'll go to this list, starting with my breathing and my footwork. I want to get them under control immediately, before they cost me points.

Your Mind Can't Think of Two Things at Once

Obviously nerves reduce your effectiveness *during* the match as well as before the match. When I feel pressure during play there is something else I consciously do to reduce my tension.

I know that nerves get worse when I think about them, when I start worrying about the consequences. I reduce that tendency by really focusing on my *game plan* at pressure points in the match: What am I trying to do with this serve? What am I looking to take advantage of in my opponent's shots? I stay focused on my game plan. I divert my attention away from nerves and toward the next point (where it should be anyway!). By thinking about that, I'm not thinking about nerves.

The Connors Approach to Nerves

There's one other approach to nerves that you can consider, but it's only worked for one player that I know of: Jimmy Connors. He has a unique attitude about pressure. His perspective is this: Pressure usually represents opportunity. The more pressure the more opportunity. And he loves opportunity.

He figures, how much opportunity can there be playing the finals of the East Podunk/Fred and Millie's Donut Shop and Radiator Repair Tennis Tournament? Not much. No fame, fortune, or flattery. How much pressure? Not much. On the other hand, how much opportunity is there playing the finals of the U.S. Open? Maximum. Careers are made there. Legends are created there. How much pressure? Maximum.

Jimmy just sees the opportunity. He doesn't focus on the pressure. He knows that in the most pressurized situations he can do himself the greatest good in terms of his career. And he really got himself jacked up when something big was at stake. Match point in a Slam event? He couldn't be having more fun. It just came natural for him. For the rest of us it's not so natural. Try my Nerve Busters. They work.

Ready for the Contest

Now you're ready to begin. You're ready to take advantage of your opponent *immediately* when the match gets going. You're ready to jump off to a dominating start; maybe up a break, with good rhythm, good concentration, a focus on your game plan, and confidence. *Now* let the games begin.

Next: A smart start to your match.

6

Start Smart:
Grabbing the Early Lead

Mental Preparation, Tools of the Trade, Stretching for Success, Winning the Warm-up—everything you've read in those chapters so far gives you the foundation for the best possible opening to the match, and one that carries forward *into* the competition. You'll start strong, physically and mentally primed to find a quick break and a pattern that can give you a substantial edge for winning the first set. *You are creating positive momentum for yourself.*

I know that if I can get off to a good early start in the match it improves my chances for winning the first set. Let me show you why statistically this is so important to me and why it can give you a real advantage.

According to the A.T.P. (Association of Tennis Professionals) a Top 20 player who wins the first set will go on to win the match 89.6 percent of the time! At the U.S. Open when Jimmy Connors has won the first set he has won the match eighty-eight out of ninety times! Winning the first set, then, carries significant weight. And getting off to a strong *early* start significantly boosts my chances of winning the first set. That's why I'm so conscientious about preparing for the beginning of a match. It's why you should do the same.

Hit the Deck Running

This next step is the point of transition from the pre-match preparation into the heart of the contest. I consider the first two games to be included in this transition. I use this period to gain an edge that may be ignored by the other player. I'm looking for those moments in a match where my opponent is probably asleep at the wheel or doesn't understand and exploit the dynamics of the situation.

At the top levels of tennis this doesn't happen often, but as you go through the ranks more and more opportunities are overlooked. The difference between a Top 10 player and a player trying to break into the Top 25 isn't tennis strokes. It's tennis smarts, the mental part of the game. I found that out in my own journey from the tennis wilderness into the Top 10. For recreational tennis players it's the same. Lots of opportunities get ignored because a player's mental game is weak.

The "transitional" period presents opportunity. Several different elements are present for the first and only time and they can be an asset or a liability depending on how you approach them. Very likely your opponent doesn't recognize them. And if they do they aren't sure how to capitalize on them.

Before you're caught up in the heat of the battle you've got this in-between period where it's valuable to know what to do to gain advantage.

How to Get the Best Possible Start
1. Never serve first.
2. Start your match like Ivan Lendl.
3. Play the first two games correctly.
4. Utilize the first pit stop.

1. Never Serve First

Here's a bet you can win 90 percent of the time with your tennis friends: "What choices does the player who wins the spin of the racket (or toss) have?" Most of the time they will say the answer is to serve/ receive or select which side to begin the match on. Wrong! There is one other option. It is to give the first choice to the other player. Knowing all of this and how to use it can be important. As you'll see.

Most club or public courts players like to win the spin of the racket so they can elect to serve first. I believe that you should almost always choose to *receive* serve first. But it's a big thing for most players, serving first. When your opponent spins the racket and informs you that your choice of "up" or "down" is wrong, have you ever caught yourself wondering if they may already have "hooked" you so they can serve first? That's okay. Let them. Don't argue with a player who wants to serve first. In fact, you can help them to do it by electing to *receive* serve when you win the spin.

They may think they get an advantage by serving first, but in most cases they don't. In fact, they get a disadvantage. At the pro level in men's tennis it's generally better to serve first in a match. With some exceptions that isn't the case in recreational tennis. Here's why.

Six Reasons You Shouldn't Serve First

1. THE FIRST SERVE IS NO BIG THREAT

You've heard the expression, "First one to hold serve wins!"? At times it's almost true at the club level. How big a weapon is your opponent's serve? Or yours? The perceived advantage of serving first may apply in men's professional tennis, but it really doesn't anywhere else. (Incidentally, if you have a great serve, congratulations, but you're the exception.) Find out for yourself. Keep track of your service holds over several matches. Here are some of the pros averages for holding serve: Edberg, 85.2; Stich, 87.2; Courier, 84.5; Agassi, 80.2; Becker, 84.4; Me, 77.9 (source: A.T.P. statistics, 1991). How do you match up?

2. THE SERVE IS WEAKEST EARLIEST

Okay, very likely the typical club player's serve isn't much of a weapon under the best of circumstances. It's even less threatening when a player isn't warmed up, isn't into the match, isn't relaxed, and isn't really comfortable with their serve, which exactly describes the conditions for your opponent serving first in the match. It's amazing anybody ever wins their first serve to open the match.

At the pro level there's a very careful approach to the serve. You'll see in their warm-up just prior to the match that the serve may get the most attention of all. In most cases it must be working and working well to win, so they make *sure* it gets lots of attention before play starts. Even then a pro isn't serving at his or her strongest early in the match and, obviously, neither are you or your opponent. A mediocre serve that can't overcome all the early handicaps becomes useless, even a liability.

3. YOU GET MORE WARM-UP TIME

The serve is a complex physical movement. It is one shot where you can't just stick your racket out in front of you and block the ball back over the net.

But one thing is certain. The serve is easier if you're warmed up. Letting your opponent serve first (and relatively "unwarmed up") gives *you* additional time to loosen up, to relax into the match, to hit more balls, *and to get ready to serve up to your potential.* You're stealing just a bit of real match play time to settle down. This will be an asset when you step up to the line to serve that second game of the match.

4. THE PSYCHOLOGICAL EFFECT

Think about how you'd react if your adversary on the court chose to let you serve first. What goes through your mind? "Hey, you don't think I can serve? I'll show you what I can do!" That, or something like it, is a natural reaction. It's also a dumb reaction.

Trying to serve harder is a big mistake. It's a formula for faulting. That's why you want to give your opponents the chance to psych themselves out by having them serve first.

5. LOSING THE FIRST GAME ISN'T LOSING

One of the easiest times to break serve is on your opponent's first service of the match. Especially if it's the first *game* of the match. However, if they hold you haven't *lost* a thing. They've simply done what they're supposed to do; namely, hold serve.

Technically, the match is "on serve" even though you haven't served a single tennis ball. Tactically, if your opponent holds in that first service game of the match it does the least damage.

6. THE QUICK EARLY BREAK CAN BE VERY IMPORTANT

My whole approach to winning is based on grabbing small opportunities as I go along—getting them, holding them, and looking for more of them. Each one separately may not seem very significant, but taken together they give you a substantially bigger chance of victory. That's why this first game of the match can be important.

Most players begin a match with a general feeling that if they lose serve it's no big deal. It was how I approached it when I played college tennis. "Plenty of time to get it back later." Maybe. Maybe not. What you do know is that by grabbing a quick service break you have given yourself a real advantage.

One of the goals of pre-match focusing, the stretching, the planned warm-up, and electing to receive first is to get this advantage. If you are successful (and you should be 25 to 35 percent of the time) you will have given yourself a better chance of winning the match *before you even serve.*

You've put yourself in a strong position for what follows. You may have a break in hand. You may have forced your opponent to get aggressive too soon (trying to break back immediately). This may help you to hold your own first serve as they force shots and commit errors. If you get lucky they may even press a little harder on their second service game of the match and give you some easy opportunities to break *for a second time.* This is your ideal scenario. And it does happen.

Think about where this can put you: up three games to none with two breaks! This is a huge advantage and puts you in a position where anybody betting ten cents on the match would bet on you. You *should* win the match. You may not, but the odds really go in your favor. A player up two breaks in the first set should win that set. A player who wins the first set is the odds-on favorite to win the second set. And unless you're playing a best of five sets that's all you need to win.

This is your goal. You're thinking, "That's no goal. That's a fantasy." Not really. It's not a simple goal, of course, but it's what you're trying to accomplish. You want to get out of the gate fast. You want to stuff your opponent as early and as hard as you can. Get them on the run. A good player on a good day might get out of your grasp. Most of them won't if you continue to exploit opportunities and avoid the temptation to get mentally lazy about paying attention to the "outer game." Instead of starting the match with the idea that you'll work your way into it, begin with the goal of working your opponent *out of it.*

I use the strategy of letting my opponent serve first about 15 percent of the time in my own matches. The reason for not doing it more often is obvious. The pros do warm up properly. And the pros do have a weapon with their serve (usually). However, there are exceptions even at the top levels of competition. I've never been concerned about letting Michael Chang or Jimmy Connors serve first. (You'll notice that Chang and Connors rarely choose to serve first when they have the option, for the reasons I've just outlined.) I've also let McEnroe and Lendl serve first occasionally just to throw them a little curve right at the start of a match.

How about letting someone like Boris Becker (with his huge serve) serve first? The potential advantage I gain when I use it is the same as the one for you. As big as his serve is, it isn't at its best in the first games. And occasionally Becker's serve acts up on him early in a match, so my choice can even be effective against him.

One other option I use (but only rarely) when I win the toss is to hand over the choice to my opponent. It's a little psychological ploy I use when things are still a little edgy at the beginning of a match. By giving up the decision to choose whether to serve or receive I may throw the opponent just slightly off balance. I'm basically saying, "Your serve isn't a threat. Take your pick." If they elect to serve first that's what I want anyway. If they elect to have me serve first they're admitting they also aren't too sure about their serve. So it can backfire if I want to receive first. But usually they'll choose to serve.

The Exceptions to the Rule

Here's when you shouldn't let your opponent serve first. Obviously, if you play someone whose serve is really big and works as a weapon right from the beginning, don't let them start using it against you immediately. Depending on your level of play and the opponent on a particular day this could be the case. But it won't happen often.

The Wind and the Sun

The other situation occurs when you're playing outside and the sun factors in. If it's in the eyes of the server at one end you want to correctly exercise your options when you win the spin of the racket. As you know, you can choose to serve or receive, or to select which end of the court you start at. The choice determining which end of the court you start at is the most important one when the sun is a problem. Select the end that puts the sun at your back for the first game. (If the elements are a factor, never hand over the choice to your opponent.)

Your opponent (if they're paying attention) will then elect to have you serve first so they don't have to serve into the sun immediately. That's okay because you have then forced them to play the first game facing the sun. Throw them a few lobs in that first game and let them stare into the sun while they're trying to hit an overhead in this earliest part of the match.

You also may get lucky. Once you've chosen to keep the sun at your back, your opponent might still elect to serve first, into the sun! If that happens you can be reasonably sure the player is brain-dead.

Wind can also be a factor outdoors. I played a match against Mark Edmunson in Las Vegas in winds that were gusting up to fifty miles per hour. On one point I ran over to hit a backhand and the wind suddenly gusted and blew the ball around to my forehand side! Later I hit a lob that went off my rim and sailed out over the side fence. The wind actually blew it back over the fence and onto Mark's court for a winner. I eventually lost the match, but not before I got a pretty good case of windburn.

If the sun isn't a factor (a cloudy day, a night match), wind becomes the first consideration. If it's blowing baseline to baseline I choose to start the match with the wind in my face. There's more room for error because the wind will knock your ball down and keep it from going long. Typically the opponent won't be as concerned about the wind as about the sun. They usually elect to serve first. This means that in the first game you've got them serving with the wind at their back. Tougher to get the ball in the service court in that circumstance. Your advantage.

So as a general rule I like to start with the sun at my back and the wind in my face if I have the options. You should do the same. If it means you have to serve first, that's okay. You've still gained the advantage.

2. Start Your Match Like Ivan Lendl

Ivan Lendl is one of the most powerful sluggers ever to play tennis. When he really rips it you can almost hear the ball say OUCH! He pulverizes it. But here's what you don't know. He never starts at full throttle. Ivan understands the importance of working his way up to maximum speed and power. He knows you're never there in the first few games of the match. Nerves, the crowd, new conditions, and other factors almost always make it impossible to really let it out right away. Ivan doesn't. He keeps his game very much under control initially.

During the first three or four games he's hitting at about 65 to 75 percent of his full power. He very consciously resists the urge to really smack it. He wants to work his way into a good rhythm. He understands the correct method is to start below it and work up to it. It's very hard to bring yourself *down* to your best pace if you start hitting too hard right away. You can spend the rest of the match looking for your rhythm. Ivan never makes that mistake.

And that goes for his serve, too. By trying to slug the ball before your body and mind are really acclimated to the match you can take your service down for the whole day. The serve is complex. Even Lendl doesn't go for it too early.

When I played him for the first time at Hartford in '82 I couldn't believe the great Lendl was hitting such manageable shots. I was thinking, "Geez, they looked a lot heavier when I watched him play other guys." This went on for about four games. In the fifth game he cranked it up. Suddenly a serve went by me that I didn't even see. I was hitting everything late. He started swinging me wide left and right. I couldn't get in position for anything. He was rolling. And he rolled right over me 6–2, 6–2. He had worked his way up to maximum speed and power and used it *when it was there*. Not before.

Lendl's approach is the correct one. Start below your maximum pace and rhythm in your first few games. Don't try to cream those early shots. Let yourself build into a solid, comfortable "power" rhythm. It'll happen if you let yourself resist the temptation to hit hard and win quick.

3. Play the First Two Games Correctly

The first two games of the match can set the temperature for what follows. The mental and physical attitude established here is valuable because it can start you on a course that makes winning a lot easier.

You and the opponent serve and receive serve for the first time. You are both getting your "sea legs" and working yourself up to attack speed. There are a number of considerations I bring to these first games that incorporate Lendl's approach and add to it.

No Unforced Errors

Remember during these first two games that you're not as loose as you'll be later. Even if you warm up correctly you still aren't really set to let it all hang out. So no unforced errors. Don't be afraid to swing at the ball, but don't try to impress the other player. Just make some balls. The pattern you want to set in place is one of consistency, of success in getting the ball back over the net and into the opposite court.

Serve Sensibly

When you're serving for the first time it's very easy to fault. Remember to avoid the temptation to try and hit big. This is the point in the match where careless flubs are made. Don't put yourself in a position where the other player wins an early game just by standing there. Don't give them freebee's. Your goals should be modest: 1. Get the ball in. 2. Get it to their weaker side.

A lot of players are lackadaisical on their first service game. They don't seem to care. If you let your opponent break you right out of the chute you've jacked them up. You've adrenalized them. You've given them the opportunity to pressure you. And pressure generally hurts your game. So be smart. Get the ball in. Keep the ball in play early on. Eliminate errors.

Don't Relax

Players who serve first and hold (or receive first and break) almost always let down in the next game. There's a sense of "Whew, I got through that. Now I can relax for a second." Bang. The other player wins at love. Don't let them off so easily.

Remember, if you serve first and hold, a subsequent break is "longer." By that I mean if you break them in that second game and then hold your own serve you're up 3–0. Psychologically that seems a lot heavier than it is. It's still just one break. But it's three games difference. It *feels* worse to your opponent. And that means it *is* worse.

If you receive first and break (which is what you should try and accomplish) don't get careless on your serve in that second game. The tendency is to get feeling a little too good a little too soon. Don't go for aces. And depending on the level of your game, don't be too ambitious. You'll be surprised at what happens in your first service game if you just get your first serve in.

Test Them Early

Also, I like to work my way to the net if I can early in these first few games. Don't force it, but if the opportunity arises take it. I look to do it when I'm up 40-love and can spare a point. The other player is a little tight. They haven't made any shots and they may jerk one that gives *you* the freebee.

4. Utilize the First Pit Stop

I get asked why the pros take a rest after the first game. Why not just change ends without sitting down for a break? Good question, because in your entire life I'll bet you've never seen a tour player skip the opportunity to sit down after playing that first game. It can't be fatigue, can it? Answer: It's not to rest. It's to think.

Changeovers are where you get yourself together mentally and emotionally. The first changeover has added value because it gives you an opportunity to check your bearings before anything too drastic has happened. I use it as an opportunity to establish again in my mind what it is I'm trying to do. I review my game plan.

I take my sip of water, wipe off the sweat, settle down, but mainly I think. I review my strategy. What am I trying to make happen? What do I want to prevent from happening? On subsequent changeovers I want to review anything that might have occurred that surprised me. Has my opponent hurt me with anything? I give myself a little pep talk: "Stick to your game plan. Don't get overeager. Be patient. Remember to get that first serve in and to the backhand."

That first pit stop is very important because the beginning of a match is a disruptive period. A lot of things are happening and a lot of adjustments are being made. It's easy to lose your focus, your plan, your attitude. This first changeover is unique in that essentially you are still looking ahead. There is no strong pattern emerging in the game yet. You aren't looking at what went wrong or right. You are still in the process of trying to force your game plan on the other player.

I realize tennis is a social event and that changeovers are where a lot of the socializing usually goes on at tennis courts. It's a chance to catch up on the latest news and gossip, or to talk about the match itself. You probably aren't prepared to put a towel over your head and start meditating. But a player dedicated to winning is willing to delay the small talk until after the match.

You are still trying to steal that early lead. If you broke serve you want to hold. If you held (or lost) serve you want to break. That initial changeover gives you a chance to approach the job calmly with your plan clearly in mind. "Get my first serve *in*. Don't get fancy. Make him play."

I think of the changeover as my isolation booth. I want to use what I'm learning in the match to my advantage. A smart tennis player is accumulating information as play goes on. And they're using that information to their advantage. The changeover is where you have an uninterrupted time to review and plan.

Watch the pros when you see a match on television. They're not sitting there looking off into the crowd or talking to the ballboys. There is heavy concentration going on. That's why the towel goes over the head occasionally. They want to really *stop and think about what's going on*. Don't waste that opportunity in your own matches.

Play Tennis Like You'd Do Business

A smart businessperson constantly tries to think of ways to improve business. It's amazing how they'll suddenly get on the court and *stop* thinking. On the changeover they'll sit there like a cow licking a block of salt. Not a thought in their head. A smart player constantly tries to improve their chance of winning. Always thinking. Always analyzing what's happening.

It can even be a good idea to have a notebook in your equipment bag that you can refer to in the beginning of (and during) a match. It can list your strengths. Your opponent's weaknesses. Your main goal against that player. Maybe a tip you got at your tennis lesson. Things you've thought out before the match. It's important information that can easily get forgotten during the match. During the changeover take it out of your equipment bag and review it.

Adults at some of my tennis clinics have told me that they're playing tennis to relax. That's absolutely okay. I tell them when they start playing tennis to win remember some of the things I've said. I've always found winning a lot more relaxing than losing.

One of the biggest misconceptions recreational tennis players have about the game is that there's not much to it mentally. Some of the big names in tennis also felt that way. Fortunately for me.

Next: Play smart during your match by taking advantage of what you see.

II

Playing Smart

Finding a Way to Win

"Brad's very cunning at figuring out an opponent; probably better at it than any player in the world."
—Allan Fox, Instruction Editor, *Tennis Magazine*

7

The Key to Victory

The *New York Times* says I'm great at making my opponents play badly. Arthur Ashe agreed: "Brad doesn't have any strokes you'd want to write home about." They're right. I don't overpower people. I don't have any flashy shots. I win because I have the ability to implement my basic game strategy successfully: maximize my strengths and minimize my weaknesses. That means I consistently get in a position where I'm hitting a shot I like rather than one I don't.

At the *same time* I want to maximize my opponent's weaknesses and minimize their strengths. I want them to be hitting shots they don't like from positions they don't want. I'll lose if I go strength to strength. I'm good, however, at working my strengths against my opponent's weaknesses.

The goal of my game plan is to turn the other player's own game against him. I did it to McEnroe that night at the '87 Masters in New York (more on that coming up), against Becker in the U.S. Open in '87, and I've done it to many others elsewhere.

Ahead are my keys for taking a player out of their A game and making them try to beat you with their B game, for picking apart a player's strokes and game plan and turning their advantage into your advantage.

Who's Doing What to Whom?

In order to follow the plan successfully you need to understand what's going on in the match, with your game, your opponent's game, and with the interaction of the two. My coach at Pepperdine, Allen Fox, used to tell me, "Always be asking yourself during a match who's doing what to whom." That means knowing how and why points are being won and lost. It means knowing what's going on out on the court.

Are you losing points because your opponent is successfully attacking you at the net or eating up your second serve? Does the other player beat you from the baseline? Is your opponent crushing overheads? Are your forehands falling short? Are you getting passed when you come to the net (and on which side)? Is the other player running around the backhand? Are they great with the groundies until you pressure them at the net? What is their style of play—retriever, serve volley, or something else?

The correct tennis response to any situation during your match can only be determined by knowing "who's doing what to whom." A successful player knows the answer. They may not know the exact numbers and percentages (e.g. 62 percent of first serves good), but they have a sense of it. It's an ability you can develop if you work at it.

Most recreational tennis players don't know who's doing what to whom during their match. They don't pay attention. They don't observe and analyze what's going on. Believe it or not, I've even had a player at one of my camps tell me he didn't realize his opponent was a lefty until the middle of the first set. "Now I know why those shots to the ad court kept coming back so good." Right! He was hitting into the guy's *forehand* thinking it was his backhand. He was not aware of what was happening out on the court.

The Combination to the Lock

Every player's game is like a combination lock. Without the combination it's tough to open, but with the combination it gets a lot easier. Knowing who's doing what to whom gives you the combination to the lock.

For me that came relatively easy once I really started applying it during matches when I turned pro. When I was a kid growing up near Oakland I was a major sports nut. I was fanatical about the Raiders, Warriors, 49ers, Giants, and A's. I always tried to figure out what was going to happen next in the games I saw, who was going to do what.

One of my idols was Kenny Stabler of the Raiders: The Snake. I'd watch him at quarterback and try to guess what play was going to get called. Would he throw to Casper or Balitnikoff, and in what pattern? Or, with the A's, would Catfish Hunter throw a knockdown pitch right after somebody hit a homerun off him? (Answer: Yes.) Or how would the infield and outfield position itself for various hitters in different situations? How would the Warriors get the ball to Rick Barry with ten seconds left in the game? It was just automatic for me. I loved to analyze what was going on out there.

Later, when I was starting out on tour, it was the same. I studied a lot—not books, but other players. Anytime I saw someone new I'd go watch them play and check out their game. Another player would say to me, "Hey, Boris Becker from Germany is on court 3," and I'd go over to see him hit.

Fat Fritz and My Little Black Book

Initially, I was watching more out of curiosity than with any great purpose. I didn't work hard on using that information in my matches. This changed one day during my third month on tour. I played a match against Fritz Buehning. He was a big guy with a powerful serve. In fact, he was too big to get around the court well, but when his serve was working he didn't need to get around the court very well. Fritz was built like a lineman for U.C.L.A., his alma mater. In fact, his nickname was "Fratz" (short for Fat Fritz). I figured he'd be a pushover.

Typical of my matches in those days I just showed up and expected that if I played well I'd win. I hadn't given any thought to Fratz, his game, or how to exploit it. I lost quick in straight sets 6–2, 6–2. What burned me up more than losing was knowing that if I'd given some thought (before and during the match) to what I should be trying to do I'd have beaten him. A big guy like that who isn't quick and doesn't like to bend his knees? Piece of cake. Just start moving him around with groundstrokes and when he comes to the net give him some dippers that drop low and throw up an occasional lob. I didn't give any thought to my tactics and got blown off the court.

After that I got serious about collecting and using information *about* my opponents *against* my opponents. After that I started writing things down. It's when I started my little black book.

Now a lot of players have a little black book with names and numbers in it. Yannick Noah's had so many in it he needed help just carrying it. But my little black book was different. It had names in it, but they were the names of tennis players. It had numbers in it, but they were the numbers of unforced errors, winners, and forcing shots on particular strokes. I counted mistakes on backhand volleys, overheads, forehand and backhand groundstrokes. I kept track of winners on those shots and watched what they liked to do in specific situations.

Most recreational players watch a match like they're looking at somebody play Nintendo at a video arcade. They just stare. I'd watch a match like I was studying for a history test. In 1984 when I first checked out Boris (in Philadelphia), I saw that when he was attacked on his backhand side he loved to go down the line. And that while he had a huge forehand, if he started to miss a few shots with it the rest of his game could suffer. As you saw, I later used that information *about* him *against* him to beat him several times, including the '87 U.S. Open.

Numbers, patterns, and tendencies. I'd see Paul Annacone always try to come to the net on a big point and make a note of it. I'd watch McEnroe swing his can opener serve wide on the ad court when he needed a point. I marked down that Connors occasionally had trouble with shots that came in low to his forehand.

The Tennis Lie Detector: Pressure

As I was watching and studying a player over several sets I'd see him fall into predictable patterns in certain situations. Especially under pressure. Pressure is the ultimate lie detector. That's when strokes speak the truth. On a big point what does a player do? They avoid (or try to avoid) the shot they don't feel comfortable with. That's when the flaws are magnified. It's when you see what their "true" game is like.

Here's how pressure works. When a player with a questionable backhand is up 4–2 in a set they may hit that backhand okay. No pressure, right? They're relaxed and ahead. When they're *down* 2-4 that backhand may get a little tentative because of nerves. And on a set point? Forget it. Pressure gets right to the heart of the matter. Under pressure is when a player will try like the devil to avoid hitting the shot they don't really trust. I want to know what that shot is so I can try to force them to hit it under pressure.

For example, if it's your opponent's backhand that is suspect, you know that they'll try to run around it on a big point. That's when I would try to set it up by swinging them a little wide on the forehand first. By pulling them wide on their forehand side and then hitting to the backhand you make it so they can't run around it. Or if they do they'll be hitting off balance. That's how you use information *about* your opponent *against* your opponent.

Agassi at First Glance

I scouted Andre Agassi in '86 at Stratton Mountain. Here was this skinny little kid with scraggly hair taking absolutely the best cut at the ball I had ever seen. Unbelievable! And people were telling me he wasn't going to do much because he had kind of flopped out as a junior. I didn't buy that.

Actually I had seen him for the first time when I was at the Alan King Classic in Las Vegas in 1981. I just happened to see him working out on a back court at Caesar's Palace. Even then his power and ability to take the ball so early got my attention. He was eleven years old.

It took me a while to put together that the kid with the bleached hair at Stratton Mountain was the same person I'd seen five years earlier in Las Vegas. Only now his hair was brighter and his strokes were bigger. In '86 I wrote down that his groundstrokes were brutal. Especially from the mid-court, where he had this great ability to take the ball on the rise and just really "de-struct" it. He radiated confidence. He was hitting the ball a ton and I could imagine the pressure he could put on a player. I also made a note that his volleys didn't look too strong, but that the rest of his game was so good it didn't matter.

When Andre lost in the finals of three slams (two French Opens and the U.S. Open) I thought maybe that his strokes were big, but his heart was small. Then he put it all together at Wimbledon in '92 and showed what he had inside. And it's a lot. Andre has a ton of heart.

It's funny. A lot of my early observations in my little black book still hold true. Some of them don't. I saw Mats Wilander for the first time in Bangkok in '81. I studied him while he played a match and didn't see anything special—no big serve, no big power, no outrageous shots. I figured he was just another solid Swedish player. I was right about Andre's potential and wrong about Mats. Seven months later Wilander won the French Open. I had to make a few additions to the "Wilander" section of my black book.

I saw that Stefan Edberg generally preferred to go crosscourt on his forehand volley. I wrote down that his one-handed backhand was one of the best in the business (Lendl's was the other). But I also noted that his forehand was not a weapon—extremely weak for a top player. His grip was bad and the whole stroke was not as impressive as everything else in his arsenal. Believe me, I made a note of that because there was very little I could write down about him that was negative.

I kept jotting down little things I noticed. Then when I had a match coming up against a player I'd check my notebook and see what was there. It was sort of like scouting reports in baseball; helping the pitcher know a batter's tendencies and letting the batter know what a pitcher likes to do in certain situations. It gave me a good idea of what to expect and helped get me thinking about what I had to do to keep that player from playing the shots he was most comfortable with.

Be a Good Scout

Do your own scouting. When you're at your club or the public courts watching a match with players you expect to face in the future, pay attention. Where do they make mistakes? What shots do they like to hit? Do they pound the overhead, but miss the volley? Do they hit a great angled crosscourt forehand, but miss it down the line? Are they fast getting to net, but slow changing directions?

Do they have a great first serve and no second serve? Are they consistent with their backhand except when it's attacked? Do they come to the net on short balls? Can they make a good approach shot, and does it have topspin or slice? What do they do when they need a forehand passing shot, crosscourt, or down the line? A backhand passing shot? How bad is their backhand? And *what happens under pressure?*

Look for patterns in their play. How do they win points? How do they lose points? What is their style of play?

Watch a set and keep track. When they lose or win a point make a note of it. Remember what they do at game point or set point. You'll see a pattern of their weaknesses and strengths. It's part of what you'll use before the match in your preparation and during the match in deciding how to play.

Know Thyself (And Thy Tennis Game)

Do to yourself what you are doing to others. Learn about your game. You may think you know your strengths and weaknesses, but you're probably not as bad (or as good) as you think. Take notes after a match or have a friend watch one of your sets and keep track of "who's doing what to whom."

Take a lesson from your club pro. But not the kind of lesson you usually take. Sit down for coffee and ask him or her to tell you what they'd tell another player about how to beat you. How are you vulnerable? What are your strong points? Have them analyze your game (and your opponent's, while you're at it). And pay them for their time—it's as valuable as hitting balls.

When you play a match have a friend keep track of your game. Find out just how many double faults, unforced errors, and winners you hit. Believe me, it's vitally important to a thinking player. In fact, a company in Florida just started manufacturing a pocket computer that allows you to do just that. The Tennis Analyst gives you information about why you won or lost. If you're too busy to write it down this will keep track of it for you. It's recognition of the importance of knowing who's doing what to whom.

"A Fool Is Someone Who Doesn't Know
What They Don't Know."—Anon.

I believe the most effective athletes are the ones who know their *weaknesses*. Of course they know what they *can* do. But, just as important, they know what they *can't* do.

The Snake was a beautiful example of that. He knew his limitations and worked around them. He knew he couldn't really throw long so he worked the fourteen- or eighteen-yard pass to perfection. He knew he had slow feet so when he dropped back and got trapped he took the punishment instead of risking a stupid mistake running around.

He'd look for his spots and if they weren't there he was willing to take the beating. He wouldn't risk mistakes trying something he knew he couldn't do. Stabler was a very intelligent athlete. He maximized his strengths.

But, just as important, Kenny Stabler minimized his weaknesses. (Sound familiar? Maximize, minimize.) And he was tough as hell. You've got to love that combination. It won a Super Bowl for the Raiders, right? All through the '80s Joe Montana did the same. He knew what he could do and he knew what he couldn't do. I tried to bring those same assets to the tennis court and so should you.

A better understanding of your own game (with input from a club pro) will give you better results. You'll have a clear understanding of what you've got to work with. Your tactics out on the court will become more calculated and less haphazard.

Take Notes During and After Class

I also recommend that you take out a notebook during a changeover and write down information as it occurs to you in a match. As you do it more often, you'll be like a computer logging information about who's doing what to whom.

And of course the best time of all for recording information is right after a match. *Always spend a little time reviewing what just happened in the match. Grade yourself and come to some conclusions about what you did right and wrong. Add information about your opponent. Why did you win or lose?* It's amazing how perceptive you can be if you just decide to focus on it.

Having collected all of this before, during, and after a match, you'll want to use it to your advantage. We'll get to that in a minute.

Drawing the Wrong Conclusions

I kept that notebook of my scouting reports going until 1986. Then I started to notice I was being influenced too much by my belief about my chances of winning. I'd see somebody out there who looked bad and I'd be thinking, "Hey, there's no way I'm gonna lose to this guy. He's playing like a plumber!"

My reaction to Wilander was an example. I didn't think he was a plumber, I just didn't think he was anything special. Wrong attitude to have going into a match. Or I would do just the opposite. I'd see Becker and catch myself thinking, "Holy Cow, there's no way I'm gonna beat this guy. He's playing awesome!" It's not good to go into a match thinking you can't win.

I didn't want to assume anything other than that I'd have a chance to win if I gave it everything I had physically and mentally, that I'd have to fight like hell in every match. So I quit scouting players myself. I asked my coach, Tom Chivington, to take over that job. He began doing my scouting and giving me the analysis of a player before a match.

For your own scouting reports just stick to the basics. Strengths. Weaknesses. Patterns. Unforced errors. Favorite shots in certain situations. You can do it while watching a match. You can do it while playing a match. You can do it after a match. But do it. By knowing "who's doing what to whom" you can capitalize on a tremendous advantage. Here's a great example of how I used that advantage to beat a good friend.

The Combination to Krickstein's Lock

A couple of years ago I faced Aaron Krickstein during a tournament in Brisbane, Australia. We get along well off the court and work out occasionally, but during a match he's just another guy trying to take money out of my kids' college fund. Just like every other player I face he's trying to kick my butt and send me home a loser. It's not hard for me to get motivated against him, but it is hard for me to face that bazooka forehand Aaron's perfected. He controls play with it by hitting routine winners from the baseline and generally putting me on the defensive in every point.

I hadn't had much luck against him over the years because I couldn't figure out a way to neutralize that power. He'd jerk me around until he'd opened up the court and then blast a winner. He was doing it to me again in Brisbane.

Then something happened during a point that got my attention. I hit a slice backhand that unintentionally landed short on his forehand side. He ran in and hit it. But nothing special, just a routine forehand and not the monster he usually unleashed. I tried it again a little later. This time I intentionally hit a soft short slice to his forehand. He ran in. Hit a return with nothing on it which I put away. A light went on in my head.

Was I on to something? Krickstein loved to camp on the baseline where the ball would sit up for him and he could knock it off with that big power spin. It was like playing T-ball for him. But with a soft slice that landed short just inside the service line he lost his favorite shot. He couldn't get under the ball because it stayed low. It meant he couldn't really crank the topspin. And it was soft, so it gave him no pace to use. He was hitting from an awkward position and he was on the run.

He couldn't hit a forcing shot and never a winner. What he gave me was a playable ball that I'd drive deep to his backhand. He was suddenly out of position playing a shot that wasn't his first choice. He'd make a weak return and there I'd be waiting. From then on it was easy.

The Payoff

I had applied part of the formula just like you should be doing with your opponents. I had minimized Krickstein's great forehand strength from the baseline and maximized a weaker aspect of his game. Suddenly I was making him try to beat me with a backhand that wasn't as strong instead of that world-class forehand. He was leading in the first set 3–2 when I made the discovery. I then won six games in a row and went on to beat him in straight sets and win $32,400. By knowing "who's doing what to whom" and being able to capitalize on it I had found a solution to his major weapon.

You're thinking I'm a little dense for not figuring it out sooner? I was so worried about his forehand that it never occurred to me that I should try and make him hit it from a different position, especially one that was *closer* to the net. I discovered that accidentally. But once I saw it I took full advantage of it.

Okay, that's how I've used information about a player's game against him. Recognize. Analyze. Capitalize. Next let me give you the combination to the locks of the players you face in tournaments, ladder matches, and just your regular Tuesday game. When facing a particular style or problem you'll know the best options for you to capitalize on.

Next: What to do and when to do it.

8

Destroying Your Opponent's Game Plan

Identify the Problem

You know who the players are who give you trouble, the opponent whose style of play or type of shots beat you more often than not. For you it may be a serve-volley player or a retriever. It could be a lefty who always gives you problems. It could be somebody who's very fast out on the court, a bloopster, or someone with a huge first serve. And, of course, you get players with combinations of these abilities.

Every player at every level has at least one opponent whose style gives them fits. You'll tell yourself, "Their game just doesn't match up very well for me." That opponent for me is Ivan Lendl. I've never beaten him. At last count I was 0 for lifetime. He's like a tennis version of Darth Vader for me. My son Zack even gave me a dinosaur toy to carry in my bag when I play against him. "Maybe it'll scare him, Daddy." I hope it does. When Ivan sees me heading out on the court to play him it's gotta be tough for him not to drool. He's beaten me sixteen straight times.

On tour, beating that "nemesis" player is more difficult, because pros develop their particular game to such a high level of proficiency that it's tough to find any cracks in their armor. Secondly, when you do force them away from their best shots their next level of shots is still pretty darn good. That's why Lendl is so tough for me to beat.

When I force him out of his A game, he beats me with his B game. And Ivan doesn't have any C game. Fortunately, I don't have to make a living playing just Lendl. And neither do you. However, there are opponents who give you headaches just like he gives me. And against those players keep what follows in mind.

The typical weekend or club player's game is one-dimensional. It's pretty easy to crack open. They've usually got a single shot they like and are fairly good at. They play a certain style and go with that. Make them change styles or take away their favorite shot and you'll win because their next alternative isn't nearly as effective. In fact, it's probably pretty bad. So how do you do it?

First, the Bad News

Here's the truth. Some days you won't be able to do anything. You *won't* be able to turn it around. Your opponent will successfully do their thing and you'll lose. They'll successfully attack your weaknesses and make you play their game at their rhythm and you'll lose. *Some* days you will not win regardless of what you do. I've learned that lesson well with Lendl.

Now, the Good News

Let me tell you something else I've learned and apply every single time I go out on the tennis court to compete. Most of the time there is a way to win. You just have to figure out what it is. Club players don't believe this. You probably don't believe it. And if you don't it's because you've fallen into a common trap.

Don't Overestimate or Underestimate

The average player tends to go into most matches thinking the wrong way. They believe pretty strokes mean something. They assume better conditioning means more than it does. They assume the opponent who's got more natural ability or had more experience will probably win. They think past results dictate future results. That kind of thinking will get you beat because it leads you to the wrong conclusions.

That's why I had to quit scouting players myself and have my coach do it instead. I started to make assumptions about who was going to win or lose. I started to overestimate or underestimate players. As a result I either assumed victory or defeat. Assuming victory will get you beat and so will expecting to lose.

The only thing I wanted to assume was this: I could win any match against anyone if I worked hard out on the court physically. But more than that, I could win if I worked hard mentally. When I go into a match I take my lunch bucket, my hard hat, and expect to work for my pay. I came to believe that it wasn't up to my opponent whether I won or lost. Most of the time *it was up to me. And it's up to you, too.*

So if that's true why haven't I beaten Lendl? Simple. I've had chances and blown them. In part III, on psyching, I'll explain how a guy like Lendl will try to beat you with his racket first. If that doesn't work he'll beat you with his gamesmanship. On those days when I could have beaten him physically he beat me up emotionally or mentally. He's a master of it. But the point is I *could* have beaten him. He knew how to take back control of the game when it had slipped away. My chance will come again.

Knowing "who's doing what to whom" puts you in a position to consider your options and capitalize on the best one. Next I want to tell you how to take advantage of the following types of players, shots, or situations that may be giving you trouble out on the court. They include:

The Retriever
The Player With Speed
The Attack to Your Backhand
The Serve
The Return of Serve
The Serve-Volley Player
The Weak Serve
The Lefty's Serve
The Heater

The Retriever

You know who the Retrievers are that you play. In fact, you may be one yourself. Don't feel bad. I've been accused of being a Retriever myself occasionally. A match I played with Boris Becker in the semis of the 1989 Thriftway A.T.P. Championship in Cincinatti was described as "like watching a man chasing a chicken around with a stick." I was the chicken. Boris had the stick.

The description may have been accurate, but the chicken won the match in three sets by getting everything back *over and over again*. On that day I was a great Retriever. In fact, I eventually won the tournament with wins over Sampras, Chang, and Edberg.

Just so we get our terms straight let's agree on what a Retriever is. The basic garden variety Retriever (also known as a Pusher, a Rabbit, or a Golden Retriever) stays on the baseline and gets *everything* back. They don't use pace. They don't use depth. They don't use spin. They don't use angles. They don't use touch. But they do drive you nuts!

Everything comes back. They chase everything down and they do it relentlessly. They're married to the baseline and will stay there all day. As Retrievers perfect their game they may start developing spin, depth, and/or pace. But their basic game plan stays exactly the same: *get everything back*.

The Bloopster or Moonballer is a variation of the Retriever, a refinement. Harold Solomon perfected this style and Andrea Yeager got pretty good at it—hitting balls very high over the net, deep in your court, with extreme topspin. Thomas Muster and Jose Higueras use this style a lot today. They stand out there and just keep hitting these hard, heavy topspin shots that bounce up shoulder high.

Moonballs are frustrating because they hypnotize you. You stand there and before long you quit thinking. The Moonballer keeps looping the ball to you without mistakes. Over and over again. They're like the garden variety Retriever because they really test your patience. The main distinction between the Moonballer and the typical Retriever is that the Moonballer hits the *same* shot back to you all the time: the big looper.

A Retriever's style of play can be very effective against an opponent who doesn't know how to break it down or gets frustrated. Boris got frustrated. Toward the end of our match in Cincinnati all he wanted to do was get off the court and take something for his headache. He was ready to lose.

The Club Variety Retriever

Here's how it looks at the club level. I was watching a match between a couple of 4.0 players at the San Francisco Tennis Club after a workout there. One of the players is a classic Retriever. His name is Mason Grigsby, but his nickname is The Great Grigsby because he's so steady at the baseline. I was just casually watching when the following point occurred. During the exchange his opponent hit a good drop shot and Mr. Retriever, The Great Grigsby, raced toward the net. I didn't think he had any chance of getting to the ball, but he did and pushed it back to his opponent's baseline.

The Great Grigsby was now at the net in position to close out the point. I thought. To my surprise (and before his shot had even landed) he turned and headed back to the safety of the baseline. A *classic Retriever*. He had gone from being three feet away from the net back to the baseline without even bothering to see what shot his opponent was going to hit. He wanted no part of the net. The baseline was his security blanket. That style of play is typical of a Retriever and it can drive you up the wall if you don't know what to do about it.

Beating a Retriever is tough because the points go on forever and they test your patience to the extreme. Bjorn Borg and Chris Evert were the greatest of all time at it. Today the best examples out there are Alberto Mancini, Todd Witsken, and Michael Chang before he added a little net game to his arsenal. All of them specialize in that "everything-comes-back" style.

Chang is particularly tough because he can get to absolutely everything. His calf and thigh muscles are so developed they look like they belong on a person twice his size, and they generate tremendous speed and give him super coverage, maybe the best of any player in the world. They say when Michael was a kid he could outrun his shadow. The problem for me is that he can still outrun most of my shots. However, speed alone doesn't win matches. Here's how I play (and have beaten) him and how you can apply my technique to your own favorite Retriever.

1. Patience Is Your Greatest Ally

The average Retriever's success is based on the same principles as Chinese water torture. It's dull. It's repetitious. It's slow. The same thing happens over and over again. And it will drive you up the wall. Retrievers love being a human backboard. Push the ball to them and they push it right back. They'll outrun you. They'll outsteady you. And they'll outlast you. Your mind begins to go.

Prepare to Suffer

If you're going to the dentist you prepare yourself mentally. You tell yourself, "It's gonna hurt, but it'll be over soon." You adopt a certain mind set. By the time you hear, "Open wide. This isn't going to hurt a bit," you're mentally set to suffer. You need to do the same against a Retriever. Prepare to suffer. The right mind set is important. It may or may not help at the dentist's office, but it will definitely help against the Retriever.

Preparing yourself mentally for what's ahead is necessary because a Retriever's style works on your head as much as anything. You must go into a match against this kind of player really understanding that every rally is going to be long. You're going to have to hit four or five or six or seven or more shots than you'd normally have to hit. *And*, when you do hit a good shot expecting a winner or a weak return, the Retriever will get it back. Mentally, you have to get ready for lots of tennis balls coming back over the net. Know it. Believe it. Expect it. Here's why.

Retrievers may be dull and repetitious, but they're also very consistent and patient. Consistency is a Retriever's primary asset. At any level of play this is a valuable tool. At the club level, among average players, it may be the most valuable tool. Consistency is tough to beat. On tour a player has to hit winners to beat another player. However, at most other levels it's the one who keeps the ball in play best who usually wins, and the Retriever really keeps the ball in play. Unforced errors determine results more than spectacular shots do. That's the key to the Retriever's game. It's also the key to beating it.

The Retriever's game may be consistent, but it's also limited. If you're patient and know how to take advantage of their game you can break them down. This is what happened to Chang. Other pros started to exploit his baseline Retriever game to their own advantage. They started to neutralize his advantage in speed (more on that coming up) and exploit his one-dimensional game. Until he developed a net game and improved his serve, Chang was getting beat. Now, he's winning again.

Why You Lose to a Retriever

The Retriever beats you because you choose the wrong game plan. As more and more balls keep coming back at you, frustration sets in.

You get impatient. You try harder. You go for better and better shots, deeper, harder, more angled. You end up trying for shots you don't have and never did. You try shots McEnroe wouldn't attempt. The Pusher keeps them coming back until you screw up.

They keep retrieving, knowing you'll eventually make an unforced error. Or possibly you'll just give up and start pushing the ball back, too. You'll lose. They're better at pushing than you are. That's why it's important to set your attitude going in. Recognize that patience is a great ally when a Retriever stands on the other side of the court.

Having prepared yourself mentally for a long day at the office with points that go on and on, here are the other tactics that can tilt a match in your favor against the Pusher.

2. GET TO THE NET

Your primary goal when playing against a Retriever is to make them hit some real tennis shots. Instead of their usual "push it back" or "keep it in play" stuff you want to force them to try something specific. You want to *get them out of their comfort zone*. The first way to do it is by coming to the net. Even if that isn't your normal game you must get to the net. That means when you get a short ball (even a medium short ball) *get to the net*. Go on the offense, but do it the right way. Not by trying to hit winners from the baseline or other low-percentage shots, but by coming to the net when the opportunity presents itself. And even sometimes when it doesn't present itself.

What this does to most weekend Retrievers is jerk them out of their comfort zone. It forces them to decide what specific shot they're supposed to make. Should they pass crosscourt? Should they pass down the line? Should they hit the ball right at you? A lob? Suddenly they face the problem of having to make quick decisions.

Hey, Retrievers don't like to have to think of all that stuff! It's easier just to keep pushing the ball over the net into that big wide open court you've given them by staying at the baseline. It gives them all that room for error. Take it away! Narrow their options by narrowing their target. I honestly believe you could almost come to the net without your racket in hand and win some points from a Retriever. Just the sight of a person standing there shakes them up a little. But take your racket along just in case they actually get the ball over the net.

A word of caution. I'm not suggesting that you should be running to the net every time a point starts (unless you're comfortable with doing that). Be selective. On shorter balls, start coming in regularly. On balls in your mid-court, if you've got a good chance of making a decent approach shot, consider coming in. A deeper ball? Occasionally, just for the surprise effect. How about on the Retriever's second serve? Good idea. On their first serve? Now you'll see them start to get uncomfortable. You'll like what you see.

Obviously, what you're trying to do is unsettle them, get them watching you instead of the ball. They'll start rushing their shots and mishitting their shots. Suddenly, they'll start giving you what at the club level is the key to victory: *unforced errors*. The Retriever who starts making unforced errors will lose.

3. BRING THE RETRIEVER TO THE NET

You have another option with the Retriever, and again it's aimed at getting them out of their comfort zone, forcing them to do something besides camping at the baseline.

This option involves drawing them in toward the net like I did with Krickstein. Bring them in close. Make them hit some shots at the net. Let them show you a good approach shot, a good backhand volley (fat chance), some overheads (not if the sun is shining), some half-volleys (call me collect when they do), and anything else you can offer up to them. By doing this you've taken a Retriever's A game away and forced them to rely on their B game.

In order to accomplish this you'll have to hit some short shots. If you don't think you can hit that kind of shot, practice it. Remember, you've done it accidentally plenty of times. Now try doing it on purpose. Because once you've done that you've effectively set your trap. The Retriever hates the net.

The Great Grigsby Attempts a Volley

Remember The Great Grigsby, the Retriever I was watching who got drawn into the net? Here's the rest of that story. After he'd raced in close to the net and pushed the ball deep to his opponent he ran right back to his own baseline. His opponent then hit *another* drop shot. The Great Grigsby came charging in a second time. And again he hit the ball over the net to the baseline. And again he turned and ran right back to his own baseline. This was getting interesting. His opponent then hit a *third consecutive drop shot*. I had never seen anyone hit three straight drop shots in my life and get away with it! Think about it. Would there be a fourth?

No. The Great Grigsby ran up to the net once again. For whatever reason he finally decided it was time to take advantage of his court position and finish off the point. He hit a volley. Or at least I think he was trying to hit a volley. From his stroke it was hard to tell. Not only did he hit the ball three feet wide, but on his follow-through his racket banged into the net. Now I was beginning to understand why he kept retreating to the security of his baseline.

Three consecutive times he was brought into the net. Twice he went back immediately to the comfort of the baseline. He was acting like it was illegal to get close to the net. Later I asked him why he didn't just stay there the first time. He told me (and this is a key to cracking open a Retriever's game), "I just feel more comfortable at the baseline." From what I had seen I could understand his thinking. Take them out of their comfort zone and you'll win.

4. Softer Is Harder

In most cases a Retriever feeds off your pace. They love to take what you've supplied (energy in the form of a hard hit ball) and turn it right back on you. The harder you hit the ball the harder they hit the ball! Only they aren't hitting harder, you are. And the harder you swing the more likely it is you'll make a mistake. They just stick their racket out (and with the new wide bodies that's *all* they have to do) and like magic the ball comes back harder. It's not magic. It's physics. Throw a ball against a wall without any zip and it comes back without any zip. Throw it against a wall *with* some zip and it comes back with zip. In the case of a Retriever they are the wall and you are the zip. The wall usually wins.

The middle-level player who faces a Retriever falls into the trap of trying to hit the ball harder and harder to win the point. The Pusher sits on the baseline blocking back hard-hit shot after hard-hit shot. They love it because they know eventually you'll overhit and make an error. Finally you hit one over the back fence or into the net. And the Retriever won't even say "thank you" for doing all the work for them.

5. HIT YOUR SECOND SERVE FIRST

Teaching pros like to say that the average weekend player has two primary serves: slow and slower. There's a lot of truth to that. While someone on tour like Goran Ivanisevic can pump the ball in at 130 miles per hour, the weekend player serves at less than half that speed. So don't worry so much about trying to serve up aces and service winners. Especially against a Retriever. In fact, think "second serve" against that kind of player.

Once again it robs them of pace, makes *them* try to generate it. It will make them actually have to take a swing at the ball. They don't like that. When they start trying to generate their own pace, watch the unforced errors start popping up. And if they just block your soft serve back it'll fall short. When it does you've just been given a ticket to the net. Use it.

No Insult Intended

Let me clear up one thing you may have thought about when I said that Borg, Evert, Chang, Krickstein, and some others would generally be classified as Retrievers. Obviously, players of their caliber don't just push the ball or block it back. I mean no disrespect when I call them Retrievers. They have taken that style of play to its highest level. Having someone come to the net doesn't bother them like it would the Retrievers you play against.

When I come to the net against Michael Chang, believe me, he's got ten ways he can beat me. The problem is if I don't come to the net he'll retrieve me to death. I played him recently in the semis of a tournament and lost the first set 6–0. I started coming to the net in the second set and came close to winning it! Why didn't I start coming in sooner? That's what I'm asking myself. In any case, unless you're better at their kind of game than they are you have to figure out another way to beat them.

Next time you play a Retriever try bringing some of what I've suggested into the match. Give yourself some time to get used to the new tactics. Develop a sense of when to do what and what works best for you. You'll like the results. And as you get more comfortable with it you'll see match point going in your favor more often than it did before.

The Player With Speed

Occasionally you face an opponent who's extremely quick. They get to drop shots. They cover lobs. Shots that pull them off the court are no problem. They're like waterbugs. They skitter all over the place and have you trying harder and harder to hit a shot they can't reach. Forget it. They'll get to *everything*. And by the time you've hit that one winner (and one may be all you'll get) you've committed lots of unforced errors.

Michael Chang has that kind of speed. I'll force him way wide on his forehand and come in behind it. He'll run it down and make a return. I'll be coming in and hit a volley wide to his backhand and start licking my chops. No way can he get there in time to do anything with it. Chang *will* get there. He *will* make a shot. He *will* beat me with a passing shot. Tremendous speed and coverage. Very quick.

Who's your Michael Chang, that player with unusual speed? Here's a very direct approach to minimizing their advantage.

DON'T LET A RUNNER RUN

Players with speed love to run and they love to hit the ball on the run. Swing them wide off the deuce court and they'll hit a good running forehand. And they'll do the same on the other side. They're real good at it because with their speed, they get to a lot of balls and get a lot of practice.

Don't let them use their speed. Take away their asset. How? Hit deep down the middle. Make them play more in the wheelhouse. Suddenly instead of running *to* the ball (which they love) you're forcing them to run *away from* the ball, to get out of its way. You're crowding them and not letting them exploit their speed. Think of wherever they are standing as a target and them as the bull's-eye.

Quit trying just to hit shots out of their range. Part of their success comes from mistakes you make trying to hit a shot they can't get to. Don't try to make it harder for them to get to your shot. Make it easier! Hit it *at* them and see what happens. They'll overrun shots. They'll start to hit shots off balance. They'll start to hit weak returns more frequently.

But remember that it's important with all of these tactics to use them intelligently and prudently. When you're on to something that works don't use it exclusively. Mix it in with the rest of your game. Keep your opponent off balance wondering what you'll do. Your results will be better.

The Attack to Your Backhand

One of the first tennis tactics any player uses or encounters is "attack the backhand". For most recreational players the backhand is usually the weakest. If you somehow had to play a match against a player you'd never seen before and couldn't warm up against (or spy on), the very first thing you'd test is their backhand. Automatic. Most players have a better forehand than backhand, including you and the players you'll face.

So what do you do if your backhand is questionable and you face a player who really exploits your liability, who knows how to get everything to your weak side and does it relentlessly? Until you get a lesson from your club pro and work on it, is there any way to minimize the damage? Yes.

1. BE CONSERVATIVE WITH YOUR BACKHAND

When your backhand is being attacked your first instinct is to attempt a better shot than you're capable of hitting reliably. You try to be an overachiever. Instead you become an underachiever. When your opponent comes to the net your mind short-circuits: "Crisis. Danger at the net. *Do something!*" The problem is you have limited resources with which to "do something" on your backhand side. Your brain tells your body to do more. You panic and squeeze off a desperate shot that goes long, wide, or into the net.

Instead, do just the opposite. Think "less" not "more." Just get the darn ball over the net and back in the court. Don't worry about hitting that great backhand return. Be conservative. Be patient with your backhand. Your first duty is to avoid the unforced error. Initially, force your opponent to make a shot, to at least hit the ball.

If the other player volleys your conservative backhand shot for a winner regularly, move on to other options. But first, *make them hit the ball*. And you do that by not trying to get more out of your backhand than is there. Make sure your mediocre backhand doesn't make world-class errors.

2. RUN AROUND THE BACKHAND WHEN APPROPRIATE

You're thinking, "This is too obvious." You'd love to run around every single backhand you get for the rest of your life. But the important thing is to understand when you can do it *most effectively*.

If your opponent is hitting constantly to your backhand, but without much *pace* or *depth*, think of it as an invitation to hit your forehand. Run around the backhand and tee-off on the ball. Smack it. When you begin to take advantage of that opportunity your opponent will start trying to hit a better shot, one with greater depth and pace. If they can do it you've got a problem, but if they could do it easily they wouldn't be hitting short or without pace to begin with. Increase the difficulty of the shot they have to hit to get it to your backhand.

Again, shot selection is important. The player who tries to run around everything on the backhand side will find themselves getting jammed, hitting off balance, and losing even more points—not to mention getting exhausted. Look for opportunities to run around the backhand when your opponent's shot lacks depth or pace.

Also, keep this in mind: Running around a ball near the alley on the ad court (for a right-hander) can pull you wide and off the court. In this situation you should go for a winner or a good forcing shot. Otherwise your opponent can put you on a string; you've given them the whole court to hit to. Running around a ball hit in the deuce court (or close to the center line) leaves you right in the middle of the court and you don't need to be as ambitious with your shot.

3. GET TO THE NET

Your opponent can't force you to hit backhands from the baseline if you're at the net. Even if your backhand volley is weak it may be an improvement over your backhand groundstrokes on that particular day. A weak or mishit volley often drops in for a winner.

If you're losing lots of points on your backhand groundstrokes get into a position on court where you don't have to hit backhand groundstrokes. Look for your chances and *come to the net*.

4. ATTACK THE SECOND SERVE

There is another way you can take the offensive before your opponent has a chance to pressure your backhand. It allows you an (often overlooked) opportunity to get to the net. Most players don't think "attack" off someone's serve. However, if your opponent's second serve is typical (which is to say a variation on the Nerf ball) it shouldn't be difficult to hit a shot that allows you to follow it to the net. Just stand a step or two closer than your normal position for receiving. When you hit your return of serve immediately follow it to the net.

You have now taken your vulnerable backhand out of play as well as forced your opponent to make a more difficult shot.

Be reasonable. Don't try for a winner when you make an approach shot off the player's second serve. Go for placement. Get it in and even go for *their* backhand. Turnabout is fair play. See if you like the results.

Remember, this is what smart tennis is all about. Testing and probing. Shrinking the gate through which a player can attack your weaknesses and finding a way to go after their soft spots.

5. Don't Forget the Lob

Many players make the mistake of hitting a shot over and over again when it isn't working for them. Sometimes they'll do it for the whole match. It may be the approach down the line, a slice serve, a forehand volley, a forehand groundstroke, or an overhead. Or a backhand groundstroke. They never give up trying to make it work. If you're going down the dumper you've got to do something else or you'll lose.

At some point it's important to quit trying to correct the stroke and start winning some points. And with a backhand that isn't working (for whatever reason) you have another option when it's costing you games: the lob.

If your opponent is coming to the net on your backhand side and you haven't made a passing shot since that accidental one in the warm-up, *remember to lob*. Find out if they can hit an overhead. Do it once. Twice. Three or four times. Maybe they'll get dizzy looking up and have to sit down. Make them show you that they can hit an overhead. Not once, but several times. And preferably throw it up to their *backhand* side.

When a smart opponent sees you having a particular problem, you have to prevent them from exploiting it. You've got to keep the flesh wound from hemorrhaging, and you can do that by knowing and using your alternatives.

The Serve

Ask the experts what the most important shot in tennis is and they'll say the serve. Is it? Maybe on tour. For recreational tennis players that answer is doubtful. How often do you or your opponents hit aces or service winners? How many times does your serve force a return that puts you in a plus position you can take advantage of? And, most important, how often do you hold serve? Probably not as often as you should.

The pros expect to hold about four out of five of their service games. My own hold percentage is 77.9 and I'm not a great server. Pete Sampras and Michael Stich can get close to 90 percent. For recreational tennis players holding serve is often a 50–50 proposition. The serve *can* be the most important shot, but for most recreational players, it isn't. Even among women pros the serve isn't much of a weapon. For Martina Navratilova (in her prime) and Steffi Graf it can be. But generally it isn't the asset you'd expect from "the most important shot in tennis."

Hey, I'm not being critical. *I* usually don't control play with my serve. However, I'm good at managing it so it doesn't get exploited badly. I do that by good placement and getting the first serve in a lot.

Most club players just use their serve to get the point started. It's one of the reasons there are so many service breaks. The serve is the toughest shot to learn and the most difficult to hit, *especially under pressure*. Most of the time your serve probably doesn't do more than give your opponent a chance to immediately take the offensive. Why? For almost all club players the return of serve is an easier shot to hit than the serve, especially with the more powerful rackets. *Especially under pressure*.

This is because it's usually easier to *react* than to *act*, and the service return is a reaction. A short swing (something between a swing and blocking it back) can often put the receiver in charge of a point immediately. Add in the occasional double faults at pivotal moments (donating points and games to the server's opponent) and you can see why serving isn't the advantage for most players that it can be for guys like Pete Sampras, Michael Stich, Richard Krajicek, or Goran Ivanisevic.

If there is one shot in your collection that you can work on that will help your cause, it's the serve. I can say that because I've seen lots of players at clubs and public parks around the world for twenty years. If you can develop a penetrating, varied, and reliable serve you'll be looking for new opponents soon. Your buddies will get tired of losing to you. But good luck. Jimmy Connors went through his whole career and couldn't develop a threatening serve. But he did develop the world's best service *return* (until Agassi came along) and with it he won over a hundred championships. So, while you're waiting for that great new weapon, the serve (the one that will become "the most important shot in your game"), there's something else to think about.

The Return of Serve

I want to tell you what *can* become the most important shot for you with a minimum amount of work. It's your *return of serve*. It's a lot easier to improve this than it is trying to learn a big serve. With a strong return of serve you are constantly putting pressure on your opponent, capitalizing on weak servers and neutralizing better servers.

The return of serve is an opportunity to attack your opponent where it hurts most, by taking the offense away from them and by constantly threatening to break their service. A player who's always struggling to hold is like a fighter on the ropes. They worry about just surviving. It's mentally and physically very damaging to know your serve is going to be neutralized or taken advantage of over and over, that you're constantly struggling to avoid being broken.

How important can it be? Ask Connors. He was able to neutralize his opponent's service and then work the point to his advantage. At the pro level he made the return of serve his most important shot. One year at Wimbledon Jimmy played Roscoe Tanner and got aced almost twenty-five times. Jimmy still won the match. He made great plays on most of the other serves and kept the points going until he could capitalize.

A more dramatic example is the '92 Wimbledon final between Andre Agassi and Goran Ivanisevic. Andre got aced *thirty-seven times*. That's *nine games worth of aces*. Then add in Goran's service winners and you've got to wonder how Andre even stayed in the match, let alone won it. He won because his return of serve is a monster, the best ever, even better than Connors'—at least according to John McEnroe, a player with a great serve who faced both of them.

So here was a great match-up between a super server who had over two-hundred aces in the tournament and a great service returner. Who won? The great service returner. Knowing what your options are on a service return can produce quick results with little effort.

What I want to do is show you how you can capitalize on your opponent's serve by knowing what to do with your service return tactically. Whether it's a big serve and volley, a weak first or second serve, or anything else, you'll be able to minimize their serve and maximize your service return. You'll love the results.

The Serve-Volley Player

The great serve-volley players are incredibly tough when they're on their game. Guys like Edberg and Ivanisevic (and McEnroe at his best) put so much pressure on you to make better and better shots that the odds swing in their favor. It's one thing to make a tough backhand passing shot when the net is covered and it's early in the match. It's something else to try and hit the great passing shot on set point or match point! On the big points I'd much rather be trying to hit a volley up close than a passing shot from the baseline with somebody all over the net.

Stefan is one of the most difficult to play. He will serve and volley on every single point. He makes you hit the difficult shot over and over again. Even though his serve isn't as fast as Becker's he gets such a jump into the court with his service motion that he's almost always hitting his first volley from inside the service line. Because his serve has such torque on it he has more time to get in behind it. And he never misses the volley. Those volleys are like having bees attack you. They just keep coming and stinging.

The hard truth of the matter is that when a serve-volley player is really playing well you may have to kiss your lunch goodbye. But don't give up without a fight, because there are tactics you can use to take the play away from that type of game. Agassi used them successfully in the finals of Wimbledon and you can use the tactics in your own matches. You won't face attacks like Ivanisevic's, but you will face capable players who get in behind their serve and cause problems for you. Here are the tactics you need to apply. I know they work because I used them against Edberg to defeat him in the semis of the '91 L.A. Open when he was ranked number one in the world.

1. WATCH THE CORRECT MOVING OBJECT, CALMLY

When someone starts attacking you at the net it's human nature to watch them and not the tennis ball. At *all* levels of play—A, B, and C—there is an automatic urge to watch the player attacking you. But the player isn't attacking you, *the ball is.* The player doesn't come over the net, the ball does. Watch the ball. Concentrate totally on the ball.

I tell players at my tennis camps to start watching the ball as early as possible. Start watching it while it's still in its can! Unfortunately, most players at most levels get distracted when a body is moving at them at the same time a tennis ball is flying over the net. Their focus shifts off the ball and onto the body.

Good contact is almost impossible when you're watching the attacking player with one eye and the ball with the other. It's why so many of your returns go wide, long, or short. You *donate* the point to your opponent. I know because I've done it a lot myself, especially against McEnroe. He'll come in sometimes and stay back sometimes. So you get caught by surprise and suddenly Mac is coming in behind a serve. That's when I do everything I shouldn't. I take my eye off the ball a little. I rush my return a little. And even if I manage to wobble the ball over the net he's there waiting. With Edberg (who hasn't *not* come in behind his serve since he was seven) you expect it and it's a little easier to make yourself focus on the ball and swing normally.

You need to block out the server like the Texas Rangers' great slugger, Jose Canseco, blocks out the pitcher. He sees only a baseball. If he didn't he'd miss every time. Ted Williams, the last batter to hit .400 in a season, said he watched the ball so hard he could see the seams turning over as it got to the plate. *That's* how you watch a moving object.

You'll notice something happen as watching the ball becomes automatic. You *do* see the server, but peripherally. Your primary focus is still the tennis ball. Increasingly you see the onrushing player with your "secondary" level of vision. For many players it's the other way around. They see the opponent with their primary focus and the ball secondarily.

When you're seeing that ball more clearly remember to stay calm; avoid the panic attack. With a player coming at you there is a great tendency to speed up your swing, to jerk it. You tend to lose balance and form. Stay calm. Your primary goal, the goal that will produce the best results, is to take a rhythmic swing, controlled, balanced, and steady. The kind of swing you would probably take if the server *didn't rush the net.*

With better focus on the ball and a less frantic swing you'll make better contact with the ball. *Watch the ball, not the person who hit it. Don't jerk your swing.* You're now in a position to begin making some choices on your service return that can cause the net rusher some problems.

2. HIT A SOFT RETURN

When you're being attacked at the net a natural response is to hit the ball harder. You want to get the ball back past the net rusher before they can cover the net. A natural reaction, the old "fight or flight" impulse. You can't take flight when you're attacked at the net, so you fight, and the normal fight response is to hit hard. Resist it. Take some pace off your return of serve. Resist that urge to hit hard and to hit quick.

First of all, swinging fast and hard causes errors. In your panic to do something immediately, you give away a point. But more than that, a good serve-volley player can handle your pace (if you manage to hit it in the court) and simply use it against you. They'll angle off a volley with a short, crisp stroke before you can even finish your swing.

A poor volleyer also gets a little advantage when you pound a return. How? The most common mistake a bad volleyer makes is taking too big a swing on the volley. When you send the ball back hard they don't have time to wind up and overswing. They just stick the racket out, make contact, and angle off a volley. You've made them a better volleyer than they are.

Returning with less pace can help you accomplish something that can be even more important. By the time your opponent gets to the ball it will be dropping below the net (or at least dropping). The net rusher will have to hit up on it. Hitting a ball that's fallen below the net is a lot harder than hitting one that's above the net. Maybe John McEnroe can angle it off for a winner, but let your opponent try it. I can guarantee that the player across the net from you won't like a low, soft return that's dropping. Their volley (if they can make it) won't be penetrating, won't be low, and won't be a problem.

Obviously, you can also get that ball dipping below the net with topspin. The "dipper" is more difficult to execute, but just as effective. Either way works. Best of all, mix 'em up. Hit with less pace occasionally. By varying your shots you keep 'em guessing.

3. BUST A RETURN RIGHT AT YOUR OPPONENT

When I come to the net against Ivan Lendl I make sure my health insurance is paid up. I call him the Terminator. One of his tactics is to "seek and destroy." He'd as soon hit you as pass you. Obviously, most players on tour can fight off a ball hit directly at them from the baseline, but Lendl will nail you occasionally even when he's up close. I got hit so hard one time I had "Wilson" spelled upside down and backwards on my chest for a week.

But it's legitimate. After all, a player who's covering the net is basically trying to limit your escape options. They're stealing the court from you (with their body) and forcing you to hit to a smaller target. One way to escape is to go right at them. A running back in football generally tries to go around tacklers. When necessary, Eric Dickerson will put his head down and go right through the tackler.

Ivan isn't afraid to go through a net rusher in his own way. He wants you to have to keep in mind that he might go crosscourt. He might go down the line. He might lob. Or he might put the tennis ball right into your belly at one hundred miles an hour. He can make someone at the net look silly a lot of ways. And by occasionally hitting at that player he's added another option his opponent has to worry about. You can do the same. Don't be polite.

A player who wants to come in behind their serve should have to factor in that you aren't afraid to hit *at* them. It means they have to consider an additional option.

When to do it? Do it when your other options are limited, when the net rusher has closed off easier shots and forced you to make a difficult one to win the point. Then they become fair game.

And, just so you don't hurt yourself by swinging too hard, remember this. When I say "bust it" I don't mean wild flailing or overswinging. Take a full cut at the ball—aim for a high-velocity swing, but stay in control. Most players tend to slap at the ball when they want to hit harder. It's all arm and hand. Bust it, but don't break it.

Do this just enough to keep your net rusher guessing. One of the added payoffs is that they will tend to hit balls that are going out. Because the ball is getting to them quicker, because the element of surprise is at work, because it's harder to judge a ball's distance when it's coming right at you, players are likely to take a fast reflex swing at a ball hit directly at them even if it's headed out.

Remember this about sportsmanship. It's not appropriate to hit *at* someone if you're looking at a sitter. In other words, if you're hitting an overhead up close, or if you have another option that's an easy shot for a winner, it's inappropriate to nail someone just to get their attention. But if they're closing you off and you're looking at tough shots to get out of the point, your opponent is a legitimate target. Put your sights on their belly button and let it fly.

4. RETURN SERVE CROSSCOURT

Let me give you a rule that applies generally *whenever* you return serve, but especially when the server attacks you by coming to the net. *Hit your service return crosscourt* when possible.

It's a good idea to return serve crosscourt because of the logistics involved. When you try to return a serve down the line you have immediately brought the sidelines into play. You are flirting with hitting the ball wide. Being just a little off means that you lose a point without even making your opponent have to hit the ball. Also, as you know, the net is higher at the sides than in the middle. Finally, you have more court to hit to going diagonally, or crosscourt. Pretty solid reasons for going back crosscourt if possible, right? More court, less net, no sideline.

But there's another advantage to hitting crosscourt. By knocking your service return back diagonally you force your opponent who's coming to the net to make a more difficult volley. If they want to hit to the open court (*away* from you) *they* have to hit down the line. Suddenly they have to make a shot that gives them less court, more net, and brings the side line into play (this applies on either the deuce or the ad court). Or they can make the other choice and hit the ball back to you. That's okay—it saves you a lot of running.

So, as a rule (and especially on big points), go crosscourt on your service returns. It'll pay off with more balls staying in for you and more missed volleys for your opponent who's approaching the net.

5. LEARN TO LOVE THE LOB

The lob is often overlooked by club players returning a serve because it's a shot that seems difficult in that situation. Give it a chance. Remember, you don't really even have to swing. Basically you just have to block the ball back using the server's pace. Always try to lob to their backhand side. You'll see good results.

The element of surprise is what is important in this response. The serve-volley player who knows you're just going to keep trying to make a passing shot will try to get closer and closer to the net. If you occasionally throw up a lob it forces that player to protect themselves by not closing to the net as much. When you've got someone who is camping on the net, hoist a lob up to their backhand side. It'll keep them honest.

This is a response you rarely see on tour because of the difficulty of making a lob off a pro's serve, and because lobs tend to get eaten up at that level. At the club level the lob can be a useful return-of-serve option.

6. MIX AND MATCH

The tactics I've suggested here will work. The serve-volley player tends to put you on the defensive and get you on the run. You never get a rhythm going and everything is reactive. By adding what I've suggested to what you're now doing you'll make yourself less predictable, less defensive, and more varied. You'll force the serve-volley player to do more and more to win a point. Eventually their mistakes will start mounting up. That's when you'll win.

Also, keep in mind that points usually end quicker in a serve-volley game. It can be extremely aggravating to have your opponent win points so fast over and over. Keep your perspective. A point is just a point, whether it's an ace or a twenty-shot rally. If your opponent is serve-volleying and winning points, stay calm and resist the urge to hit out in anger.

Andre Agassi never lost his cool when Ivanisevic was throwing all those aces at him during Wimbledon '92. Andre kept looking for his shots on the service return and didn't let Goran's service winners break down his composure. You should do the same. Stay in control when your opponent starts ending the points quickly. Make them hit a variety of shots. Don't give them freebees. If they can counter what you're doing for the whole match, they deserve to win. But chances are they won't.

The Weak Serve

The player who can take their opponent's weak serve and use it to their own advantage has a tremendous asset. In my own game my serve works *against* me like this. My first serve is good enough. On a day when I'm "on" it can be effective. I played Agassi in a Volvo semifinal match in 1991 and aced him fifteen times and hit a bunch of service winners, beating him in straight sets (6–1, 6–2) because of it. But that's my first serve. My second serve is another story.

The second serve has me psyched out. All my career I've had a weak second serve. It's just something I've never been able to overcome. There's a little more pressure with that second serve especially on big points or when I know the receiver is good at capitalizing on my weakness. My second serve stinks, and it has really cost me against the players who know how to take advantage of it.

Lendl is the best (or worst) for me. He's like Freddy Krueger when he's waiting for my second serve. He absolutely eats it up. Becker is another one who feeds on my weak second. McEnroe does, too—not by using power like Lendl or Becker, but by taking the ball early, chipping, and charging the net. Either way I'm immediately playing catch up.

So what happens? To protect myself against a player who can take advantage of the weak second serve, I'm forced to make sure my first serve gets in. To do that I have to take something off of it. Doing that reduces its effectiveness. You can see the progression. By knowing how to capitalize on a weak second serve (mine) the receiver (Lendl) has forced me to change my first serve or suffer the consequences. Fortunately, I'm good at working the first serve to my advantage; not necessarily with power, but with good direction, consistency, and movement. I maximize the first serve because my second serve often makes me vulnerable.

That's what you want to do to the player with the nothing second serve. You want to force them to get more cautious on their first serve.

The Nerf serve is probably the one you'll have to receive most frequently at the club level. Whether it's a second serve that's weak or a first serve that has nothing on it, you will see the Nerf serve often. You'll see it most of all at important moments in the match. That's when the player serving to you is most likely to get nervous and develop The Elbow. The tennis ball comes over the net with nothing to it, no pace, no depth, no spin. It's like watching sand go through an hourglass. It takes forever. And it's a son-of-a-gun to take advantage of. Here's opportunity waiting and you can't capitalize.

The problem is that a ball just sitting there waiting to be creamed brings out the beast in you. You know it's opportunity knocking. But instead of just opening the door you try to tear it off its hinges. BANG! As hard as you can! BANG! As big as you can! BANG! As deep as you can! BANG! It goes in the can. Unforced error. Dumb mistake. In golf they'd say "too much club." You do that a few times and you get gun shy and change your tactics.

Pretty soon you see a Nerf ball serve and you hit a Nerf ball return. You get timid. You had opportunity staring you in the face and you handed it right back to your opponent. Back and forth you go. Every so often you get up the courage again and take a ferocious cut at a weak one. Into the back fence. Then it's back to the pattycake return. There is a solution. Here are the tactics you should use to capitalize on a weak serve.

1. Move Inside the Baseline

Waiting for the weak serve in your usual spot on or behind the baseline means you have to be running forward to get to a weak serve. You have made the shot more difficult by making yourself go farther to get to the ball. Step inside the baseline two feet, maybe three feet, depending on how bad the server is. Now you're in a position where you only have to move forward slightly to get the weaker serve and you can swing normally.

2. Keep Your Feet Moving

The easier the shot, the lazier the player. It's not that receivers don't try to kill the ball, it's that they quit doing what's necessary to hit with force. They swing at the ball with a swatting motion like they were trying to catch a hummingbird with a butterfly net—all wrist and arm. It's like the brain is telling them, "Hey, this is no sweat. An easy one. Take a break!" With a weak serve coming, the tendency is to let up. Bad thinking.

The laziness first shows up in your footwork. I see big lunging steps or no steps at all. A player will stand there waiting for the ball to arrive or wait until the last second and lurch at the ball. Instead, you should keep your feet moving with short peppery steps. Watch Connors's feet, or Lendl's when he's getting ready for the weak serve. Light, quick, and on their toes. They can get to and set up for the ball with much more consistency, much better balance, and much better timing. Start the feet moving before the toss. Stay light and loose on the balls of your feet when you smell the weak serve coming.

3. Shorten Your Grip and Your Backswing

The urge to overhit a ball that looks easy (the "sitter" or "duck") will be reduced if you grip down a little on your racket. That will shorten your swing and help you maintain control of the racket. I've seen players grip down five or six inches. That's too much, or at least unnecessary. Just move your hand two or three inches up toward the racket head. You're much better able to control things that way. And psychologically the shorter grip tends to reduce your urge to overswing.

4. Hit With Your Racket, Not Your Ego

Having done all of the above you're still going to make unforced errors if you don't control your urge to kill the ball. I call it getting "big eyes"; the player sees that soft serve waiting to be destroyed, the eyes bug out in anticipation, and the mind short-circuits. Result? Unforced error. Keep your eyes in your head. You just want to make a good return, so hit it with your racket, not your ego. And that goes for any sitters—volleys, overheads, groundstrokes. Manage your shots. Power is usually less important than placement. When you start seeing the pattycake second serve make it a priority to "place" your return to the opponent's weak side. When the player across the net sees you successfully and consistently capitalizing on their weak second they will start taking something off their first serve. You have made them change their game. Your Advantage!

The Lefty's Serve

The left-handed player has two advantages over you if you're right-handed. One is in your head and the other is on the court. Let's look at the court advantage first.

A left-handed server's strong side is the ad court. This is the court where they can more easily serve to your backhand. They can really move you off the court if they're able to swing their serve wide. A right-handed player's strong serving court to a Lefty is the deuce court. Again because it's easier to serve to a Lefty's backhand on duece court with a spin serve.

So it all evens out, right? On one side you have a serving advantage (the deuce court), and on one side the Lefty has an advantage (the ad court). The problem for a right-handed player is this: more ad points come up on the ad court than on the deuce court. How do you think it got its name? This means that in every match a Lefty has more game point opportunities on the court that favors their serve. They can swing a right-handed player off the court on those points when it counts most.

A right-handed player has a much more difficult time trying to exploit the Lefty on the ad court. If you do *try* to move a Lefty wide off the ad court you're forced to hit a more difficult serve (less court, higher net, tougher angle). And even if you succeed, the ball is still coming to the Lefty's forehand (and presumably stronger) side. If you hit to their backhand you're serving up the gut and leaving your left-handed opponent in the middle of the court. Not the best options when you want to get the point off to a good start.

Again, you're going to have to take away the Lefty's advantage by minimizing their strength. Here's how to do it.

1. BE AN ALLEY CAT

If you face a Lefty who's consistently able to swing you off the ad court by serving wide to your backhand, you have to cheat. By that I mean you have to take away that wide serve by moving closer to the ad court alley. It reduces their target area dramatically when you start cheating to your backhand side. Get closer to that alley (and a few steps forward, or closer to the net) when receiving their serve.

The Pie Chart for Tennis

This might explain it better, and it applies elsewhere. Depending on where you are positioned during a point, you give up parts of the court in greater or lesser degree. I think of it like the pie charts in *USA Today*. If you're standing exactly on the center of your own baseline the opponent has two equal pieces of pie to hit at: the deuce court and the ad court. If you move to your right, what happens? The left side of the pie gets bigger. If you move left, the right side gets bigger. Obviously the bigger side is an easier target for your opponent.

So when you face a Lefty's serve on the ad court move to your left and give them a sliver of pie on your backhand side and a nice chunk of pie on your forehand side. You've made it harder for them to serve to your backhand, to swing you off the court. You tempt them with more court on your forehand side, but to take advantage of it they will have to hit a more difficult flat serve up the middle.

You'd probably make this adjustment somewhat anyway. What I'm suggesting is that you "overadjust." Don't try to be secret about it. Don't try to sneak over a little bit. Do it big-time. Let your opponent know you're taking away their advantage. *Force them to serve to your forehand. Force them to serve up the center of the court on the ad court.* And force them to do it on big points when you've got a two or three point advantage. At 0–40 stand in the alley (or even *outside* the doubles sideline). See what they do. You'll love it. Adjust somewhat if they can effectively hurt you down the middle. Find a receiving position where they have trouble swinging the serve to your backhand and can't get it by your forehand.

You are disrupting their preferred routine. You have taken away what they would like to do and forced them to accept a secondary option. You have denied them the chance to routinely hit their strength to your weakness. You have forced them to hit a more difficult serve to your stronger side. This is exactly what you want to accomplish.

Now for the consequences. Will you get aced down the middle? Of course. But challenge your opponent to make that move. The Lefty will see the huge opening, that big piece of pie you've conceded, and start changing their game. Initially, they'll get greedy and go for the big ace down the middle to teach you a lesson. "You can't step around your backhand on me, buddy." Remember, you're challenging them. Disrupting them. Probing them. If they don't get the ace it'll either be out or in your wheelhouse. If it is in, nail it. The Lefty may now decide to try your backhand side even though you've given them only a sliver to hit to. A couple of faults and they'll be trying to go down the center again.

If they happen to be sharp that day you'll have to give up some of the alley you've claimed. You'll have to give them a smaller piece of the pie to hit to on your forehand side. But it's more likely you'll start to see mistakes. They'll try to steer the serve into that little opening on your backhand side (producing faults) or blast the ball down the middle for an ace. You've made them change their game from something that works against you to something that isn't as effective.

Does it work all the time? No, but it works often enough to be a disrupting factor that can change their game, especially if you keep adjusting. Keep mixing your position up so your opponent has to react to what *you're* doing and not the other way around. Keep changing the pie chart. Give them a big chunk on your forehand side one time and less the next time. One time make your move when they can see you. The next time move just after they make their toss and can't see you. Take their mind off the ball they're trying to hit and move it onto you. Especially at 40–love or love–40. Now you can really throw it in their face.

2. Don't Give Credit to a Lefty

So the Lefty has a court advantage that you have to deal with. What about the psychological advantage? This second advantage is more subtle, but just as common. Both club and pro players tend to get bent out of shape at the prospect of even playing a Lefty. We tend to put ourselves under the gun and expect to lose. I used to worry about it a lot. I just felt that a McEnroe or a Connors had so much to start with that to have the added advantage of being a Lefty was almost unfair.

While Connors didn't really maximize his serve potential, McEnroe did. His great hook serve was hellacious. It would swing wide (the can opener), bounce low, and run you off the court into the stands. Try and hit a winner with him at the net when you're sitting in the first row of seats. Tough. I'd get myself in a losing frame of mind just thinking about it.

What I had to do was tell myself that the court advantage could be minimized somewhat. That I could reduce the effectiveness of his best serve with proper positioning. From that point on I thought the Lefty and I played on an even field. I simplified it. Once we got into the point we were playing even. I quit telling myself that the Lefty had such a big advantage. I quit worrying because I knew the Lefty was at a disadvantage when I was serving to the deuce court.

The best thing you can do to neutralize the psychological advantage is to play more Lefties. Get used to knowing that when you hit a forehand to the deuce court against a Lefty it's going to your opponent's backhand and probably weaker side. Know that throwing up a lob on the alley side of the deuce court is going over their backhand side. The usual tactics you use are reversed against a Lefty. When you include Lefties in your regular schedule of partners, suddenly the perceived advantage evaporates.

Putting It Into Practice Against McEnroe

Remember the '86 Masters match against McEnroe at Madison Square Garden? (He retired for six months after I beat him.) The reason I won that match was because I used the strategy I've just outlined. I had played and lost to him several months before, but the match had been close. I lost 6–4 in the third, but for the first time I really felt that I could beat him. And I thought about it a lot heading into that match at the Garden.

In preparing my game plan I decided to do exactly what I've just outlined. I intended to crowd the alley on the ad court when he served. In addition, I wanted to step in slightly closer to the net when I got a chance to see a second serve. I knew that by coming in a little I'd get more aggressive. This was good. If McEnroe senses that you're tentative about what you're trying to do he smells blood and takes advantage of your indecision.

In that match I had two goals: take away his can-opener serve on the ad court and be more aggressive. What happened? By the end of the second set his serve had started to weaken. He was trying to force it up the middle on the ad court (I was giving him that bigger piece of pie) and he started missing it. Just a little, but missing it nevertheless. I was challenging him so much that on his first serve I'd be standing halfway in the alley. Just tempting him to go up the gut. And on that day he couldn't do it enough to hurt me. He was missing enough so that he had to let up on his serve and bring it in to my forehand. Then I'd mix up my returns, busting it one time and massaging it back the next. It kept him off balance.

I had minimized his strongest weapon in serving and made him try to beat me with something else. On most days Mac could adjust. But not that night at the Masters in New York. If it worked against him, believe me, it will work against the Lefty you play.

The Heater

The Heater. The Bomb. The serve with a lot of stick on it. These days, at least at the pro level, serves are coming in faster and harder. The new rackets are making ballistic missiles out of fuzzy balls. In fact, the tennis balls themselves seem different from a few years ago. I believe they're harder. That combined with the newer rackets means there's just more firepower available to good servers today. Stich, Krajicek, Wheaton, and a lot of the other young players are changing tennis with that power. Believe me, it's not just the result of their service motions.

On grass it can become almost a joke. At the 1991 Wimbledon Men's Finals between Stich and Becker the average point lasted less than three seconds! In the semis that year Stich beat Stefan Edberg and Edberg *never lost his serve once.* Power serving.

When I run into a guy who's in the zone with his serve on a particular day, just firing aces like it's nothing, there's not a lot I can do. I mean, in order to return a serve first you have to see it. When a ball is coming up the gut at 131 miles an hour it's by me before I can wink. It's like the story of the cowboy who said he was the fastest gun in the West. Somebody at the bar said, "Prove it, partner. Show me that fastest draw in the West." So the cowboy got up, put his hands above his guns and stood there motionless. Five seconds later he asked, "Want to see it again?" That's how it is playing against a Heater by Pete Sampras. "Want to see it again?" And my answer is "No!"

It's unlikely you'll ever be on the receiving end of a serve that breaks the sound barrier. But you will face some serves that are big enough to put you on the defensive, forcing you to make errors or throw back weak returns. In that situation there are a couple of important tactics to keep in mind that I use when necessary.

1. Move Back Three Steps

When someone is beating you with a particular shot or style of play it's important to change what you're doing. Give the player who's cruising along on the other side of the net a different look. Make them react to what you're doing. That's true in almost any situation in tennis and it's true here. When someone comes in with a serve you can't handle, change your court position for receiving serve.

First of all, move back. Don't fall into the macho mindset where you're thinking, "Hey, I'm gonna stand my ground. I don't care how hard he's serving!" Don't be proud. Back up. Maybe five feet. The extra distance will give you the time you need to react to the ball.

2. Move In Three Steps

Then move in closer. Get inside the service line closer than you'd normally position yourself. You'll try to block the ball back. Grip down on the racket and make contact in front of your body. The idea, of course, is to start disrupting your opponent's smooth ride. You're making him think. You're trying to get him to change what he's doing. And believe me, moving up or back will do that.

When a server sees you standing up close, challenging him, the result is predictable. They'll try to hit even harder. And when you move back behind the baseline five feet they start trying to take advantage of the angles available by going wide on either side of you. In both situations, do you see what happened? You got them to change their game.

Sounds too simple, doesn't it? It works. Bjorn Borg often stood twelve feet behind the baseline at Wimbledon and he won it five times in a row. Michael Chang stood *almost on the service line* because of leg cramps and forced Ivan Lendl to double-fault on match point in The French Open. Michael did a major number on Ivan's mind with that move. Yes, it does work.

3. Make Your Racket Shorter

The big serve gets on you too fast. You don't have time to react. It's even more difficult if you're swinging the racket with your hands at the end of the grip. Make your racket more manageable by shortening your grip; hold it two or three inches closer to the head of the racket. You'll have better control and be able to move it into position quicker.

4. CUT YOUR SWING IN HALF

When you're getting pounded by a big serve, shorten your swing. Think of taking half of a swing. If that doesn't work, think of just blocking your return back. Agassi blocked serves back *for winners* several times in earning his first Wimbledon title. Use the pace your opponent is supplying and just make good contact. This is very effective at all levels of play and is usually ignored by recreational players. They love to hit a hard ball hard. That's why there are so many mishits, late hits, and donated points.

Messing With Their Mind

If you can diminish the effectiveness of your opponent's best serve you've really given yourself a big boost toward winning the match. If it's a Lefty with a good can-opener serve, cheat to the alley and force them to try to beat you up the middle. If you're playing a righty who can pound it down the middle on the deuce court move to your left and give them just a sliver of the pie to hit to on your backhand side. And mix it up.

If someone's beating you consistently with their serve, you've got to work on their mind. Move to your new position when they can see you (but before they settle into their pre-serve motion). Then later move after they toss and can't see you. Exaggerate the move so that you force them away from their preferred shot. It's poor sportsmanship to be hopping back and forth simply to distract your opponent. It's legitimate to move with the purpose of taking a new position.

It breaks up their rhythm, the mental groove that they have. Instead of tearing you up with one particular serve you make them beat you with something else.

When you watch a match on the tube think along with the receiver. Watch how they position themselves to force an opponent away from a damaging serve. Then do it in your own matches.

Next: Recognizing opportunity during a match (the smell of blood).

9

The Seven Hidden
Ad Points

Deadly Dynamics

Recreational tennis players tend to consider most points and games in
their match as being roughly equivalent. The second point of a game
is about the same as the fourth point, 15–15 is no different from 30–
30. The third game of the opening set is no different from one played
at 4–all in the second set. With the exception of ad points it's all
pretty much the same on their scale of importance. (**Note:** For brevity
ad points and break points are *both* referred to as ad points. Any point
that can win a game for one of the players is called an ad point.)

But the differences in the impact specific points and games can
have on the momentum and outcome of the match are significant.
There are certain moments in the match that are dynamic and
volatile. They have both psychological and strategic weight that can
really help or hurt your cause.

Ad Points Get Attention

We know that an ad point presents opportunity. The player who has
one and converts it (wins it) secures a game. It's the kind of opportunity that every player from Mack The Hack to the number one
player in the world understands. On an ad point (especially for the set
or match) you sweat, your heart starts pumping, and your blood

pressure rises. At least it should. Most players wake up for an ad point (even the very first one) because a *game* is on the line, for them or their opponent.

Since just about everybody recognizes the impact of an ad point, players get a little pumped when one arrives. You're not going to catch your opponent unaware very often. When was the last time you won your ad point and didn't know what you'd done? ("That was for the game?") Rarely. And if it was for the set? Never. The same goes for the people you play. Ad points get noticed. They're obvious and they get treated with respect.

Learning the Moment: "Sleeping Booty"

In my own approach to building victory I seek those dynamic or "impact" situations that get *overlooked* by the other guy. Ad points aren't included because players are alert to them. However, there are important moments during a match that significantly affect its dynamics and that aren't appreciated. I call them Hidden Ad Points. They are situations that allow a player to *get* to an opportunity like an ad point, produce or deny momentum, reestablish their presence, or continue their dominance in the match at critical times.

Often they're moments your opponent won't regard as offering any special reward. So when they come up your opponent is asleep. The booty is unguarded, especially at the club level. That's when you can do yourself some real good *just by being alert* to the potential of the situation. I call it *learning the moment*, recognizing the dynamic importance of crucial junctures in the match.

These undervalued swing points and games can have a tremendous impact on the outcome of your match if you're aware of them. If you do nothing more than *recognize* them when they occur (and they occur frequently) you'll be giving yourself a significant advantage. And if you play them intelligently, your winning percentage will go up.

Your Tennis Security System

When those moments arrive an alarm goes off inside me. Just as getting off to a dominant start can have a great effect on what follows, I know that these hidden, or overlooked, opportunities can also greatly influence the outcome. I want to recognize them when they arrive, be alert, and capitalize on them as best I can. Here are the ones I've singled out over the years as being especially important to me, opportunities where I don't want my mind to drift, where I want to be totally engaged and play smart tennis.

The Seven Hidden Ad Points

1. The Set-up Point
2. The Set-up Game
3. The Dictate Games
4. Stretching a Lead
5. Stopping the Match From Slipping Away
6. Tiebreaker Tactics
7. Closing Out a Match

These are specific situations that come up, must be recognized, and need my full attention. Let's translate.

1. The Set-up Point

For some pros (the ones not making any money) and most recreational players there are two kinds of points: ad points and all the rest. Wrong. I treat the point that can *get* me or my opponent to an ad point as a major moment because it offers a major reward. That reward is the *opportunity* to win (or convert) a game. I call any point that *precedes* an ad point a Set-up Point. The point played at love–30, 30–love, 15–30, 30–15, 30–30, and deuce are all Set-up Points for one or both players.

When I'm looking at one of those scores bells are ringing inside me, especially at 30–30 (or deuce) when we *both* have a chance to step up and get to an ad point. Those are the points that really get the juices going. Each one is a big swing because it decides who gets a chance to cash in on the game. And if the set or match comes with winning that game the Set-up Point's value is multiplied (I think of those moments as Super Set-up Points).

If I win a Set-up Point at 30–30 or deuce I'm only one point away from winning the game. My opponent is three points away. A big difference. If I win a point at 30–15 (to go up 40–15) the spread is even bigger. Psychologically it's all positive. Winning it allows me to move into a strong position mentally whether I'm serving or receiving. In fact, often at the club level if your opponent is serving and you win your Set-up Point (moving to ad out) it may be all you need to do. A double fault can give you the game.

I know if I get enough ad point opportunities (while limiting those of my opponent) I'll probably win the match. And the Set-up Point is where those opportunities are created. In baseball you can't get a hit until you come up to the plate with a bat in your hands. In tennis you can't win a game without a convert opportunity. The Set-up Point can give you the chance to come up to the plate (or to keep your opponent from doing so). It's very important and it gets my respect.

And what's best about the Set-up Point at the club level is that your opponent is usually unaware of the weight it carries. They tend to play them just like any other point, without a great deal of thought or focus: 30–15 just doesn't get their attention, 30–30 doesn't alert them. Their wake-up call is the *ad point*, not the point preceding it, the Set-up Point.

Now is when you make sure *your* mind is focused, your body prepared, and your plan is in place. It's when you can catch them unaware.

RULE 1: GET IT IN OR GET IT BACK!

When a Set-up Point arrives (either for me or the other player) I pay attention. The primary goal I have in mind is this: *Get it in or get it back!* That means if I'm serving I want to *get the ball in.* If I'm receiving I want to *get the ball back,* and preferably to a spot that forces my opponent to hit a weaker shot. And it's even more important at 30–30 or deuce. These points require more caution. Or, to put it another way, they require less casualness or carelessness.

Serving at 40–love you might want to try busting one in, going for your annual ace. If you're receiving maybe you'll try a spectacular return. Not at 30–30 or deuce. Let your opponent go for the glory. Serving at 30–love the server tends to get careless because that score feels like it's bigger than it is. Pay attention! Win that point and you get three straight convert opportunities. Get that first serve in. Don't double-fault.

What's surprising is how often club players *will* double-fault or carelessly slam a service return long or into the net on a Set-up Point. They've just given their opponent a convert opportunity (or denied it to themselves) free of charge because they didn't understand the significance of the point and what it can mean to the dynamics of the match. That's unintelligent tennis.

RULE 2: BE SENSIBLE AFTER THE SERVE

Once the point is under way, be sensible. Don't get fancy. Don't get brilliant. No stupid errors. It's amazing how often recreational players will go for the "miracle shot" in the middle of a rally when neither player has any advantage. That may be okay with a big lead, although even then I dislike seeing it and absolutely hate doing it. At crucial moments a risky shot is a sign of a player who doesn't understand the game. Let your opponent play brain-dead when it counts.

This doesn't mean you should play pattycake tennis. It means you should manage your shots, avoiding low-percentage shots that carry unnecessary risk at inappropriate times. And that's the strategy you should apply to all of the Hidden Ad Points.

Pressure Paralyzes

Winning the Set-up Point can create pressure. All players are most tense when something is at risk. Losing that Set-up Point can put your game, set, or match at risk. Pressure will be layered on your strokes and confidence, and to some degree pressure paralyzes most recreational players. Recognizing the importance of winning a Set-up Point and approaching it correctly will consistently keep pressure off you and place it on your opponent.

2. The Set-up Game

Any game that can move a player to within one game of the set is a Set-up Game. It's similar to the Set-up Point in that it's generally not viewed as anything special, just another game. But it *is* special. It isn't just another game, as I'll demonstrate with the '92 Wimbledon final.

And the Set-up Game at 4–4 or 5–5, when both players have a chance to move up to a set game, has tremendous dynamic value. If you break serve you are then serving for the set. Or if you hold serve (at 4–4 or 5–5) your opponent has the pressure of knowing if they *don't* hold serve they lose the set or match. Knowing that they *have* to hold serve or lose is significant pressure for most recreational players.

It can also be significant pressure for a professional. All Goran Ivanisevic had to do to stay alive in the fifth set against Andre Agassi in the '92 Wimbledon final was to hold serve. But Goran knows if he doesn't hold serve at 4–5 he loses the match. Pressure? Even though he had over two-hundred aces in the tournament and thirty-seven aces up to that point in the match, he began that service game with four consecutive faults! On match point his first serve went eighteen inches below the top of the net. That's the pressure of knowing you have to hold serve or lose the match. And that's the kind of pressure you can put on your opponent by winning a Set-up Game.

Goran told the press later, "For the first time all match I was thinking in the air. Instead of thinking about my plan before I tossed the ball I started thinking when the ball was in the air." Pressure did it and it was the pressure created when Agassi won the Set-up Game. Andre understood fully the dynamics of winning the Set-up Game when he was serving at 4–4 in the fifth.

Agassi said later that he "wanted to hang in long enough to make Goran think about it, *to serve to save the match.*" He knew what enormous pressure would then fall on Ivanisevic's shoulders (and elbow). Andre played a very effective and solid Set-up Game at 4–4, holding at 15. He played very alert, stable, and *sensible* tennis. No shots with unnecessary risk. It was a classic example of understanding the dynamics of the situation. Underneath the long bleached hair was a brain thinking like a wise old Professor of Tennis. You can do the same in your matches if you pay attention.

When a Set-up Game arrives (especially at 4–all or 5–all) a flashing red light should go off in your head and signal: "Pay attention. The stakes have been raised. Don't be casual. Stay alert. Opportunity beckons." Your concentration level should notch up considerably. Every point here is a big point. Every point helps or hurts a lot more.

THE "CRITICAL" SEVENTH GAME ISN'T SO CRITICAL

Here's one of the reasons I don't agree with the common notion that the seventh game is such a critical game in a set. It is critical if it moves one player to within four points (one game) of the set. This it can do at 4–2 or 2–4. But it doesn't have nearly that importance at 3–3 at the club level. The "critical" game of the set for me is the Set-up Game, which moves one player to within striking distance of winning the set.

Play Like a Boa Constrictor

In those important swing moments of a match I want to play like a boa constrictor. Do you know how a boa constrictor kills? It doesn't crush its prey. The victim suffocates. Each time the victim exhales the boa constrictor tightens its hold slightly. The prey can't *inhale* as much on the next breath. Each time it breathes out it can't breathe in as much. Soon it can't breathe in at all. Suffocation. Nothing flashy there. Just constant steady pressure. And that's my approach on the Set-up Games where winning moves one player to within four points of the set (or match).

Don't force shots. Don't get impatient. Don't try to make something out of nothing. Just keep squeezing. When I'm playing the Set-up Game I'm trying to get the other player to make mistakes, to get impatient, to go for the brilliant shot. And at a pivotal moment when a player can get to within four points of the set by winning the game I put a premium on steadiness. I want my opponent to earn everything they get. Agassi played like a boa constrictor when he was serving at 4–4 in the fifth.

Most of the time in recreational tennis Set-up Points and Set-up Games are played loosely and without much consideration for their weight. A player who recognizes the potential in these situations will often have to do no more than get the ball over the net. The opponent will give up the points because of sloppy play and sloppy thinking.

3. The Dictate Games

The first two games of the second set (in a best-of-three match) are my Dictate Games. It's when a player has an opportunity to continue their dominance over the other player after winning the first set, or to reestablish their presence in the match if they've lost the set. Here's what I mean.

Win the first set and the percentages say you should win the match. (Remember: that happens almost 90 percent of the time for the top pros). Lose the first set and you've got problems. However, there's a reason the contest continues after the first set. Winning it doesn't guarantee victory. Losing doesn't necessarily mean defeat. But, win or lose, those first games of set two can significantly affect the dynamics of what follows.

RULE 1: BEWARE THE WOUNDED BEAR

Let's assume you've won the opening set. Your opponent understands that it's a long road back to victory. Depending on their attitude or character one of two things happens. They may get a little bit discouraged, figure it's not going to be their day and quit trying. If they do, great! The meek may inherit the earth, but they won't win many tennis matches. More likely you'll have a Wounded Bear on your hands. And a Wounded Bear is dangerous. You've injured them by winning the first set. Now their focus is sharp and their motivation is high. They *have* to get something going and they know it. They are prepared to dig in and fight at the beginning of set two.

For your part, it's critical that you continue the momentum you've created by winning the first set. Starting *immediately* in this second set you want to stuff them. You want to slam the door on any hope they have. They're motivated and energized. They're looking for quick blood. They want to hurt you fast and turn this thing around. And *they think they can do it!* Of course they do. A good competitor believes he or she can turn it around. You want to puncture those hopes. And nothing hurts (or helps) their attitude and their game as much as losing (or winning) early in the new set.

The Dog in a Player

Competitive spirit is an interesting quality in a player. Everyone has it, some more than others. Your job is to squash that spirit in the other player, to destroy any idea they might have of beating you on that day. But even quitters usually have a little fight left in them. They think they can win. It's just that it doesn't take much to convince them otherwise. A cloudy day can be enough to discourage them. With quitters that first set loss may be all the convincing they need. With most others it takes more to get them thinking "I'm gonna lose today." *How much more you don't know.*

Against Jimmy Connors it's a *lot* more. I know from experience. After I beat Jimmy in straight sets during the '87 Masters we almost got into a fight in the locker room. He started yelling at me about how I'd never beat him again (so far he's almost been right). How my win was an accident. How I didn't *deserve* to beat him. Sound familiar? He's standing there in his jockstrap telling me how I can't win even though I just canned him.

Connors is a rare bird, though. He doesn't believe he should ever lose and he wanted me to know he didn't accept the fact that I could beat him.

But I'll tell you this. Nobody you play thinks like Jimmy. After losing the first set a lot of your opponents look at the beginning of the second set as a barometer of what's to come. If they lose early they may quit early. If they win early they think they're back in it. A lot of players will dog it if you can stick them early in that second set.

Even among the top pros you see it. Ivan Lendl was accused of tanking a match occasionally early in his career. He would just decide at some point (like early in the second set) "it's not my day" and throw in the towel. Goran Ivanisevic does it occasionally now. Mentally he's not as tough as he should be. He'll let something bother him, a bad line call or something else, and decide to check out for the day.

Get 'Em Down and Keep 'Em Down

I've seen, in the course of hundreds of tournament matches, that the beginning of the second set is often when a big psychological shift can occur. It's a new beginning for your opponent who's just lost the first set. You can smash that new beginning with a strong start. Even a quitter can get their hopes up if they get going early in set two.

But most of all you must beware of the Wounded Bear. When you win the first set tell yourself you've just created a big problem—you've hurt your opponent and motivated them to come clawing out after you. You must pay attention or you'll get hurt.

RULE 2: BEWARE THE HAPPY CAMPER
or
Don't Have Your Victory Party
Before You Have Your Victory

Players at every level of tennis are susceptible to relaxing a bit when they achieve something during a match. You know that one of the Laws of Tennis is this: The time you're most likely to lose your serve is right after you've broken serve. It has nothing to do with mechanics and everything to do with attitudes. A player who breaks serve tends to let down or get careless. The player who's been broken plays harder.

The end of the first set is often when this attitude adjustment happens most dramatically. Winning that set creates a natural feeling of achievement accompanied by a false sense of security. After winning the opening set a player becomes a Happy Camper, relieved, pleased, and satisfied. With this new attitude comes a decline in mental alertness and a temporary and subtle lessening of competitiveness.

When you're a Happy Camper, that's when you're vulnerable. That's when you'll play a loose game or games at a critical time. That's when you'll give your valuable advantage right back. It's truly a great player who gets *hungrier* with a lead, who doesn't get complacent and relax. There are three of them out there and I'll get to them in a moment.

The Wounded Bear
and the Happy Camper Go Together

Of course, the Wounded Bear and the Happy Camper often appear at the same time. When you're feeling good and getting a little comfortable because you've won the first set you can bet you're opponent is feeling wounded and threatened. They are going to fight back hard. And, conversely, when you get hurt and your system is on "emergency" (because *you've* just lost the first set) your opponent is across the net gloating just a little, relieved to be ahead.

The Window of Opportunity:
Close It, or Jump Through It!

If your opponent (having lost the opening set) comes out and immediately breaks you, the first set is erased in their mind. It's history. They feel the match is essentially even. If their attitude *was* negative, now it's positive. Just like that the momentum shifts. And when momentum swings to the other player it can be tough to get back. Don't let them crawl through this window of opportunity at the start of the second set because you've taken a little mental vacation. Slam it shut with alertness and solid tennis.

And, of course, it works the other way. If you've lost the first set the beginning of the second set is when you look to strike back immediately, to reestablish your presence in the match. You want to take advantage of your opponent's more casual attitude and "stick it to 'em". Your biggest window of opportunity exists right at the start of the second set: the Dictate Games. Jump through the window. Get back in the match.

McEnroe Understands Dynamics

You'll see McEnroe become unhinged at this point occasionally. He's won the first set and is looking good. Then his opponent starts strong in the second set. McEnroe understands that you don't want to give the other player any hope at all of winning. This is why McEnroe really wants to drive the nail in the coffin. Instead his opponent starts crawling out.

The crowd is wondering why McEnroe will get crazy with himself when he's just won a set and loses serve early in the second. Doesn't he have a big lead? Isn't there plenty of time to get the break back? McEnroe understands the dynamics of the situation. He doesn't want to let the other player out of his grasp and he knows that the psychological advantage he gained by winning the first set can evaporate with a bad start in the second.

Be a Good Doubles Partner to Yourself

Sports psychologist Dr. Jim Loehr has found that a pro doubles team talks to each other an average of eighty-three times during a match. Eighty-three times! That's a lot of talk, and we're not discussing where to have lunch. One of the most important things we talk about is those moments in the match where we have to be sharp and play heads-up tennis. It's easy to forget in the heat of battle.

In singles nobody is out there to remind you. You have to be your own doubles partner. Talk to yourself. Tell yourself what's going on and what you want to do.

I mention this because the beginning of the second set is a dynamic moment in the match; one of those times when you've got to remind yourself to be alert. Great gain can be made or damage done psychologically. If you know that and remind yourself to play accordingly you'll capitalize on the moment more often than not. And that applies not only to this particular Hidden Ad Point, but to all of them. Talk to yourself. Be your own coach.

I do exactly that. If I get ahead I force myself to get my mind right back into the fight. I don't want to feel any sense of relief that I've won the first set. I don't want to be comfortable. I don't want to feel like it's okay to relax a little bit. I don't want to enjoy the moment. I want to be afraid of what the other guy might do. In fact, I get nervous when I can sense that I'm feeling too comfortable in the match. I want to come out fighting. I know my oppoent will.

In those situations (and the other Hidden Ad Point moments) I want to play blue-chip tennis—no speculating on fancy shots or high-risk tactics. It's when I remember the tactics of the boa constrictor: squeeze a little. Then squeeze a little more.

Those early games of the second set can make winning the match easier if you've won the preceding set. They can get you back into the match if you've lost it. Don't these same dynamics occur at the beginning of the third set? Not usually. Beginning a set where both players know they can win the match by winning that set usually alerts and motivates *both* players. If one of them gets broken early they understand they only have to recover that break, not a break and a set. Psychologically there's a big difference.

(I'll admit that sometimes the beginning of the third set can create the same dangers or opportunities as the beginning of the second. In '93 I faced Andre in the finals of the Volvo/San Francisco Tournament. He won the first set and should have won the second set. I managed to fight back and win the tiebreaker even though he had a couple of match points in it. He *immediately* broke me in the first game of the third set partially because I let down a little. I was so happy to still be alive. From that point on he ran with his lead and won easily. I let myself get vulnerable at the beginning of the third set and he took advantage of it. But usually it happens at the beginning of the second.)

4. Stretching a Lead

Holding a lead once you've broken serve is often more difficult than getting the lead in the first place. Actually *increasing* the lead is really tough. Again it has to do with the psychology involved. It's the habit most of us have of getting comfortable after we've achieved something, whether it's winning a set *or* breaking serve. But this is the time when the alert player will get their head right back into the game.

Any time you break serve the alarm inside your head should again start ringing. Concentrate on that first game after a break like it's the most important game of the match. Get the ball in play and keep the ball in play. I want to play more solid tennis—no mistakes, no unforced errors, no stupid shots. I want to squeeze my opponent more and more. I want to raise the degree of difficulty of the shots the other player has to make to beat me. This is when I tighten up the focus mentally and get more aggressive. I guarantee the other player is doing it. They want to get that break back right now.

Aggressive Doesn't Mean Hitting Harder

What do I mean by aggressive? When I tell you to play more aggressively you may think I mean run faster, hit harder, and get to the net. Attack.

But playing aggressively doesn't necessarily mean hitting everything harder. It *may* mean hitting harder. But it may mean hitting softer. It can be the placement of the shot (down the middle or swinging wide). It can be the type of shot (topspin or underspin). What I mean by playing more aggressively is being mentally more alert, aware of the significance of the situation and intent on not losing your advantage through sloppiness.

I tighten the noose slowly. Michael Chang and Emilio Sanchez are experts at this approach. Once they have a lead they just wait you out. They're very strong mentally with a lead. It is very difficult to get that lead back from them because you know they won't give you any easy points.

You have to know your own game. If you do play better with a lead, with less tension and pressure, go ahead and press the issue. If you make mistakes with that approach, stay with what got you the lead in the first place. Just concentrate on doing it better. As the saying goes, "Dance with who brung ya."

In either case a primary factor is mental alertness and an understanding of the dynamics of the situation. You've *got* the lead with that break. Avoid becoming careless. Don't make stupid mistakes. Don't give up your advantage by getting mentally lazy.

MY MOTTO: D.R.M.

As I mentioned, my motto is D.R.M; "Don't Rush Me." Tennis players tend to speed up when they go ahead (or fall behind). It hurts their game. You feel good when you grab a break to go ahead. You're pumped. It's natural to step up the pace. But be careful. That's when mistakes happen. A double fault. An ill-advised attempt at a forehand winner. An approach shot at the wrong time. Bing. Bing. Bing. You've lost the break. So be deliberate. Don't race to the line and jump into the next point. Think a little about what you're going to do next. Don't slow it down. Just don't speed it up.

Here's my antirushing device. I'll pick out a spot on the back wall (in front of the spectator seats) or a mark on the court five or ten feet behind the baseline. Between each point I will actually go to that mark and touch it with my racket or hand, or at least look at it. I walk back to it, touch it, and then go back to the baseline. It prevents me from jumping into points carelessly. When I've got a lead I want to avoid getting careless.

THE BEST AT STRETCHING A LEAD

Jimmy Connors, John McEnroe, and Ivan Lendl are the absolute masters on tour when it comes to holding and stretching a lead. Nobody else in tennis even comes close, although Jim Courier is showing signs of wanting to join the club. When I'm down a break at 2–4 against Lendl the next time I look up at the scoreboard it'll say

6–2, 3–0 Lendl. Before you even know it's happening he's turned the match into a rout. Connors and Mac do the same.

Most players don't feed on a lead like they do. There's something inside them that gets absolutely bloodthirsty when they go ahead. It's one of the reasons they're such great champions. When they've got you down and their foot is on the back of your neck they're not satisfied. They want to get both feet on the back of your neck. And when they've got both feet on the back of your neck they want to start jumping up and down on it. They are unique. And very dangerous.

Connors and McEnroe instinctively pound on the opponent even harder when they get ahead. I believe they avoid getting casual with a lead because they enjoy the thrill of beating on an opponent more than the feeling of being comfortable. They go for the throat when they have the chance. When they get up a break they never think about just holding serve to win the set. They want to get another break. And another break.

They don't want you to get another point. Lendl, too. They get into a feeding frenzy with a lead. It's almost scary how focused and intense they can get. Courier now shows it in his game. Watch him play when he's ahead. He hits harder and goes for more at critical times than almost anybody else out there.

BE A GOOD LIAR

Very few players are like those guys. And just like most others, I tend to get comfortable when I'm ahead. The reason is simple and straightforward. Pressure makes us feel uncomfortable. We don't like it. So our mind will seize on any positive development as a reason to worry less, to feel less pressure and subsequently think and play with reduced intensity. So when I do get up a break I try to provide myself with a mental attitude that keeps me in a "hungry" mode. Here's what I do: *I lie to myself.*

I'll think, "Brad, pick it up now. You're down a break (even though I'm not). Don't fall behind. Work harder. You've got to break him back. This isn't going to be easy." It works. I feel like I'm fighting to catch up instead of sitting on and relaxing with a lead.

In fact, the bigger the lead, the more I want to be concerned. I keep telling myself that unless I work even harder I'll lose. The bigger the lead the more consciously I work at being mentally engaged. When I'm behind it happens automatically, the emergency alarm goes off by itself. When I'm ahead I have to work on myself to keep my nose in the fight. I believe most recreational players are exactly the same way.

What Connors, McEnroe, Lendl, and increasingly Courier do is very difficult to accomplish, and I don't recommend it. They increase the risk level of shots they take. They go into attack mode with a confidence that's really amazing. You've heard the phrase, "protecting a lead"? Not these guys. They're out to *stretch* their lead. And they do it because somehow when they get ahead they aren't afraid to start taking risks. And they can do it without making many mistakes.

My approach is different and I believe better for the average club player's game. Most players make mistakes when they start getting aggressive and hitting harder. My goal is to continue doing exactly what I did to get ahead, only better. I don't work on increasing my power. I work on increasing my awareness and concentration. I don't want to change my game (after all, it got me ahead). I want to work on my mind so that I stay on track. You should do the same.

Players at all levels start feeling a great urge to experiment with new tactics and shots when they get ahead. It's strange thinking. They get a lead doing one thing and then want to hold or increase that lead by doing something else, usually something they're not as good at or they'd have done it originally! When you're ahead, keep doing exactly what worked to get you ahead.

I go even farther than that. I don't change *anything* when I'm leading. I usually keep the same shirt (even if it's soaked), the same racket, the same towel to wipe off sweat, and I want to keep the same ball in play after I win a point. *Change nothing*.

5. Stopping the Match From Slipping Away

When I feel that a match is slipping away from me (or in danger of slipping away) I want to make changes, strategically, mentally, and physically. In order to do that I have to be observant. I have to ask, "Who's doing what to whom?" If I can answer that correctly I'll know where the adjustments in my game plan need to be made.

First I ask myself:

1. Am I following my game plan?

Then, if I *am* following my plan I ask:

2. What is my opponent doing to defeat my strategy?

Obviously, if for some reason the answer to the first question is no, I'll want to get back to what I said I would do in my pre-match preparation. I'll want to at least try and give my game plan a chance to work. Most recreational players tend to give up on their strategy too soon. They lose a few points or games with it and abandon ship. Give it a chance to work! Stay with it long enough to test your opponent.

However, if you continue to struggle you will need to address slippage. When a player breaks you and consolidates the break (holds serve) you have to be very sure it doesn't get any worse. I always figure I can come back from a break down; two breaks down is serious trouble.

It's at that point in the match when D.R.M. (Don't Rush Me) is again very important. I know that mistakes tend to come in bunches. Suddenly, I'm not a little bit behind—I'm a lot behind. It's like stepping on a banana peel. Just like that you can fall on your butt. And it's right at that point that I want to control the tempo of the match. I want to be deliberate. I want to avoid rushing. I don't want my opponent to cruise on that momentum they've built.

That's when I'll make sure to walk back and touch the mark on the court or back fence between points. During that time I'll be giving myself a pep talk, "C'mon Brad. Let's go! Work a little bit." Or I'll towel off. (You'll often see a player take a towel from one ballperson and after using it walk to the other side of the court and hand it to another ballperson. It's just a mechanical device to slow things down and stop the slide from turning into an avalanche.)

Tying shoes, talking to the chair umpire or line officials, straightening strings, bouncing the ball before a serve—these are often just devices to cool the heat the other player has created. All done within the legal time limits (usually), but just bringing the tempo of the match back down a little. In Part III you'll see how McEnroe, Connors, and Lendl do this with great results.

When a player starts to break open a tennis match (as Lendl does so effectively) it can turn into a stampede. You can lose control of things quickly, just like a car that hits a patch of ice and is suddenly skidding out of control.

When that happens to me I make the tempo of the match more deliberate. Most opponents will come out of their rhythm. They'll drop out of the zone they're in if you interfere with their momentum. This is going on constantly among the pros.

Pay attention during a televised match to the tempo between points. Watch what a player does when they're behind or ahead. When they're ahead they want to keep playing along at that same winning tempo that has given them the lead. When a good player starts falling behind watch them slow things down.

CHANGE YOUR SHIRT

When I'm behind and looking for a change, I shake up my attitude. And I do that by going to my equipment bag, my Tools of the Trade. I may change into a dry shirt. Or put on a fresh pair of socks, have a Jolly Rancher, or just put a new sweatlet on my wrist. Just a little change to feel like it's a new start, a fresh beginning. When I'm trying to get a break back I'll often tie both of my shoes. I'm telling myself it's time to bear down and work hard.

Remember the old right tennis shoe that helped me win $114,000 against Jim Pugh at Stratton Mountain? I actually carried it around with me for a couple of years. I thought of it as my rally shoe and would change into it when I needed a little psychological boost. I want to feel positive and confident about my chances. I want to avoid that sense of being on the run. A little equipment change helps.

A CHANGE OF PLANS

At what point do you have to go further and actually change strategy? It varies from match to match and player to player. If you want a specific point in a match it's this: when you're down a set and a break. That's not always the time to change, but it's a good guideline. You may have lost the first set in a tiebreaker and then lost serve because of great shots by your opponent. This is still a close match. But if your opponent won the first set easily and is doing the same in the second, you better change. Wait much longer and you're terminal.

Occasionally you will want to make a change in the first set. If you're down 0–5 and just getting wiped out, make some adjustments to see if they work. Get them going before you start the second set.

If you want a specific point at which you should generally make a change, though, that's it—down a set and a break. At that point something has to change or you will lose. The match has been underway long enough to establish a trend. And the trend shows you congratulating the winner. Change your strategy. Analyze your options and give your opponent a different look.

If I've been losing by staying at the baseline I'll try to upset my opponent by coming to the net. If my second serve is getting bossed around I'll know it's because my first serve isn't going in and I'm letting my opponent see second serves. (Remember the '87 Open against Becker? I was very conscious of keeping him from seeing many second serves.) If I'm getting passed when I go to the net I'll either attempt to improve my approach shot or decide to stay back at the baseline. If my opponent is attacking my backhand successfully I'll take action to reduce my vulnerability there (see The Attack to Your Backhand in chapter 7).

My coach, Tom Chivington, actually believes I play better when I'm behind than when I've got a lead. He may be right and if he is it's because I'm better at handling things. I know what to do when I get behind. It's never a panicky situation. I recognize what needs to be done and do it. Perhaps the most important thing is to do it before it's too late. That's how you'll start climbing back into matches.

6. Tiebreaker Tactics

During the 1993 A.T.P. tournament in San Francisco I had to play a total of three tiebreakers. I won them all, including one in the finals against Andre Agassi. My success in those tiebreakers and others was because I had a plan. Here it is.

I think of a tiebreak as a mini-set. Everything is compressed, but the components of a set are all still present. During a tiebreak you serve for the first time and receive serve for the first time. You need to break serve (a mini-break) to win. The tiebreak has a Dictate Game (or Dictate Points) at its beginning, it has the Set-up Point, and it often requires that you hold a lead or stop the tiebreak from slipping away. The dynamics are very similar to those in a regular set, but condensed and more potent.

Because the results of a tiebreaker decide who wins the set and because it's so compressed I'm extremely aware of the tempo of the match during this period: D.R.M. is my watchword. Playing quickly and carelessly can immediately put you at a disadvantage from which you won't recover. Three double faults in the third game of the first set may only cost you the game. Do the same during a tiebreak and the consequences will almost always be much more severe.

I approach a tiebreak just as I do the rest of the set. You should do the same.

Approach the beginning of a tiebreak with the thought in mind that you are going to play blue-chip tennis. Let your opponent be spectacular. The first two points of a tiebreak are Dictate Points. You can seize control and put your opponent at an immediate disadvantage, in a position where they may pressure themselves into making mistakes because they're behind. Those first two points bring increased tension to the match and so I want to be extremely careful not to go for a high-risk shot just because I'm nervous and want to end the point quickly.

Separate those first two points of the tiebreak from the set you just played. Don't just glide into them. Gather your thoughts and refocus (walk back and touch the mark on the court while you think over what your game plan is). This is not just an extension of the last game of the previous set. Make yourself isolate those first two points and play them with renewed alertness; get it in or get it back.

You don't want to "play afraid," but you don't want to introduce loose shots or new tactics unless you're *very* comfortable with them. Continue to use what was successful in getting you to the breaker.

The tiebreak is a separate entity and needs attention. Don't rush. Be deliberate and know what you are going to do, especially at the beginning.

Each player's initial serve in the tiebreak is performed under high pressure. So again my goal is to *get it in*. I don't like to try to do too much. I think of those first points as being similar to the start of the first set. I want to be sure early in the tiebreak to play within my game. I want to avoid being too ambitious. Often with the increased pressure of a tiebreak a player's nervousness will cause him or her to try an inappropriate shot. I want to *play steadier tennis, not flashier tennis*, at this time.

Too often players will approach a tiebreak less with the thought of winning it than with the hope that their opponent will lose it for them. That's not conservative play; it's constricting play and it will hurt you. Go for your shots if they present themselves, but don't try to jam in a winner just because you get impatient.

The tendency to just hope your opponent "loses it" is especially common when you get a lead during a tiebreaker. You go ahead 4–1 and suddenly get nervous, hoping the opponent will just hand it to you. This is when I will lie to myself, tell myself that I'm behind so I don't get complacent and lose my intensity. It's when you have to talk to yourself about what you want to do.

And of course the point in a tiebreak that precedes a set point is one that I treat as very special. A Set-up Point in a tiebreak (for example, 5–3) is almost always undervalued at the club level and even sometimes at the pro level. It can move me (or my opponent) up to an opportunity to win the set or match. I want no stupid mistakes, no unnecessary risks. Squeeze your opponent like a boa constrictor. At this crucial moment in a match, where you can move up to a set point, make sure your game is under control and you're thinking correctly.

7. Closing Out a Match

It may seem out of place to include tactics for closing out a match in a chapter called "The Seven Hidden Ad Points." After all, what's so hidden about the opportunity presented when you're serving for the match? The reward is obvious: winning the match. While the reward is obvious, the dangers aren't. Closing out a match is a delicate time for the player who has the chance to do it.

One of two attitudes usually prevails in the recreational player at such moments: an assumption that the job is almost done and victory is in hand, or a subtle fear that they won't be able to finish the task.

More dangerous than either of those mindsets is what is going on across the net with the player in danger of being *closed out*. One of the most common mistakes tennis players make is to underestimate the opponent who is in immediate danger of losing the match. It's an extension of the Wounded Bear syndrome. That player is a lethal weapon. They will frequently play their best tennis just as you are in a position to win the match. Always remember: *A fish fights hardest when you get it next to the boat!* And a tennis player (at any level) does the same.

Regardless of what they may have done previously in the match, expect the worst. This means expect their best. Assume they're going to be faster and tougher, to hit deeper shots with fewer mistakes. They will fight their hardest as you try to drag them in.

The way I prepare myself is to lie a little (again) to myself. I tell myself I'm the one in trouble. I'm the one who has to work to save the match. I'm the one who needs to be most alert. I want to feel that just when I'm closing in on victory I'm at the most dangerous point. I also remind myself to expect my opponent's best tennis to surface at this time. I don't want to be surprised by outstanding efforts.

I'll be sure to keep nerves under control by monitoring my breathing and footwork (Nerve Busters #1 and #2). D.R.M. is my tempo. I don't want to drag along, but I want to be very sure that I'm mentally and emotionally under control before a point starts.

And when the point starts I return to my basic concept of winning tennis: no mistakes, no free points, no stupid shots. *I want my opponent to get his points the hard way. I want him to earn them.*

Donate to Charity
Not to Your Opponent!

One basic element of my approach to a tennis match (and especially to the Hidden Ad Points) is to be very stingy when it comes to giving my opponent free points. I work hard at managing my concentration and making sure I understand the dynamics of the match. The Seven Hidden Ad Points are recurring swing moments in the match where I want to be especially connected to what's going on.

I want to make my opponent have to do something *special* to win the point or the game. I really batten down the hatches and try to produce my most focused thinking and smartest tennis. Is the first point of a game important? Yes. Is a game played at 3–2 important? Of course. All games are important. But for me the Seven Hidden Ad Points are the points that have the greatest potential for gain while being the most commonly overlooked or undervalued, *especially* among recreational players.

If you recognize them as they occur in your matches and respond as I've suggested you will win more often. You'll be taking advantage of the dynamic swing moments in the match. Improve your results there and you'll improve your results when it comes to winning.

Next: What to do when your shots fall apart.

10

The Player's Pit Stop: Stroke Repair

Tour players who are ranked in the Top 20 or 25 play a few matches each year where they're in the zone. I mean totally in the zone. When nobody on the planet is going to beat you on that day. When you feel no pressure and know you'll win. When shots come off your racket with a sweetness and power that almost makes you laugh (or cry, because it doesn't happen more often).

When it *does* happen you hope it happens in the finals of a grand slam event. It did for Sampras against Agassi in the '90 U.S. Open. Nobody was going to beat Pete that day. And late at night over a cup of coffee he'll tell you that. Michael Stich against Becker at Wimbledon in '91. Boris could have stayed home, Stich was in the zone so deep.

Sometimes the zone lasts longer than one match. It happened for me during the summer of '89. It started in West Germany where I won both my Davis Cup singles matches. I had just won the tournament in Memphis in the spring. Then I got into a serious zone. I won tournaments in Stratton Mountain, Vermont; Livingston, New Jersey; and Cincinnati. Along the way I defeated Jim Pugh, David Wheaton, Jim Courier, Boris Becker, Michael Chang, Pete Sampras, and Stefan Edberg. At one point my match record was 17 and 0. I became the first player since Becker in 1986 to win three consecutive tournaments. I was scorching the tour.

Then I went into the U.S. Open and lost in the first round. Nerves? No. Food poisoning. Some bad shellfish the night before I played Todd Witsken. It was bad luck, but I still stayed hot after the Open. Two weeks later I got into the finals in Los Angeles, and later I won the tournament in San Francisco. It was a phenomenal summer and an unforgettable year—five tournament victories plus the Davis Cup wins. That's what you call really being in the zone. But it doesn't happen often, and it usually doesn't last that long.

The No-Zone: What to Do With Dog Meat

Usually when a match is underway there is an ebb and flow to the quality of your play. It's true for everyone at all levels of tennis. The dynamics are changing constantly. A single player rarely performs at their highest level of play (in the zone) for the whole contest. Your game varies in effectiveness and reliability. Sometimes you're seeing and hitting the ball just fine. Then suddenly the wheels come off some part of your game and you're dog meat.

This book isn't aimed at improving your strokes. Go to a good teaching pro for that. They can see exactly what your particular problem is. They can evaluate your swing and give you specific ideas on how to improve. I want to give you some tips on what you can do *during* a match when a particular stroke suddenly goes sour. It may be that you start faulting on your first serve. Maybe your forehand groundstrokes are falling short or being netted.

Whatever the problem is it's good to have an idea or mental image you can use to bring that stroke back to life before it costs you the match. These are tips that have worked for me over the years and have been effective for the players at my tennis camps. But like so many tips you read or hear about, some will work for your game and some may not. The next time the wheels come off try these and see if they help.

The Failing Forehand

If there is one stroke the majority of recreational tennis players feel comfortable with it's their forehand groundstroke. It may not be great, but it's greater than the rest of their shots. You run around your backhand to hit it. You stay away from the net to hit it. You'd eat breakfast with it if you could. So when it gets wobbly you're in trouble.

Better Late Than Never? Wrong!

There are a lot of things that can go wrong with any stroke, and the forehand is no exception. Without question the most stabilizing thing you can do to restore it when it gets in trouble is to check out your racket preparation. Are you getting your racket back in time? Probably not. More than likely you're taking the racket back late. And the reason is usually understandable. We tend to get casual or careless on those physical movements that we're comfortable with. Hey, we *know* that we can hit the shot with our forehand. No sweat.

When you take the racket back late (when the ball is almost on you) everything else in the swing is thrown off—footwork, balance, timing, and options. This can happen because of carelessness, casualness, fatigue, or the other player's forcing shot. When you suddenly find yourself missing that forehand, focus *immediately* on an earlier takeaway.

"It's at the Net. Am I Ready Yet?"

The racket should be back when the tennis ball coming toward you is at the net. When that ball crosses the net you should be ready. Can you take the racket back too early? Maybe. But better too early than too late. For every player who takes the racket back too soon I see a hundred who take it back too late. When your match is under way and suddenly you find yourself cussing at your forehand, say to yourself, "It's at the net. Am I ready yet?"

Backhand Blues

Most recreational players have low expectations for their backhand groundstrokes. They expect a certain (modest) level of production and are willing to tolerate mistakes, up to a point. That point differs from player to player, but it usually ends up with this statement uttered in total frustration: "I know I haven't got much of a backhand, *but this is ridiculous!*" It's the backhand blues. Some C level players have such a poor backhand they can't even tell when it goes bad. That's the exception, however.

When your backhand gets so bad you're running around it even to pick up a towel, it's fix-up time. The most useful checkpoint I have concerns how much you're trying to accomplish with your backhand groundstroke.

Don't Ask a Skinny Dog to Fly

We all have a tendency to ask for more than a shot can give us. With the backhand groundstroke, asking for even a little more than it can give is usually a mistake. Recreational tennis players with a questionable backhand (if yours is solid, congratulations) tend to try to do too much with it, *especially under pressure*.

As I mentioned in chapter 8 (Destroying Your Opponent's Game Plan) it's very effective to come to the net against a weak backhand simply because a common reaction by the other player is to panic, to try and hit that darn backhand better than they've ever hit it in their life. Result? The attacking player didn't even need to bring their racket to the net. The opponent's backhand self-destructs.

When your backhand starts to hurt you more than it usually does, lower your expectations. Stop trying to do more with it than you can reasonably expect. Get it over the net. Keep the ball in play. Go for placement instead of power. Keep your head when your backhand is under attack. Make your shot and force your opponent to at least make a play on it.

If I put you in front of a ball machine and said to just hit backhands over the net and in the court you'd do okay. Why? Because you'd be just trying to hit the ball over the net and into the court. When your backhand bites you during a match, remember that goal. Hit the ball over the net and into the court. Make that the goal. You'll achieve it and the backhand will start to improve.

Your Serve Goes South

When the serve disappears it's the most frustrating of all stroke breakdowns because you can't really blame anyone but yourself for the trouble. When your backhand, forehand, volley, or overhead come apart at least you can look over the net and blame it on your opponent. They had to hit the ball before you could screw up, right? Not with the serve. All they did was stand there. Tough to blame them for your double fault when they're just standing there.

(Note: I don't underestimate the effect that "just standing there" can have. Don't forget Chang beat Lendl in the quarters of the French Open by "just standing there." On match point Michael was cramping up so bad he could hardly move. To cut off Lendl's serving angles Chang camped on the service line. The mighty Lendl collapsed. He double-faulted his way out of the French Open. It was an unbelievable tactical move that had an unbelievable psychological effect. So there are exceptions, but generally you've got nobody to blame for your service fault but you.)

LOOK IN THE MIRROR—DO YOU SEE PETE SAMPRAS?

Start correcting the problem during a match by remembering this. Your best serve may not be as good as you think it is. It isn't a cannon. It isn't an ace machine. And it isn't worth double-faulting for. And that's what you risk doing. Most recreational players (especially guys) believe if they can get everything right on the toss, the extension, the wrist snap, and the follow-through, they'll have a super serve. So they pursue that elusive monster at their own expense.

Here's an indication of how it works. At the recreational level a very common time to double-fault is after a service ace. Reason? The player who serves up that ace loves it and figures the puzzle is solved. "Hey, I've got it working now!" Bang. Fault. Bang. Fault. Double fault after the ace. Which was the accident, the double fault or the ace?

My suggestion is to get a realistic view of your serve. As for my own serve, I occasionally get my first working and it can spit out a few aces. But a lot of the time I know I have to manage it. It isn't going to overpower my opponent and I hate donating points. So I keep a realistic view of what I can accomplish with my first serve. And I've told you how my second serve is—the worst. So I don't get into a macho mindset of trying to show the other guy how "big" my serve is. And neither should you.

Downshift From Fourth to Third

When you start missing that first serve I want you to downshift. Let's call your "maximum" serve fourth gear. That's when you're going full out and really taking a big cut at the ball. What usually happens is a player who is missing that serve will *keep* missing it because they don't want to back away from the challenge. They keep banging their head against the wall time after time hoping the serve will come back. Forget it. Shift gears. Not from fourth to first suddenly, but from fourth to third. Downshift slightly. Don't try to do as much. Don't worry about the ace. Don't worry about service winners. Worry about starting the point without a fault or double fault.

Does that mean you should just bloop it over the net? No. That's going all the way down to first gear. Remember when Mecir had all those double faults and started serving underhand? He went from fourth to first. Mentally, you should just drop it down to third gear. Get some balls in and some rhythm back. *Then* move back up to fourth. You'll like the results.

The Vanishing Volley

The easier the volley is, the lazier the player gets. Watch the players at your courts. When anyone gets a "duck," the kind of ball that's just barely flapping its way over the net, they get lazy or passive. They wait for the ball to arrive. They don't move forward. They assume it's going to be easy. And of course they blow the shot. Usually with a huge last-second swipe at the ball that goes long, wide, or into the net.

Move to the Ball

The closer you are to the net, the better your chance of making a successful volley—the net is less of a factor, you have better angles to use, and you have more of your opponent's court to hit to. Never wait for the ball to arrive. This isn't the Post Office. You don't wait for delivery. In tennis you've got to go pick it up. And with a volley, that's especially true. The quicker you pick it up the better. The extra step or two into the net will improve your percentage of successful volleys dramatically.

So as you're going in to hit a volley, get close to the net. Every step you take closer to it improves your chance of success. Watch John McEnroe or Stefan Edberg. Both of them close out points by getting so close to the net they could lick it. And they do it with great swiftness, like a hawk swooping down on its prey.

The Underachieving Overhead

So you take my advice and now you're on top of the net for those volleys. Only you're not getting a chance to hit any volleys because your opponent realizes you're up so close even rimshots off your racket can dribble over the net for winners. So they start lobbing you and now it's your overhead that is missing in action. You're snapping them into the net. You're pushing them deep. They're going so wide they'd be out even if you were playing doubles.

Go for Placement

When that happens it's because you are usually thinking "power" instead of "placement." Most of the time when an overhead is coming towards you the goal becomes to end the point, to hit an outright winner. Again, it's the trap of asking more from a shot than one can reasonably expect it to give. If your overhead gets shaky during a match, you've got to regroup. Don't try to do so much with it. Resist thinking, "I've got to end it." Go for *placement* instead of *power*. You'll have immediate results because you've taken the pressure of hitting hard off your swing. It will be more rhythmic, more loose, and much more effective.

Playing in Wind

The wind can affect your strokes because it works on your mind. If you're uncomfortable in the wind, here are some ideas that will help you neutralize its negative effects.

1. Start With the Wind in Your Face

Sun is the most important factor to consider when electing which end of the court to choose. As I mentioned in chapter 6, "The Smart Start," if the sun is a problem I'll start the match with it at my back so my opponent has to deal with it first. However, if the sun isn't an issue (at night, or not in the line of sight) the wind is the next consideration. If it is blowing north to south (baseline to baseline) I will elect to start the match with it in my face. That first game is shaky enough without having the wind push my shots long. Hitting into the wind allows me to hit out and I have the assurance of the wind knocking the ball down a bit.

2. Lower Your Toss

A tennis ball doesn't weigh much. A windy day can make it seem like it's a leaf blowing around, especially on your toss. If the wind starts to affect your serve, bring your toss down. Reduce its height a few inches (or more) and you reduce the wind's effect.

3. Shorten Your Strokes

The same goes for your groundstrokes when you're playing in a real breeze. Try to make your shots more compact and concentrate on good contact. You'll reduce the number of mishits and increase the number of shots that go back over the net on a windy day.

4. The Best Weapon Against Wind

Finally, remember that if wind is making your tennis life miserable the ultimate wind cheater is this: Build your own indoor court. Then invite me over to play. I don't like playing in wind either.

A Final Fact About Footwork

Tips are tips. You'll find one in *Tennis* magazine that works for you and you'll tell a friend. It won't do anything for them. Players differ so much in their physical skills, the amount of time they play and practice, and their motivation level that it's rare that a tip will help *everyone*. But there is one tip I'll give you (again) that does work for everyone. It's this: Good footwork improves your tennis.

All of the problems you face with strokes have many solutions. But the first and most important thing to check is your footwork. If it's bad it can hurt every shot you hit. *Or*, it can improve every shot you hit. Whenever you start having a problem with any shot, check your footwork. You know how to do it: get on your toes (the balls of your feet). If you stay light and on your toes you will increase your chances for good stroke execution significantly.

Practice Doesn't Make Perfect, but It Helps

The real key to improving any of your strokes is to work on them when you're not playing a match. Most players think they'll get better if they just play tennis. They play and play and never can figure out why they don't improve. Practice may not make it perfect, but it sure makes it better.

In golf if all you do is play and never hit a shot out of a sand trap except during the round, you won't get better at sand shots. In fact, you'll probably get worse because as you miss some you'll start to get nervous about the shot.

PRACTICE LIKE JACK NICKLAUS

The greatest golfer in the history of the game may also have been the greatest practicer in the history of the game. He practiced with a purpose. He knew what he wanted to work on and he isolated it on the practice range. He was very methodical about fixing the problems that occurred during a match by addressing them in his practice session.

You can make a great improvement in your tennis game by doing the same. Working on a specific problem even for thirty minutes *once a month* will give you terrific results. If you can do it twice a month you won't believe what can happen.

HOW TO IMPROVE?

1. Check on swing mechanics by taking a lesson. Your club pro will get you swinging correctly.
2. Practice what you learned during the lesson. Use a ball machine, the backboard, or a wall. Don't just flail away without a plan. Start by swinging easily and go for consistency. Play little games with yourself. Try to hit the shot you're working on two times in a row. Then three times in a row. Isolate it and concentrate on it. When I was a kid I spent hours and hours hitting against backboards and walls in Piedmont, California. I would play entire imaginary matches in the U.S. Open against an imaginary Ilie Nastase. The wall was Nastase and it was great practice because the wall would never miss.
3. Play someone you know you can beat without much trouble. Look for opportunities during the match to work on the shot that you practiced against the backboard. You may lose. Don't worry about it.

    If your backhand is weak, make sure that you never run around it in this practice match. If your backhand volley is in question, *look* for chances to hit it. Club players don't like to do this because they're afraid their friends will find out about the results. Don't let your ego get in the way of progress. You'll be winning points from those same friends with what you've improved.
4. Bring the shot into your regular matches. You'll find that instead of expecting difficulties on the weak stroke, you'll be looking at it with more and more confidence. Both your shot and your attitude about the shot will be better
5. Play against someone who is better than you are, who will beat you. Playing your buddies all the time gets you into the habit of putting your mind and your game on automatic pilot. Go against someone better and you've got to dig down inside yourself. You've got to work harder, think more, run more, and *you're still going to lose*. Great. That's why you're there. It'll pay off when you go back to your regular opponents.

A little attention in the form of practice will produce big results in your game. Winning is a lot more fun than losing, and improving your weakest areas will make winning easier.

Next: Stealing from the superstars.

11

Learning From the Legends

The superstars of tennis exhibit physical skills that are almost uncanny. In his prime, John McEnroe's eye-hand coordination was equal to any athlete in the world—if you've ever watched a cat's paw toy with a ball of string (or a mouse), John's hand on a racket had the same delicate grace and deadly purpose. Boris Becker's overwhelming physicality would make him a superstar in almost any sport he chose. Early in his career when he was diving after shots he almost made tennis a contact sport. Boris as a star quarterback, home run king, or basketball hero? No problem. And what about Andre Agassi? How can a player take the ball that early and hit it that hard? His timing is better than a Rolex. The same level of outrageous physical gifts applies to all the great ones: Sampras, Edberg, Connors, and others.

So, can you learn anything from them? After all, they're blessed with physical gifts most people only dream about. You can't "learn" a natural gift can you? Yes, you can, but not necessarily in the way you think. Obviously, certain mechanical fundamentals apply to all levels of tennis—turn your shoulders, use your legs, keep your eyes on the ball. All stuff you've heard before.

I'd like you to think about a different area when it comes to learning from these tennis superstars. It is this: their attitude and tactics during a match and how these apply to your tennis.

Keep in mind that very few rules apply to everyone. What works for you may not work for someone else. As you think about what these superstars bring to their game remember they've often succeeded with totally different approaches. Study what they do and look for what can help your own approach, given your style of play and temperament.

Andre Agassi

It's showtime when Double A arrives. Neon clothes. Neon hair. He's like a rock star. He gets away with it because when it comes to tennis he delivers the product.

I've never seen a guy his size get so much stick on the ball. It's really unbelievable. He's just got serious heat. Because of it, he puts immediate fear into you because you know he can just rack the ball and control play. When he's on his game, he just moves you back and forth at will. It's no fun to play Andre when he's "on."

He also is a guy who plays on emotion. If he's feeling mentally, emotionally, and physically good, and things are working for him, he is definitely the best player in the world. (Except for Jim Courier, who when he's "on" is also the best in the world. Two best in the worlds? Right. I think that one of the great rivalries of the '90s is going to be Agassi and Courier, two phenomenal athletes who go back a long way with each other. They battled when they were Juniors and then at Nick Bolletieri camps. On the court against each other they take no prisoners. When they meet in the finals of a Slam event—and I don't think it will be long from now—be sure you stop whatever you're doing and watch it on the tube. There'll be blood on the tracks when they're done with each other.)

One of Andre's greatest assets is his ability to take the ball extremely early, on the rise. Connors has also done that throughout his career, but Andre takes it even earlier and hits it harder. The way he does it is almost impossible to copy or more pros would. Many times his groundstrokes are virtually a half-volley, he takes it so close to the bounce. However, the basic idea is something you should keep in mind for your own game.

Taking the ball early means sending it back to your opponent harder and sooner. It's devastating to hit a shot to Andre and have him blast it back to you before you've even finished your swing. It seems like it happens that quickly. Your own opponents won't like seeing the ball come back at them sooner either.

For your own game don't think about hitting the ball early. Think about hitting it *earlier*. Normally you'd wait for the tennis ball to land on your side of the court, bounce, rise, and start to fall before you hit it, below the top of its arc. That's because it's easier to hit that way; it's moving slower and you've had more time to get to it. But that strategy also gives your opponent more time to get set, attack, or recover. It also means you have to swing harder to create pace or get depth because the ball is losing speed by the time you hit it.

So think "earlier" instead of "early." Here's how to start.

When you get a ball that's coming deep to you the natural tendency is to back up and wait for the ball to drop before you hit it. Instead, force yourself to move into the ball and take it just slightly earlier—10 percent earlier. When practicing make it a goal. Look for balls that you might otherwise be a little lazy on. Step into them and hit 10 percent sooner than you normally would *after* they start descending.

Get used to it and then start looking for an opportunity to take the ball right at the top of its arc. Now you'll see some results (both good and bad). You'll have your share of mishit balls, but as you get comfortable with taking the ball earlier you'll see it go back harder, deeper, and faster.

The other thing to notice about Andre when you watch him play is the way his feet and racket are moving together at all times. They don't move separately and neither should yours. Don't move your feet and then suddenly jerk your racket into position. Bad timing is guaranteed. That's a pretty basic idea, but Andre really is the best example of how to do it. When you see him play on television watch that great early racket preparation.

When Andre swings wide to either side his racket moves back almost immediately. When he is receiving serve his racket moves back as soon as the server makes contact with the ball. It's why he can take the ball so early and with such precision—his racket preparation is excellent. It's unsurpassed on the tour.

The Lesson From Agassi

1. Practice taking the ball 10 percent earlier for more damaging groundstrokes.
2. Move your racket and your feet simultaneously.

The results will show up in your scores. Who knows, you may even start wanting to bleach your hair. Believe me, if I thought it would give me Agassi's groundstrokes I'd do it.

Ivan Lendl

Ivan Lendl hits the ball harder and *with more accuracy* than any player on the planet. He just knocks the cover off the ball. The major difference between him and Agassi is that Ivan is usually four or five feet *behind* the baseline when he makes contact. Andre is often *inside* the baseline so his shot gets to you sooner and is going faster. But there are three other elements of the Terminator's game that you might want to incorporate into your own approach.

First of all, Ivan is known for his consistency. It is something he is careful to establish at the very beginning of a match. As I mentioned, when he comes out and begins the first several games he will not miss a ball. That's because he's hitting at only 65 percent to 70 percent of his full power. You should approach the beginning of your own matches the same way. Set your timing, rhythm, and confidence in place before going for more power.

Second, Ivan has a favorite little spot on the court that is sort of his own personal pitcher's mound. Have you noticed how he likes to move about four feet left of center on the baseline? He is actually running around his backhand just slightly (sometimes more than just slightly). He just loves to park himself there and start cranking the forehand. From that spot he loves to move you back and forth as he opens up the court.

When I've played him he'll settle in on that spot and start moving me right and left, wider and wider. Finally, I'll hit one short and he bangs out a winner. He feels very confident and strong in that position.

In your own game look for the spot on the court that gives you your favorite shot and work to get there. If you love the forehand, set up your own pitcher's mound and fire away. If it's the forehand volley, start *really* looking for opportunities to come to the net. Don't wait for an invitation (a very weak shot). Force the issue a little.

That personal pitcher's mound for me is just behind the service T. It sets up my best weapon, the forehand approach shot to the ad court. I'm always looking to get that shot. I call it my equity shot because if I get it enough I'll usually own the match. When I do get it I have great confidence in hitting it. Most players are the same. Know what it is that works for you and then actively try to get in position to use it.

Another element that Ivan is a master at is stretching a lead. He may be the best there is at staying ahead when he gets ahead. And one of the reasons he's effective at it is that he takes intelligent risks when he's got the cushion of a lead. Not wild shots, but ones that are more forcing, more angled, more powerful. He likes to build on the momentum of getting ahead by upping the level and range of his game. He does it in a measured and calculated way. When he gets a lead the pressure he exerts is very noticeable, but he always operates within the boundaries of his game.

When he's ahead he starts going for his aces with more regularity and with more confidence, because he trusts his second serve. If he's receiving serve he really tries to punish the ball, especially on his opponent's second serve. Lendl waiting for a second serve is like inviting The Alien over for dinner. You know it's not going to be fun. Ivan will totally destroy a weak second. It's one of the reasons I've never beaten him. I'm forced to go with a weaker first serve to insure that I don't let him see a second.

How does what he's doing apply to you? When you get ahead increase the pressure on your opponent. Don't be careless or swing wildly. Seize the opportunity to press your advantage and force your opponent to come up with more difficult shots.

Finally, I want to stress Lendl's great patience during a match. During the '80s he maintained a mental discipline that was almost like Borg's. Lendl never rushed into a point or through a shot. He was very methodical. Almost *all* recreational players are just the opposite. They (this means *you*) get impatient. They attempt to hit the winner too soon. They want to make an approach shot more than it's supposed to be (the approach shot sets up the winner—it isn't supposed to be the winner).

I'll watch two club players during a point and suddenly one of them will try and end it when they had no advantage, no opening, no reason to do so. They just got impatient. Lendl in the '80s knew when to strike. He was patient. In fact, one of the reasons his game has suffered in the '90s is that he *isn't* as patient as he used to be. Maybe he just can't wait to get home to his family, but he definitely doesn't have the patience that he used to possess.

Learning From Lendl

1. Start the match at 65 percent of your power potential.
2. Know where your own "personal pitcher's mound" is and get to it.
3. Stretch a lead by taking intelligent risks. Pressure your opponent when you're ahead.
4. Be patient. Don't force a shot that isn't there.

Ivan is great at maintaining an advantage, not so good at coming back when he's behind. In fact, early in his career he would tank it occasionally when he got behind or didn't want to play. Different players have different tendencies. I get cautious when I'm ahead and try to squeeze my opponent with steady tennis. Lendl likes to up the level of his game. It's worth trying with your own tennis.

Boris Becker

Boris is an out-and-out superathlete, maybe the best one in pro tennis. You can just sense his eagerness to compete. He also has tremendous presence out on the court. By that I mean he plays big, and he plays big off of *everything*. He has heavy artillery, and with it he's constantly putting pressure on you. It's right here right now! The Becker serve is humongous. You can't really get a sense of its weight watching him on TV. It just goes right through you. In addition, if his serve is on it allows him to take chances with other parts of his game because he knows he can come back with the Heater.

Having said all that I haven't even gotten to the strong part of his game: his self-confidence. At his best he's so confident in his ability to come back or dictate play that he never doubts that he can win. He may get mad at himself, but he never thinks that he's outgunned. He not only thinks he can beat you with his strengths, he believes he can beat you with his weaknesses. Total confidence. And Boris is similar to Lendl when it comes to stretching a lead. In fact, he will go further than Lendl and actually take more risks.

Basic Becker

1. Believe in yourself. Think positive thoughts about your game and your ability to win.
2. When you get a lead, go for it. Don't be timid.

John McEnroe

When he was playing, John McEnroe's hands had the precision, soft touch, and dexterity of a brain surgeon's. He invented and started routinely using shots that most players had previously seen only in dreams. For example, in the early '80s Mac would occasionally come to the net behind a weak approach shot and his opponent would absolutely crush the ball! Four or five times a match John would desperately lunge at the passing shot and not only get his racket on it, but he'd hit a soft, drop-shot winner. This is not taught currently by any tennis coach in the world. Try it. Believe me, if you succeed in doing it it's an accident.

But there are two tactical elements that John was known for that are worth considering. First, McEnroe played aggressively. He took the action right to his opponent. When he was playing well you felt the pressure before he even hit a ball because you knew he was going to start attacking. He wanted to see you make the passing shot against him. He wanted to see *if* you could make the passing shot against him. He got in close behind the net because he knew it was easier for you to choke at the baseline than for him to choke at the net. You knew that John was going to put his game right into your face.

Secondly, McEnroe was flexible. If you did start passing him or lobbing him successfully he adjusted. He could be an all-court player when it suited him. If you showed him the passing shot he would stay back and come in very selectively. His game (and mind) were very adaptable. He was a very smart and observant tennis player. He was always aware of the dynamics of the match and was looking for ways to exploit your weaknesses.

Mac's Attack

1. Probe. Aggressively search for your opponent's weaknesses. Put pressure on them.
2. Be flexible. If what you're doing isn't working, change.

One of the remarkable things about John's game was that his great tennis skills were complemented by his intelligence on the court. He knew what he had and how to *use it most effectively to exploit his opponent.*

Stefan Edberg

Stefan's tactical approach is the opposite of McEnroe's. This is a good example of how different styles can be equally effective. McEnroe will test you here and test you there, trying to find a weakness and exploit it, coming in, staying back, constantly probing. Edberg's approach is blunt: "I will serve and volley on every single point and attack the net constantly. If you want to beat me you'll have to do it with me at the net."

He has polished his serve-volley game until there are no cracks or rough edges on it. His movement off the serve is just terrific. He jumps into the court on the serve so that he's hitting his first volley from inside the service line most of the time. And he doesn't miss that volley.

Stefan will serve and volley twenty-two consecutive times. You can pass him cleanly twenty-two consecutive times. What'll he do next? Number twenty-three will be a serve and volley. Whereas McEnroe will retreat to the baseline and look for something else to hurt you with, Edberg will force you to make the difficult shot one more time. And one more time. And one more time. You have to be very solid to pass someone like Edberg for the entire match.

He has no fear of anybody. Even if he's getting passed regularly he *knows* he's better off near the net. It takes a lot of pressure off him when it comes to deciding what to do next. Edberg's fellow Swede (and my coauthor's tennis hero) Bjorn Borg would stay on the baseline as relentlessly as Stefan attacks the net. He knew his game and he made you try to beat him when he was playing his strength.

Stefan Edberg also has a great ability to cover a weakness. He has probably one of the weaker forehands of any number-one-ranked tennis player in the history of the game. He basically uses a backhand grip to hit a forehand groundstroke. He understands that and also has the ability to limit any damage it might cause.

He offsets the damage in two ways. He takes his forehand out of play on his service games by coming to the net. The rest of the time when Stefan hits a forehand he doesn't try to do more with it than he has to. He understands what it can do and doesn't try to push more out of it. And he gets away with it. Remember the old saying, "Don't fix it if it ain't broke"? Well, his game "ain't broke" and neither is Stefan. In 1990 he was ranked number one and earned $1,995,901. By 1993 he had won over $13,000,000. Maybe that's why he hasn't bothered to improve his forehand.

Also, like Borg, Stefan Edberg has total control of his emotions. Have you ever seen him get rattled or mad out on the court? On his way to winning the '92 U.S. Open he was down a break in the fifth set both to Lendl in the quarters and to Chang in the semis. The look on his face was no different then from what it was at the start of the match. It told you nothing.

He understands that for him getting emotional doesn't work. He's in total control, and when you're on the other side of the net it's discouraging. You never get a chance to see Edberg get discouraged. His composure is the same whether he's ahead or behind. He won't allow you the boost of seeing him get down on himself mentally.

Edberg's Excellence
1. Develop a style of play that best fits your strokes. Have a clear idea of who you are out on the court.
2. Have a plan. Stay with it. Don't get nervous if it doesn't work immediately. Make your opponent beat you at what you do best.
3. Don't let your opponent know you're discouraged. Your body language (and your verbal language) can give a boost to the opposition.
4. Know where you are vulnerable and reduce your exposure there.

Stefan is workmanlike in his approach to playing. His game can be almost boring to watch because it's so predictable, but he gets fantastic results. He has a very simple strategy based on his strengths and he pursues it relentlessly.

Jimmy Connors

Jimmy Connors is the pit bull of tennis. Even today, past his prime, he is a great, great competitor. He is tenacious. He is a super tactician. He is opportunistic. He is smart. He is ballsy. He is relentless. Jimmy plays tennis like he's in the Roman Colosseum fighting for his life—he would have been a great gladiator.

Until Agassi came along Connors had the greatest return of serve in the history of the game. He used it to take away the big serve advantage of guys like Kevin Curran, Ivan Lendl, and Roscoe Tanner. He would make a play; get the ball back, and force the big server to hit some additional shots. Guys like Curran were used to getting two or three points a game off their service. Jimmy made them play a couple of extra volleys per game. That eventually would translate into a break.

Jimmy starts a match looking immediately for weak spots in your game. If he senses a flaw in some part of it he's like a shark in bloody water. He'll attack until you show him that you can beat him with it. Connors will find out in the first couple of games what your problem is that day and immediately start ripping at it.

His tenacity and grit are without equal. He goes full tilt from the opening bell. With Jimmy it's war. With Jimmy *it's personal*. He gets cranked up like nobody else in the game. He really was—and is—one of the great acts in tennis.

Learning From Jimbo
1. Never give up. Repeat. Never give up.
2. Aggressively search for your opponent's weaknesses. When you identify them, keep attacking them.
3. Improve your service return. You can turn your opponent's serve to your advantage.

Jimmy Connors is the tennis version of a hired gun. He comes out with one purpose: to win. And so should you. That may sound obvious, but with Jimmy you can just feel the incredible desire to beat the other guy. He cares only about winning.

Jim "Terminator II" Courier

A ton of game is what Jim Courier has and he brings it to the park with him every day. He tries to the maximum on every *single* point of every single game of every single set, whether the score is 5–0 or 0–5. He just has an amazingly consistent, high level intensity during a match. Watch him and you'll see just how totally focused and committed to victory he is.

You used to see that look of ferocious desire in Connors's eyes all the time. Obviously, all great players have that desire. But few of them have it *all the time*. Courier does. I get the feeling he probably brushes his teeth ferociously.

Another aspect of his game you should be aware of is his willingness to really go for the shot that's in his range. When Jim sees a ball that he likes, one that he can open up the court with, make a strong approach shot off of (or one that he can just really lay into), he *fires* away at 110 percent. He's not afraid to *take his shot when he sees his shot*. He's not bashful. He doesn't wait until he gets the perfect opportunity to whack the ball. Jim bangs it if it's even close to being in his range. And he does it without getting careless. When he smells a chance to start taking control of a point he immediately seizes his opportunity.

He's also great at mixing up his shots. He drives the ball hard and flat, he loops the ball, he hits great angles, and he gets depth on his shots. You never see the same thing over and over, so you can't get into a groove with one type of ball. He keeps varying the program. And he can mash his serve! Believe me, this is a package of stuff that is going to win him more Grand Slam titles.

Finally, I want to get back to something I mentioned earlier: pressure and nerves. Jim Courier handles them in a very unique way, totally the opposite of what I do. When the points are big, when the pressure is on, Jim hits the ball harder and harder. You don't see him getting conservative or playing it safe. That's why I call him Terminator II (Lendl is the original tennis Terminator).

When you're across the net from Courier you know that on big points (Set-up Points, Game Points, Tie-breakers, Match Points) he is going to hit harder and let it all hang out. Knowing this really puts you under the gun. You know Courier is going to blast away with all his firepower and it tends to get you trying to do things you shouldn't (going for aces, trying to end points too soon, overhitting).

Jim Courier was the number one player in the world in 1993. He's fallen off that peak as he's struggled with his game a bit, but Courier has dedication and heart. On any given day he can light up just about anybody.

Copying Courier

1. Desire. Come to play. Give the match everything you've got. Lock into the match from the very first point and don't check out mentally or physically until after the last point.
2. Mix it up. Use all of your shots and work on developing more weapons. And then incorporate them into your game. Don't let your opponent see the same thing over and over.
3. Guts. Don't back away from opportunity. When the points or situation are big tell yourself to hit away. Try Courier's approach. If you go down, at least you go down with your guns blazing.
4. Take your shot when you see your shot. This really is part of number three, "Guts." When you get a chance to make a play, to start taking charge of a point, *take it*. Develop your sense of smell. Then when you even sniff a little opportunity, capitalize.

Jim Courier doesn't have the same level of natural physical gifts that Pete and Andre have, but he neutralizes that small difference with desire. He plays red hot. So if he doesn't burn out he's going to be a force in tennis for years to come.

Pete "the Heat" Sampras

Pete the Heat comes to the tennis court bearing gifts—his gifts as an extraordinary athlete. He's right at the top when it comes to talent. Like McEnroe he can hit shots other players only see in their dreams. He'll attack the net and his opponent will whistle a near perfect passing shot down the line. Pete will dive at the ball and on the absolute full stretch hit a soft drop volley for a winner. Cruel.

His techniques are hard to copy because he's so relaxed when he hits shots with what I call his "loosey-goosey" technique: wristy, flashy strokes that call for tremendous skill. But there is a lot in his tactical approach that you can think about.

Pete serves big and knows he has a dominating weapon at his disposal. On those days when he's serving up aces (and service winners) like he was picking grapes, he starts taking chances on his *return of serve*. He puts big pressure on the other guy's serve because Pete knows he's going to hold his own serve without trouble. He starts attacking serve by taking some risks and pressuring you on every serve. When you're serving against him in that situation you suddenly face enormous pressure. It really destabilizes your serving game.

But, just as important, when Pete starts missing his first serve he isn't afraid to back off of it, to spin a few first serves in and get his rhythm back. He doesn't just keep pounding the Heater over and over again unsuccessfully. He goes from fourth gear to third gear (or second). Then, when he gets his rhythm going again, it's back to Pete's Heat. Good mental management.

One other thing: Pete doesn't get caught up outside the lines. He's always composed and doesn't let himself get concerned with the crowd, bad calls, disruptions, or anything else. He won't let what's going on outside the lines bother him. You'll see him settle himself down with a few deep breaths and a couple of ball bounces. Very cool. He refuses to waste energy or emotions on anything except what's happening *inside* the lines.

Pete's Principles

1. When you're holding serve easily, increase the pressure you put on your opponent's serve. Take some chances and get more aggressive.
2. When you miss three or four serves in a row, shift gears. Don't be as ambitious with it—instead, spin a few serves in and get a little rhythm and confidence going.
3. Play inside the lines. Don't let outside distractions bother you. It takes energy and it breaks your concentration.

Pete the Heat is one of the great ones out on tour. He has great skills, great composure, and he's a smart player. That's the combination for becoming a legend.

Brad Gilbert

From Tom Chivington, Brad's coach, Foothill Junior College tennis coach and 1992 N.C.C. Men's Tennis Coach of the Year

When Brad came to me at Foothill College from A.S.U. in 1980 it took me a while to figure him out. The first time I saw him hitting on a court I made a mental note: "No forehand. No backhand. No volley. Weak serve." I also made note of something else: "Wins matches."

This is what's known as a coach's dream, a kid who can figure out how to win without any outstanding weapons. Brad was doing that.

Through his college career it never occurred to me that Brad would make it as a pro (or even try to make it). However, he did something right after he left Foothill that told me he had a future.

At that time (early '82) he had to qualify to get into tournaments. In case you don't know about it, qualifying is where the stars of tomorrow fight for the two or three available openings in that week's tournament. The ferocity and intensity of those matches is legendary. The kids are desperate to get in and it is bloody. In 1982 Brad won twenty-eight qualifying matches in a row against players like Pat Cash, Guy Forget, Miloslav Mecir, and others.

They don't keep records on things like that, but I doubt if it's ever been done before or since. That showed me Brad had something special going for him.

Many of the experts have criticized Brad's abilities because they don't see in him the kind of obvious brilliance apparent in players like McEnroe, Becker, Agassi, or Sampras. When he played as an amateur they said he couldn't make it as a pro. When he turned pro they said he wouldn't make a living out there. When he got to Number 4 in the world and earned $4 million he started to make believers out of a lot of people. They admired his ability to find a way to win. That's when he got tagged with the label "Winning Ugly."

However, before you dismiss Brad's shot-making ability let me assure you that he does have some assets in that department. He works with a broad range of shots that are dependable. Brad is a counterpuncher. He's at his best when he's being attacked.

His physical condition is also important. After surgery in '88 Brad began working exclusively with Mark Grabow on conditioning, and he improved his strength and stamina dramatically. The longer the match, the better I like Brad's chances.

He also has great anticipation. He is almost always prepared for what happens on court.

But where Brad excels, where he is as good or better than anyone in the world, is in his mental approach to the game. He understands *the importance of matching up your strengths to the opponent's weaknesses*. He knows when to attack and when to be cautious. He has great court awareness and really understands the dynamics of the match. His pre-match preparation is superb. When Brad arrives at the court he is totally prepared for the task ahead.

Brad's basic approach to the game is one every club player should copy. Brad Gilbert *abhors unforced errors. He hates stupid mistakes. He absolutely can't stand to give his opponent the free point.* When you play Brad Gilbert you have to provide it all yourself. You can't borrow anything. For a recreational, high school, or college player I believe there is nothing that could improve results sooner than fully understanding and applying that philosophy. Don't donate points. Brad makes very sure he gives away a minimum of points.

Brad gets described as a very conservative player, one who doesn't do much. But Brad is actually doing a great deal. It's just not flashy. He is extremely analytical with opponents. He knows what to expect, what a specific player will do in a specific situation. What the player's favorite shots are and what shots aren't so hot. He plays smart at important moments in the match.

In working with my students I've found that those who apply Brad's thinking and approach to their own games improve a great deal.

It sounds easy, but it's not. Most players are mentally lazy out on the court. I've always felt that maybe the reason Brad tended to excel in this way was because as a kid he couldn't fall back on the kind of astonishing physical gifts that so many athletes are blessed with. Maybe he realized early on that in order to win he needed to develop the analytical, mental side of the game. I believe he proved to a lot of average players how valuable this part of the game can be.

Basic Brad
1. Learn to hate your unforced errors.
2. Be observant of your own game and your opponent's. Know what's going on during the match.
3. Try to play your strength to your opponent's weakness.
4. Read number one several more times.

Brad Gilbert understands the great degree to which a tennis match is played in the mind. Observation and analysis are fundamental to his success. He may have more in his approach to the game that the average tennis player can learn from than anyone else on tour. He doesn't win with superstar strokes. He wins because he maximizes what he's got in that department. He does that because he's a good thinker. He understands how to get ready for a match and how to recognize and capitalize on the dynamics of a match. He's brilliant at bringing down the effectiveness of his opponent's game. If the typical club player would do the same the improvement would be dramatic.

Next: Gamesmanship ain't no game!

III

Mind Games, Psyching, and Gamesmanship

Tales From The Tour

"Better parking."—Brad Gilbert, when asked what being seeded eighth in the U.S. Open meant

12

The Masters of Rage:
Connors and McEnroe

Go out and buy the most expensive tennis racket on the market.
Practice until your hands bleed and take lessons until you're broke.
Then take some vitamins and get a good night's sleep. You can do all
this, but it won't do you much good if your opponent psychs you out
during the match. Or before it even starts. And I know. I've been
worked over by some of the best in the business. In fact, John
McEnroe pulled one of the greatest psych jobs in the history of tennis
on me and he wasn't even on the court when he did it. He psyched
me out before the match started—the *day before.*

We were scheduled to play in the finals of the TransAmerica/San
Francisco Championship in 1984. I was starting to get some attention
in the tennis world by then and since I'm from the Bay Area I really
wanted to look good in front of my hometown fans. And what better
way to do it than by beating the number one player in the world,
John McEnroe. However, Mac had other ideas. One of them was to
work on me before we ever hit a tennis ball.

The night before our match McEnroe was quoted by the *San
Francisco Examiner:* "Brad Gilbert doesn't swing at the ball hard
enough to break an egg. He doesn't hit the ball. He waves at it." I
read his quote that night at my apartment and got so mad I couldn't
finish dinner. "He wants to see a little power? I'll show him some
power. I'm gonna knock that little s——— off the court!" Needless to
say, the outcome of the match had just been decided. McEnroe had
gotten to me in my own home.

The next day I went out on the court at the Cow Palace and tried to smash the fuzz off every single ball I hit. I whacked serves and pounded groundstrokes. I went for aces on my *second* serve. I went for winners off his *first* serve. I wanted to show the hometown fans that McEnroe was wrong, that Brad Gilbert was a big power hitter. What I showed them was that John McEnroe is a great con artist. He had pulled me out of my game. I lost in straight sets.

McEnroe had to love it. He won the match 6–4, 6–4, and the psyching had been the difference. Later he told a reporter, "Brad seemed to be playing a little more aggressive than usual. I think it hurt his game." And he said it with a straight face. Great psyching by Mac.

Two Kinds of Psyching

There are two types of psyching that can hurt you. The kind that your opponent does to you and the kind *you* do to you. Both can hurt your game if you don't understand what's going on. With McEnroe in San Francisco I didn't really think about what was happening. He laid out the trap and I fell right into it.

The mental games that get played during a match can affect the outcome just as much as the physical and tactical part of tennis. Remember this: The mind games the other player uses all have the same general purpose—to disrupt your concentration. They upset your emotional equilibrium and tempo, they pull you out of your game. You become the one getting jerked around. Instead of controlling the tempo, pace, and "attitude" of the match, you're being dictated to.

Here are some specific things you can do to counter the tactics, psychological and otherwise, intentional or not, that come up most often in your own matches. I say, "Beware the Turtle, the Rabbit, and the Hooker" (as in slow play, quick play, and cheating). Also, I want to mention a couple of special psych jobs that I've run into that you might learn something from. But I want to start with the most common mental "disorder" that occurs in tennis: anger, in you and in the other player. Both can take you out of your game and destroy your chance of winning.

The Best at Being the Worst

The two greatest "game"-players of all time were John McEnroe and Jimmy Connors. When it comes to controlling what's going on out on the court they ruled; they controlled the crowd, the umpire, the linesman, the referee, even the ball boys and girls. They controlled the altercations and disputes and, just as important, *when* in the match they occurred. They were great at dictating the tempo of play, speeding it up or slowing it down depending on what they were trying to do to the other player. They could control the energy, the atmosphere, and the attitude on and around the court.

In a long match they could take you through more ups and downs than an elevator. And at their best (or worst) they could do more to hurt you without even hitting a tennis ball than most players could do with a racket. They were like Bart Simpson's evil twins. Here's how the King of Gamesmanship, Jimmy Connors, manipulated things to make anger (his and mine) his weapon of choice.

Connors Goes Ballistic: Chicago '85

Jimmy and I have had some unbelievable battles and come close to bumping heads a few times (remember the locker room screaming he did after his '87 Masters loss?). He takes no pushing from anybody, and I hate to get knocked around too, especially by someone who'll use their "legend" status to get an advantage. And Jimmy would do that any time he could. He pulled something in Chicago that got me as angry as I've ever been during a match.

In 1985 we were scheduled to play in the Windy City at an important point in my career. Keep in mind that I'd just broken into the Top 20 but still didn't have any wins against big name players. I'm moving up in the rankings little by little and suddenly here I am in the quarters against Connors, who's ranked number three in the world. A win against him would be a big notch. I also thought I could beat him. Let me get to the good part and show you what happened. And why.

We split the first two sets 6–4, 4–6 and I'm really playing my tail off. The third set is tough tennis, neither one of us wanting to give an inch. We keep holding serve until it's 4–5 in the set, Jimmy serving at 30–40. I can't believe it. I've got a *match point* opportunity looking at me. I know the sports psychologists say you're only supposed to think of winning just "one point at a time" and all that stuff, but I couldn't help myself. I'm wired and thinking, "Gilbert, you're going to take out Connors. You're moving into the big time, baby!"

With a match point facing him Connors gets ready to serve to stay alive in the match. He's very deliberate. Bouncing the ball eight or nine times. Focused. Patient. I'm thinking if I get a chance I want to attack him before he can attack me. "Come in first chance," I tell myself. Then he serves. Nothing special (his specialty). It comes into my backhand and I hit a slice right back down the line. And deep. I race in behind it. Jimmy covers and hits a lob up on my backhand side. I'm not expecting it and get caught. But the lob is weak, not very deep. I backpedal a couple of steps and do kind of a twisting leap. I stretch up, swing hard, and pound an overhead right back down the line on the deuce court. Connors guesses wrong. He was heading east and the ball's heading west. It hits the sideline behind him and the linesman signals good.

I've done it. I've won match point and beaten a legend in a big tournament. I start jumping up and down and pumping my fist in the air, excited, exuberant, and proud of myself. I run to the net with my big paw out and get ready to shake hands and accept the congratulations. But Jimmy isn't in a congratulating mood.

Before I can even take two steps toward the net, he starts freaking out. He's screaming and yelling at the linesman, pointing at the line and pointing at a spot outside the line. He's like a wild man! So mad he's got stuff coming out of his nose and spit coming out of his mouth. He slams his racket into the court and runs back to the chair screaming about the call. He's holding his head in his hands and shouting stuff you'd get arrested for if you said it to a cop. He points back to a "spot" he thinks he sees outside the line.

Meanwhile I'm standing at the net like a kid waiting for Santa Claus. I was going to have to wait for the congratulations. I honestly didn't know what was happening. The match was over, wasn't it? Was he putting on a little show so he could claim I didn't *really* beat him? In his mind did he want to claim it wasn't a legitimate win? Was this a variation of what he pulled in the locker room after his Master's loss? What was going on?

Jimmy keeps up some unbelievable heat, literally screaming in the umpire's face from a couple of feet away. He's just really roasting him with a tirade about the ball being two inches out! He runs back and points to a "mark." The crowd is whistling and booing and stomping. They're in an uproar.

I've got both hands on the top of the net and am just standing there a little confused. Waiting for things to quiet down. Things didn't quiet down.

Suddenly I hear what I can't believe. The umpire turns on the microphone and says, "Overrule. Ball was out. Mr. Connors serving. Deuce." *He overrules the linesman's call on a match point!* You could have stuck a fork in my eye and I wouldn't have screamed any louder. Only you couldn't hear me. The crowd drowned me out. The screaming fans—8,321 of them jammed into the University of Illinois Arena—let out a noise like a bomb exploding. The place went absolutely wild.

It meant more tennis for them and they felt great. I felt like I'd been mugged. They love Jimmy in Chicago (these days they love him everywhere, but back then only a few cities had taken him to heart) so the crowd was in total pandemonium. First they were booing the original call. Now they're wild for the overrule.

I completely lose it. I race over to the chair screaming, *"How the hell can you overrule five minutes after the point is over!"* I was crazy. The umpire sits up there like nothing's happened. He's looking down on me like I'm a ballboy who's not doing a good job.

I was so furious that I started shaking his chair. I'd completely gone over the edge. He's alarmed because he's sitting up there ten feet above the ground and a guy who's obviously out of control is shaking his chair and screaming at him like a madman. He looks like he's just seen the ghost of Bill Tilden, hanging onto the arms of the chair like it's a carnival ride. I was furious.

It didn't help. The overrule stood. The match continued. Jimmy serves at deuce. I didn't win that point. Or the next point. It's 5–all. Now I serve. Lose the first point. Lose the second point. Lose the third point. Lose the fourth point. Jimmy serves at 6–5. I lose the first point. The second point. The third point. The match point. Match point! I just lost match point. I lost the match. A total nightmare. I hadn't won a point in three games. And Jimmy had grabbed the match from me. Jimmy had gotten to an official at my expense. Just a complete disaster. I was destroyed.

Here's the point. Jimmy *had* intimidated the umpire into giving

him another chance. The ball was very close. Obviously I thought it
was in. And the linesman thought it was in. On a ball that close on
match point you generally don't get overrules. Unless it's Connors
who's yelling in your face demanding an overrule and 8,000 fans are
backing him up. The chair umpire caved in to Connors's pressure.
But that wasn't where Jimmy did the worst damage. The worst
damage was what he did to me. The worst was that I folded.

The overrule completely destroyed me, my thinking, my emotions, my control. I came apart from the anger and never got my head
back on. I was so upset I lost control of what I was doing on the court.
I felt like I had been robbed and became a complete basket case. I
knew it was asking a lot of myself to beat Connors once. I figured it
was asking too much to beat him twice on the same night. I hate to
admit it, but for one of the few times in my life during a tennis match
I quit caring. I felt like I'd been cheated out of victory.

Jimmy got to an official and he got to me. In his prime he was
willing and able to do anything he could think of to win. Remember,
the point of this little incident isn't that Jimmy is a bad guy. Jimmy is
Jimmy. Anger is the point here, uncontrolled anger. It happens on
the pro level and it happens on every level. Uncontrolled anger
happens for a variety of reasons and at strange times. But when it
happens you have to be ready for it. You have to recognize it and you
have to be able to regain control or it's like playing with a broken
racket.

In this case I was unprepared mentally. I'd never had an opportunity like that in my career. I didn't anticipate that what happened
could happen. That was my mistake. I learned from it.

Anger out of control kills you (unless you're like Connors or
McEnroe). Anger for the right reason helps you. Against a master
like Connors I needed to tell myself going in to be ready for anything.
My pre-match mental preparation was weak. Remember what I said
about Connors's ability to "control the elements"? I wasn't ready
for it in '85. I needed to tell myself that he was capable of doing
anything. And when he did it, not to play into his game. Of course,
I had a right to argue my point with the umpire, but when I started
shaking the chair Connors had won the mind game. If I had been
prepared mentally I could have won the match. My game didn't
fail me. My mind did.

And to add insult to injury, I got fined $1,500 for abusing the umpire.

But as you'll see later, I learned a valuable lesson.

To Scream or Not to Scream? That is the Question

So, how is anger ever good? I repeat, uncontrolled anger is what destroys your game. Anger for the right reason and kept under control will work for you.

I do my share of complaining during a match. Some people say too much. I hear, "Brad you're too hard on yourself. You whine about everything." They're probably right. But what I'm usually doing is trying to crank myself up after I've made a mistake in execution or strategy. When I get casual, or miss a sitter, or try too much at the wrong time, when I get impatient, or keep repeating the same mental or physical mistake, *I get mad at myself.* And so should you. That kind of anger can work *for* you.

It's like a high school football coach who kicks you in the butt to get you going. Get angry at yourself when you screw up. Show yourself that you care. Your game will listen. But then move on. Look at what's happening right in front of you. You have to forget about what's just happened.

You cannot look ahead and behind at the same time. If you grind on a point (or problem) that's over, you can't be in the point facing you. You're distracted and a distracted tennis player makes physical and mental mistakes. With Connors that night in Chicago I couldn't look ahead. I couldn't take my mind off what had happened and focus on what was going to happen. And it cost me the match.

So anger—controlled anger—can be a great motivator, a great way to get your own attention. It can get the juices going. Use it and don't be afraid of it. Control it. Don't let it control you. I've never understood how a major player like Bjorn Borg could be so cold during a match. It was like he didn't care. He got robbed on calls plenty of times and he knew it. I never saw him get upset even once. It worked for him. It doesn't work for most people.

How to Control Your Anger

I've gotten better at controlling my anger over the years, better at moving on and away from the problem that gets my fuse lit. Remember the difficulty here is controlling being out of control. If that sounds like a contradiction, it is. But you'll see what I mean when you read my rules.

1. Put Out the Spark, Not the Fire

Learn to recognize anger when it starts. Anger sneaks in on you before you recognize it. It can build slowly, or it can happen quickly (like it did against Connors). But the time to do something is before you're consumed with it. That takes discipline, great discipline. You have to override your natural emotions and use rational thought. That's tough for most of us to do. Anger feeds on itself and the longer you grind on something the harder it is to stop. Don't let the spark turn into a blaze.

2. Channel Your Anger

It's important to be able to channel or tunnel your anger toward a specific cause. Identify the source. Was it a bad call or calls? Was it a missed shot or series of missed shots? Isolate it. Understanding the cause helps create the solution. Get good at spotting anger early. Ask yourself: Why is this happening? What can I do to change what's happening? If your forehand is driving you up the wall, look for ways of correcting it.

If your opponent creates the anger in you, let it make you stronger. I know some club players who have told me they can't really get into a match until something the opponent does upsets them—a bad line call, playing too slowly, something to get them irritated. When your opponent has gotten you upset, turn the negative into a positive. Don't think, "I'm gonna lose this match because of the stuff he's pulling." Tell yourself, "I'm going to beat him for doing that. He's gonna pay a price." You'll work harder to win.

I used to get mad at my opponent *personally*. I'd forget about tactics and strategies and just think about what a jerk the other guy was, or how the linesman had missed a call. Here's how bad it was for me. I used to *stay* mad about a bad call for three or four *days*. I'd be in Europe and call my brother, Barry, in California two days after a match and he wouldn't know what I was talking about. "Brad, didn't that happen last week? Get a life!" I'm getting better. I work hard to forget about the personal part now and concentrate on trying to do to the other player what I don't want him to do to me.

Anger is volatile. Like gasoline it can run your car or explode in your face. Clark Graebner supposedly got so mad at Ilie Nastase during a match that afterwards he picked him up and hung him from a hook in the locker room. Even though I've heard the story a couple of times I doubt it's true. Graebner *is* big enough to do it, though. So who knows? I do know that with the exception of McEnroe and Connors, unchecked anger usually throws a player off their game. If you contain it the results can save you points. I'm sure that's what Borg was doing, containing it and using it for motivation.

3. Don't Beat Up on Yourself

You know you're in trouble when you start yelling at yourself like you'd yell at a dog that bit your leg. Don't do it. You already have one opponent on the court trying to beat you. If you gang up on yourself there will be two people on the court trying to beat you. So don't pound on yourself. I still do it too often and it doesn't work. It's a bad habit and it hurts my cause. "I'm the worst. I really stink up the place. *Moron!*" Those are typical of my complaints on a bad day.

First of all, the opponent loves to hear it. When a player hears me yelling "I can't hit a backhand!" he's going to hit more to my backhand. Besides, it pumps the other player up to see the competition totally lose it. You make them feel more positive about their chance of winning that day. When you start belittling yourself like that it's hard to turn it around. When you start digging that rut it just keeps getting deeper. And you stay in it. When you start yelling at yourself about how lousy you are it's amazing how often you'll continue to match that description.

So be careful with anger. It can really hurt your chances. You're there. You're on the court. You're not going to walk off and go back to work. If anger is a problem for you, channel it. When you get angry, think about what you're going to do next, *not what you did last*.

4. Have a Safety Valve

A good way to divert anger is to divert your attention. Develop a specific procedure you go through when you're upside down with anger, when you know you need to settle yourself. I could give you fifty little "busy work" things that I've used, but here are the ones that I've gone to most often when I need just a couple of moments to stall and get myself together. Tie your shoes. Straighten your racket strings. Towel off. Then do it again.

Nothing complicated. Ultimately it comes to internal control, mental or emotional management. Just like you want to control the quality of your tennis strokes or your footwork, you should try to control your anger, and you can do it in a straightforward and logical way. That is, until you go up in smoke the next time.

Anger Part II
The Good, the Bad, and John McEnroe

John McEnroe decided to hold up a match against me at the Olympic Tennis Stadium at U.C.L.A. while he protested a call that he didn't like. It's a great example of how he used to take control of what was going on out on the court when he felt it was necessary. And how anger was his weapon.

We played the match in '86 on a night when the temperature was in the mid-40s. The crowd was drinking to stay warm and a fight even broke out in the stands. The umpire had to stop the match and call for security guards to break it up. Paper cups and programs were getting thrown around and people were screaming and shouting during the changeovers. It was like being at a Raiders' night game at the Coliseum. That was the kind of rowdy scene it was.

McEnroe started out just tearing me up; 6–1 in the first set and up 1–0 in the second. I was losing so bad I didn't blame the fans for drinking just for something to do. Sometime early in the second set I looked over at my coach, Tom Chivington, and kind of gave him a look like, "Hey, what am I gonna do?" He's not supposed to do any coaching during a match, but he nods his head toward McEnroe a couple of times. He might have just been trying to stay warm, but I took it to mean that I should start rushing the net. Why not?

I start coming in on everything. I start serve-volleying. And on some of McEnroe's second serves I start chipping and charging. Out of desperation I started coming in on everything, just trying to get him out of his game. You know what? It does some good. He starts making a few mistakes. I start feeling better and making a few shots. I win the set 6–4 and suddenly we're heading down the stretch. Third set: three games a piece.

As you know, this is where things get interesting during a match. Mistakes are costly. Rewards are great. Mac is serving at 15–30, 3–all. I'm thinking this is a Set-up Point and if I win it I should win the game, then hold serve twice and I'm home free.

He serves and we go into a long point. Finally, he hits a backhand slice down the line. I rip my backhand right back down the line at him. Only he's not there. I wrong-foot him just enough and he can't get to it. The ball lands just inside the line and is called good.

Now, some line calls are close and you can make a case either way. This ball didn't catch the outside of the line and it didn't land on the line. It was *inside* the line. You're thinking, "Gilbert, here you go again. Every time a call goes against you it was a bad call. First the Connors story. Now this with McEnroe!" Okay, I don't blame you for thinking I'm paranoid. Only this time I know I'm right. And so did the linesman. And so did the umpire. So did the crowd. Only one person didn't think it was good: John McEnroe (and I've got to believe even he knew it was good).

When McEnroe hears the call, he erupts. He drops his racket and falls over on his back like he's been shot. Right away he jumps up screaming (it's tough to scream at the umpire lying on your back). He's acting like it's the worst call since they invented tennis, *even though I'd stake my life on the fact that he knew the ball was good.*

But here's what was going on and where psychological warfare comes into play. John could see the match slipping away if I won that Set-up Point. He was thinking *exactly* the way I was thinking. If I won the point, I'd be up 15–40 and looking at going up a break late in the match, a match where I hadn't been broken since I got on track. He knows I'll probably serve out the match if I break him. We both know that the point I just made is a monster in the dynamics of the match. He sees I'm playing good and figures he's got to do something, anything to take the momentum back. And when I say *anything* I mean it. It's time for a Mac Attack.

Tatum O'Neal was in the stands that night, and even she must have been impressed with her husband's theatrics. Absolutely Oscar level: "Best Performance During a Tennis Match in 45° Weather."

He's storming around raving at the linesman about how he missed the call. He goes after the chair umpire, Zeno Fau, a guy Mac thinks he can work on, and pleads for an overrule. He begs for an overrule. He demands an overrule. The crowd gets into the act, whistling into the night (even though they don't really understand why the point means so much to McEnroe). At least this time I'm not standing at the net with my hand out like with Connors. I keep my head together. I'm not going to get caught up in the turmoil. This call I know is not going to get overruled.

Meanwhile, McEnroe somehow manages to turn the point dispute into total mayhem with the linesman, the umpire, and the referee. *We don't play another point for over ten minutes.* I don't notice it, but I'm starting to cool down. I stiffen up slightly. After ten minutes I feel like I've been hanging in a meat locker. Sweat turns cold real quick in that temperature.

McEnroe keeps up the mayhem and I'm losing my concentration, my focus, my match energy. Anger wasn't the issue for me. I didn't let myself get mad (maybe I should have) but I did let myself get taken out of my game. I became a spectator watching a performance by one of tennis's great actors. Mac had gotten me good. Even though he didn't get the overrule, he got what he wanted.

Fau orders play to resume. It's now 10:15 at night and people are starting to stream out of the place, probably because the vendors have stopped selling beer. I head to the baseline cold, upset, mentally out of it. John is just the opposite. He is fired up and ready to roar. Nobody, but nobody, uses turmoil, commotion, disruption, and disorder to their benefit like he did. His game actually got better in the midst of chaos.

I'd like to know how many times he's come back from a blowup on the court to immediately serve an ace. You've seen him do it on the tube plenty of times. Guess what? He does it again. Goes into the most recognizable service motion in the world and zips one right by me. Ace! 30–40. I'm too cold to get upset. Then a serve-volley winner. Deuce. Then another ace. And then a service winner. Or was it an ace? Now it's a blur. Mac has come thundering back, and I feel like I'm catching a cold. I wish that had been the worst part. It wasn't.

The match is at 3–4 in the third. My serve. McEnroe wins a couple of points and I get a service winner. Now something happens at 15–30 that effectively ends the match. I'm serving. Big moment in the match; Set-up Point, Set-up Game. He wins it and he's looking at two break points. Win one of those and he's serving for the match. Major moment right here. And I do what I'm supposed to—D.R.M. I steady myself down. Tell myself, "No stupid mistakes. Take your time. Don't rush."

I realize the match is in danger of slipping away, though it hasn't yet. I collect my thoughts. I slow down. I go to the ball boy for a towel even though I'm not sweating (I need a hand warmer, not a towel). I wipe off my grip and my hands. Give the towel back to the ball boy. I walk back to the service line. Bounce the ball and look over at McEnroe. Suddenly I hear Mr. Fau turn on the P.A. system: "Game delay warning, Mr. Gilbert." Is he talking to me? This can't be happening!

McEnroe has just shut down the match for over ten minutes and I get a warning for game delay? It was torture. And it was all over for me. I scream at Fau. He looks like he might give me another warning or a penalty. I have no place to go. I'm finished. McEnroe breaks me. Holds. Game. Set. Match. Oscar. McEnroe.

Why did he beat me that night? Very simple. I wasn't smart during the delay. I let myself get caught watching and doing nothing. It was John's show and I couldn't stop that. But I should have seen to it that I stayed physically warm, hit some serves, put on a jacket. Asked to go to the locker room until the McEnroe Show got to intermission.

What I should have done is anything except stand in 45° weather cooling off. Whose fault? Mainly mine, for not thinking smart during the delay. For not ignoring the game delay warning (after all, it meant nothing). I let myself get taken out of my game both physically and mentally. And it cost me.

Here's the great ending to the story. Later, in the locker room, Mac comes up to me with that little sheepish grin on his face. I think maybe he's going to apologize for his tirade and delay on the disputed call. I'm wrong. He looks over at me and says, "Brad, you've gotta be more careful about delaying the game like that. In this weather I could have caught a cold." John does have a sense of humor.

Tempest on A Tennis Court

The fact was McEnroe was always looking for an excuse to disrupt play when he was behind. Here's the best proof. Did you ever see him blow up when he was *ahead?* It had happened, but almost always when the dynamics of the match were starting to go against him (like early in the second set when an opponent started to climb back into the match after losing the first set).

Otherwise, if something bothered John, he might jabber for five seconds just to get the crowd stirred up, which he liked. When he was ahead, he wouldn't risk changing his momentum by causing a ruckus. If he was *behind,* or if his opponent started to rally in the match you had a different story. That was when you got the four-act play.

McEnroe knew that he could deal with the commotion. He knew that it helped him. And he knew it hurt his opponent. And he knew he could get away with it. Umpires and officials were not going to mess with McEnroe when he was on top. The match on that cold night at U.C.L.A. stopped dead in its tracks for about ten minutes because he needed some help in turning things around. And I'm the one who ended up with the warning for delaying the game!

Did he do it intentionally? Of course! Is it fair play? No way. Fau and many others recognized the stature of McEnroe and Connors when they were on top of the tennis world. They allowed them to get away with stuff that would be unthinkable from other players. Can you imagine any other pro being allowed to shut down a match for that long on a 45° night? I can't think of one (other than Connors). Mac and Jimmy used this to their great advantage against opponents over and over again.

It wasn't until the 1991 Australian Open when officials booted McEnroe out of the tournament for his behavior that tennis took a real stand. Until then they were cowards. When he was a major attraction and a force in any tournament he entered, they were afraid to put a stop to all of his baloney. When he was no longer that draw or that force, they finally summoned the courage to do something. It was too little too late. Had they done it sooner, it would have been better for tennis and better for John.

He paid a huge price for his behavior. McEnroe lost a lot of friends and a lot of respect among players on tour because of his tactics. Had he kept a lower profile on court, he would have been subjected to a lot less heat and his life in and around tennis would have been a lot more productive. How much more productive? John McEnroe could have won one or two additional Grand Slam titles. Who knows, maybe even the Grand Slam itself. Forget money. Forget the lesser titles. I'm talking about making tennis history.

It's too bad, because he was a true tennis genius. The tennis gods blessed him with a gift for the game that few, if any, ever received. Hockey had The Great Gretsky. Basketball had Magic. And tennis had the awesome talent of John McEnroe.

When he was on top of his game through the '80s, what he did with a tennis racket was beautiful. It was really like art. But his antics started to hurt his game. The press, the crowds, the publicity, and the image affected his nerves and his head.

Wimbledon became an annual nightmare for him. The British press worked him over like he was Jack the Ripper on parole. The crowds everywhere came ready to taunt and yell at John like he was some kind of circus freak. He became everybody's whipping boy. Here was maybe the greatest player in the game being held up as an example of what was *wrong* with the game. Eventually it got to him. The constant controversies he created derailed him, and he had to leave tennis for half a year.

And you'll remember he blamed his retirement partially on me (when I beat him in the Masters, he said it was time to reconsider why he was even playing the game). I was just the straw that broke the camel's back.

John McEnroe established himself as one of the greatest players ever in tennis. He had a terrific career, but he might have been the greatest. John didn't give himself the chance to reach his full potential. But it wasn't only his fault. The tennis establishment shares the blame. They didn't have the guts to deal with him when they might have done some good for John and for the game of tennis.

McEnroe came to understand very early that all of his belly-aching worked for him. He was able to bring the fury of hell up onto the court and then walk away from it as if it hadn't happened. He did it to me that night at U.C.L.A., just as he had done it to others throughout his career. What he didn't figure on was the toll it would eventually take on his head, his game, and his life.

Beating McEnroe is Heady Stuff

And while we're on the subject of John McEnroe, remember when I said my win against him in the '86 Masters was "too great"? Here's what I meant.

After that match at Madison Square Garden the press got excited about me. I did interviews with all the national media. "Good Morning America" wanted me for an appearance. The local sports shows were speculating that I might be the next American superstar in tennis. In just a few hours I became a somebody. In my own head, as well. It sounded great to me: "The Next American Tennis Star!" It was a long way from the foggy courts at Golden Gate Park in San Francisco. Unfortunately, I fell for it. Briefly.

In just twelve hours I went from a player who never took anything for granted to a guy who assumed victory. From a player who always took his lunch bucket and hard hat onto the court with him to one who wanted to have his socks ironed before a match. From a player who assumed he was going to have to grub it out and work his behind off to have a chance of winning to one who thought he could keep sweat to a minimum and still win. Big mistake. The next day I got my butt kicked by Anders Jarryd 1–6, 1–6.

I learned more from that match than any other I've ever played. I learned the hardest possible way that you must know who you are and stay with that. I've won by understanding my game and the game of my opponents. I realized I'm not going to overpower most players. I'm not going to outserve most players. I'm not going to outvolley most players. What I *am* going to do is make them play their weakness to my strengths more often than they want to. And, with occasional exceptions (like the TransAmerica/San Francisco tournament against McEnroe where I wanted to impress the fans), I've stuck with that plan.

In that '86 Masters match McEnroe tried to get me out of my game by insulting me during a changeover, saying I didn't "deserve" to be on the same court with him. When I heard that I was smart enough to recognize that he was in trouble, that he was trying to beat me psychologically because he wasn't doing it with shots.

I knew he was thinking maybe he's going to lose to me for the first time ever. And in front of his hometown New York fans! I go to my chair, put the towel over my head, and talk to myself. "McEnroe's worried. Stay in your game, dammit. Be prepared for anything. Steady tennis. Keep the ball in play. Steady tennis." His psych job didn't work because I knew what he was doing. When the disruptions started happening I was ready. I won the match because I had good mental and emotional management.

That day John couldn't take me out of my game. The next day I got taken out of it by me. I went into the match with Anders thinking the frog had become a prince. I was brought back to earth by 1–6, 1–6. I learned my lesson very quickly. The next week I got to the semis of the U.S. Indoors. A few days after that I was named to the Davis Cup team. And the following week I won the U.S. National Indoor Championship, beating Connors, Edberg, *and* Jarryd. A month after that Jarryd and I played again in Memphis. I beat him 6–3, 6–0. I've never lost to him again. I wish I could say that about McEnroe.

13

Lendl's Lethal Weapon

I call it Turtle Time—slowing the match down so much that it seems like you're playing in quicksand. It's like one of those dreams where you're running as hard as you can, but you're not going anywhere. Everything is in slow motion. The Master of Turtle Time is Ivan Lendl.

Turtle Time is designed (like any psych job) to change the dynamics of what's happening out on the court. There, in a variety of ways, a player can make time stand still. The victim (you, or in this case, me) gets impatient. When you get impatient you tend to rush. When you rush you make physical and mental mistakes. Make mistakes and you lose points. See how it works? Your tempo is rearranged. Your concentration drifts. It can destroy your game if you don't know how to respond.

Ivan isn't generally a slow player; deliberate, yes, but not really slow. It's when things aren't really going his way that he uses this tactic. He used it successfully on me in a match when he was on top of the tennis world and I've still got a headache. If you remember that I've never beaten him, you might think this is sour grapes. Hey, you might be right. But mainly it's an example of how you've got to know what to do when you're getting psyched or you'll lose. Here's how it went.

Lendl vs. Gilbert: Stratton Mountain, Vermont, $315,000 Volvo International Quarter-finals, 1986

I put a lot of pressure on myself going into this match because I knew a win here would be a huge victory for me psychologically. I had never beaten Lendl. He was number one in the world and I was struggling at twelve or thirteen. I had a feeling that I might just be able to sneak up on him in the quarters and knock him out. And, as it turned out, that's what was happening.

Although Ivan won the first set I started to find a tempo and really got going in the second set to win it 6–3. I carried it over into the third and was rolling along up a break and a hold, 2–0. Ivan knows we've reached a pivotal moment. The set and match could slip away. If I hold serve the rest of the way I'll win. He appreciates the dynamics of where we are in the match and understands if he's going to do something he better do it soon.

He also knows I'm cruising right along, in a nice zone where everything is working for me—solid strokes, good footwork, concentrating, positive attitude. I can almost hear my victory speech. As it turned out, the speech was to be delayed. Ivan had a few tricks up his short sleeve.

You'll remember that I said Ivan is one of the greatest when it comes to holding and stretching a lead? He's also one of the greatest when it comes to stopping his match from slipping away. Like McEnroe and Connors he has a keen sense of when this is starting to happen. His response, however, is totally different from theirs.

This match was in danger of slipping away and Ivan was not about to let it happen. He knew that at this point one of my greatest assets was momentum. The energy I had created was carrying me along and I was winning points smoothly. I had won eight of the last eleven games, so Lendl understood that for once I was beating him with my strokes. He knew that to win he had to upset those strokes and the best way to do that (at this point) was to upset my composure, to break up the momentum I was riding on. Ivan knew it was Turtle Time!

Again, here's where we are in the match: third set, my serve at 2–0. I step up to the baseline and get ready to serve. Ivan has other plans. First he makes a little fuss just before I start my service motion. He's asking the umpire to tell the crowd not to use flash cameras. Now, after more than two hours of tennis and two and a half sets, plus several reminders, the crowd is definitely *not* still taking pictures. How could they be? By this point they don't have any film left. His complaint is just a little interruption designed to jerk me out of my motion.

We play a point. Ivan walks over to a linesman and questions him about whether he's sure of the call. He asks him about a previous call and suggests perhaps the linesman should pay more attention. Lendl stands there shaking his head with that long look on his face like he's just lost his favorite dog. Slowly he heads back to the baseline.

He's shaking his head like life is very difficult for him. No big deal. Just a little delay to interrupt things. Perfectly legitimate. Gradually . . . slowing . . . things . . . down. Gradually . . . changing . . . the . . . pace . . . of . . . play. On the way back to the baseline he stops to towel off.

Now he adds a little more to the routine. I'm getting ready to serve again. Just as I'm ready to go into my motion, Ivan holds his hand up and slowly walks halfway over to the chair umpire. Ivan points at me. I hear him ask the umpire to tell me to quit taking so long to serve, it's disrupting play. Good move! Catches me a little by surprise. He's the one slowing things down and he accuses me of doing it. I complain to the umpire that I'm serving exactly like I have the whole match. I'm ticked. The umpire agrees. But I had started to fall into Lendl's trap.

Almost imperceptibly he's breaking down my rhythm and my concentration. He wants me out of the mental zone I'm in because it's gotten me ahead in the match. He wants me to start thinking about how he's jerking me around by complaining to the umpire. He wants me to think about whether I *am* taking too long on my serve. He wants me to think about anything except what I have been thinking about, because it's beating him!

His gamesmanship is working, too. Instead of thinking about winning one point at a time (confident and positive input) I start thinking about the interruptions and delays, the possibility that this match could slip away (negative input). I'm letting Lendl's actions intrude on my concentration. I'm getting a little edgy. I want to get this match moving along faster. I'm getting impatient.

I start speeding things up a little to counter his slowdown tactics. I'm rushing just a little bit. This is the wrong response. It's exactly what he wants, and it works.

Lendl breaks me right back. We're on serve and I'm mad as hell. I had slipped off my focus. I had failed to follow my rules. Ivan's distractions had kept me from doing it.

I had started to play from an emotional stance. I was reacting in the wrong way to what he was doing. Instead of telling myself that I was was winning and that patience would get me a victory I was worrying about whether he'd steal the match from me.

Turtle Stew at Its Finest

Lendl has gotten the break back and is serving at 2–1 in the third. I am furious and determined to get the break back again, and immediately.

He gradually edges up to the line to serve. I get ready, but he's not quite set to go into his motion yet. He has some business to take care of first. He begins with his eyelash routine. You've seen that on television. He plucks an eyelash and looks at it. Then he plucks another one and looks at it. Then another one. How he can have any eyelashes left at this point in his career I don't know. He's been plucking and looking at them for fifteen years. On this night at Stratton Mountain he starts plucking again.

Next, he deliberates over which ball to serve with. He looks at one. Then he takes a long look at the other one. Then back to the first one. Then he starts rolling them around in his hand like dice. Again he looks at them individually. Finally he decides on a ball. I'm still in the ready position.

Time to serve? Ivan starts bouncing the ball he's finally chosen. Once. Twice. Three times he bounces it. Four times. Wait a minute. Must be some sweat in his eyes. He's wiping off the sweat and running the sweatband over his eyebrows. I'm still in the ready position. He bounces the ball again. Here we go. Once. Twice. Three times. Hold everything! The grip must be slippery.

Ivan goes to his pocket for a handful of sawdust. Rubs it on the grip. I'm still in the ready position. He spins the racket a few times. Taps his shoe. Bounces the ball one more time. Stares over at me. I'm still there.

He serves. Ace! Lendl leads 15–love. I'm still in the ready position.

Ivan goes through the whole act again on the second point. I've been in the ready position so long my legs could cramp. First the eyelash routine. Then rubbing the sweat off. Bouncing the balls. Putting on the sawdust. Bouncing the ball. Finally he serves. *Fault!* Into the net.

Ivan walks away from the baseline. Straightens the strings on his racket. Wipes off the sweat. Checks the balls. The whole thing all over again before his *second* serve. Maybe even longer.

Here's a fact. Rules or not, Lendl has been timed at fifty seconds between his first serve and his second serve when it's suited him. This is Turtle Time tennis and it's lethal. I'm starting to lose it. Ivan slows his way through the game to hold. The match is dead even.

Ivan worked his plan to perfection. From 2–0 in the third I didn't win another game. He won the match going away, six games in a row to win the match 6–2, 3–6, 6–2.

The next time you watch him slow things down, study his strategy. Think about what it means if you're on the other side of the net waiting. Waiting. You know he's playing games out there and those games can beat you. You end up beating yourself.

That night in the quarters at the Volvo International at Stratton Mountain Lendl managed to break down my concentration, rhythm, and timing. If I'd been smarter he wouldn't have been able to do it.

He kept up Turtle Time until he was up a break and then returned to his usual pace. I had been psyched out by one of the finest psychologists in the game. I had forgotten the rules about countering this tactic. If I'd remembered them I could have won.

How to Beat Slow Play Tactics

I've already mentioned that gamesmanship or psyching is designed to upset your concentration, to disrupt what you're doing. You'll rarely see a smart player who's ahead do anything that could change the pattern of play. We want things to stay just the way they are. It's when someone falls behind that they'll try to get under the other player's skin. The goal is to divert attention, to get the opponent thinking about the wrong things.

The slow play tactic takes a variety of forms—all of the Lendl routine, plus tying shoelaces, walking over to get the farthest ball to serve with, or doing just about anything to stall before playing. One weekend player I've seen has a unique method of slowing things down. When he's behind and serving he'll toss the ball two or three times before he actually hits it. It's like he's practicing his toss. Every point. Not exactly illegal, but a major annoyance and one I hope Lendl doesn't hear about.

Remember, no smart player starts changing things when they're ahead and rolling right along. But when your opponent is behind and starts playing little games to upset you, it's good to have a plan to protect yourself. When it comes to slow play, here's how to keep it from damaging your game.

Fight Slow Play, Slowly

Turtles know you have to wait for them to start play. It's tough to do, but you have to be patient. When you notice what looks like a slowdown in the action, be flexible. Don't press. Don't force it and get impatient. There's no way you can make someone play faster if they're intentionally (or even unintentionally) slowing down the match tempo.

Let the Turtle crawl through their whole range of business. Wait. Wait. And wait. When they've finally gotten around to beginning play, just before they serve, it's your turn to slow things down. Hold up your hand and step away from the line. Tie your shoe. Step away from the line and adjust your strings or wipe off the sweat. Let the Turtle wait for you. Then when it's your turn to serve, give them a taste of their own slow medicine. Bounce the ball eight or ten times. Do your own version of Turtle Time. They'll usually get the idea.

I know what you're thinking. All this game playing is going to disrupt your thinking and rhythm. You'll still come out behind. Not necessarily. You are now taking the initiative. You're not just being passive. You're not standing there being worked over. You're doing something to defend yourself. It can be a big psychological boost.

I have a little rule I follow. Before a point I don't like to stand at the baseline waiting for my opponent to arrive and get ready. It creates tension and makes me rush into the point once they do get set. If the other player is not ready to proceed when I am I take a few steps away from the line and bounce the ball several times if I'm serving. If

I'm receiving I'll back away and straighten my strings. Then as they approach their line I'll do the same. But I don't just stand there and wait. Neither should you. Whether they're making you wait for them intentionally or unintentionally doesn't matter. You're still just standing there waiting, and that doesn't help your game.

Lendl is one of the best at maintaining a good pace when he's leading in a match. When he gets ahead he's methodical and merciless. But when he's behind, or it's close in the third, fourth, or fifth set, it's like watching water evaporate when he goes into Turtle Time. He'll drive you bananas, and in the process get you totally out of your game. And officials through the years have cut him more slack, as they have with McEnroe, than they do for most other players.

I've found that it helps a great deal if I can do something myself when I'm being worked over by a psych job. Instead of just standing there absorbing the routine my opponent is putting on, I want to respond. How? By doing to him what he's doing to me. With Lendl that time I let him get inside my head and destroy my composure. He acted. I reacted.

Against Lendl it didn't work just to stand there and do nothing. When he took fifty seconds to get ready (twenty-five seconds is allowed) for his second serve, I should have asked the umpire to keep him to time. If that didn't work, the next time he went through the whole pre-serve routine I should have stepped away from the line when he was all done with it and toweled off (or tied my shoes, straightened my strings, plucked my eyelash, anything). I should have slowed the match down and forced *him* to stand around.

But here's why Lendl is a master. He started working on me before I recognized the tactics. And before I knew it I was acting out of anger and frustration. I was ready to scream, he tied me up so bad.

Is that why I lost? No. But it was part of the reason. Match dynamics are volatile, and Lendl had taken control of them at a crucial moment. I lost because I didn't respond correctly.

And just so you don't get the wrong impression, at last count Ivan Lendl "owned" me. He's mentally and physically very tough. Most of the times he's beaten me it's been because he's so doggone good. However, my point is that on those occasions where I've had a chance to win he knew how to use another aspect of the competition: gamesmanship. I'm not complaining. It comes with the territory.

Ivan understands the psychological aspects of the game very well.

Here's a small example. Early in my career when he didn't view me as a threat to him I was occasionally invited to his estate in Connecticut to be his hitting partner. We'd work out on his court (the one he has resurfaced each year to exactly match the court surfaces at the U.S. Open). When I began to start playing him tougher in tournaments, taking him to three sets occasionally, the invitations stopped.

Ivan knew (and so did I) that the sessions were helping my confidence in playing him out on tour. He was losing his aura because I was getting familiar with his game and forgetting any sense of awe his image might once have created. When he recognized that it was happening he found a new hitting partner. He's smart, both on and off the court.

It Can Happen to You, Too:
Windmill and Dr. J

You're thinking that that kind of stuff (slow play) never happens where you play. Great. And I hope it never does. But it can. I've saved the greatest "slow-down-the-match" gambit I know of for last. In case you think Turtle Time only goes on at the professional level, you're about to see that it can occur at every level of tennis, including tennis clubs and public courts. If something like this ever happens to you, just admit you've been outfoxed and go home sadder but wiser.

Again, it's at the San Francisco Tennis Club. Dale Crase and Julius Colbert (their real names) are playing the semifinals of the club's B tournament. They call their own lines and enforce their own rules (which is what led to the problem). Let me describe their styles of play.

Crase is a born Retriever whose nickname is Windmill because of his strange serve. He stands with his serving arm straight down at his side holding the racket. Then he tosses the ball up, and without bending his elbow he swirls his arm around to hit it. He never bends his elbow. It looks like a windmill, hence the nickname.

Colbert (nicknamed Dr. J) is a good athlete who played minor league baseball before an injury stopped his rise to the big leagues. He plays full throttle, all or nothing. Goes for everything and makes spectacular shots occasionally. Occasionally. But let's get to the match.

Windmill wins the first set easily 6–2, and is ahead in the second

4–1. Looks like a quick win and a trip to the finals. But Dr. J starts to get it going. He makes a few of those spectacular shots and gets his energy level and attitude way up. Suddenly he's won six of the next seven games to win the set 7–5! Sets are even at 1–all. The momentum has changed dramatically, and Windmill knows it.

Now it's the changeover. (Club protocol was to break out new balls and make a changeover before the third set in tournaments.) They sit down for the break. Windmill asks for a little favor. Would it be okay to run up to his locker and get a dry shirt? Dr. J has no problem with that. They're buddies and who's going to tell a friend they can't put on a dry shirt. Windmill leaves. It takes Dr. J a little time to sense that something is going on. Four minutes go by. Seven minutes. Thirteen minutes. Dr. J is starting to boil. He can't believe what's happening. Eighteen minutes and still no Windmill.

Finally, after twenty-two minutes, here comes Windmill, looking like he's just had a good night's sleep, a massage, and a cool drink. And it was almost true. He *had* gotten a dry shirt. He *had* put it on. But not before he'd taken a shower, shaved, relieved himself, and eaten a candy bar.

Dr. J was seething. His buddy had "gamed" him. What does he say when Windmill gets back to the court? Nothing. Ego gets into it. He refuses to declare a default because he'd rather take it out on Windmill on the court, really pound on him, nail him 6–0 in the third. You can guess the rest. The score *was* 6–0 in the third. Only Windmill had the 6. Dr. J had the 0. He couldn't hit a ball within two feet of the court. He was out of his skull and lost it. He didn't know how to deal with slow play and delay tactics. And he didn't know how to deal with anger.

Maybe Dr. J should have disqualified Windmill (although he gave him permission to leave). Maybe he should have complained or left the court himself. Maybe he should have gone home for lunch. Instead, he got his lunch handed to him. He got psyched out, and he paid for it. Just like I paid for it against Lendl. If it ever happens to you, be ready. Don't let a Turtle break down your concentration and your game.

14

Agassi: Breaking the Speed Limit

Andre Agassi moves faster *between* points than some players do during points. He's rushing all the time. He's got so much energy he could make a hummingbird nervous. But he lives on caffeine and sugar, so I guess you'd expect him to be a little on the quick side.

I like Andre and think he's great for the game. Some players resent his Las Vegas flash and the showboating, but it brings people through the gate. Plus, Andre doesn't intentionally screw around with you out on the court. Unintentionally, he does, because Andre moves you through a match faster than anybody in the business. That can destroy your game.

Rushing into points is bad. Rushing into points means you're rushing through points. As we saw with Lendl, rushing creates both mental and physical mistakes. It throws off your rhythm in serving. It creates all kinds of timing problems. It just takes you out of your game totally. Unless you're Andre Agassi. Andre likes rushing.

The quick play artist doesn't necessarily catch you by surprise during a match (e.g. by serving quick). Instead, what throws you off is the general tempo at which they do things between and during points. You never really get comfortable, set, and focused. They move you into the point *immediately*. Andre gets it going so fast when he's serving that you feel like you could miss something if you blink. He doesn't walk. He trots. He could be the poster child for the caffeine industry.

Fast play is common at clubs and public courts. You'll often run into players who are moving along just enough faster than you to throw you off. They serve immediately when you get to the line. They don't sit down on the changeovers. One club player used to spin the racket for the serve while he and his opponent were still in the locker room! He'd have the other player rushing before they even got to the court. It does happen. And when it does it requires a little management.

Know Your Speed Limit

It's easier to deal with a player who's rushing you along—a Rabbit— than with a Turtle. The main thing you have to be aware of is that it's happening. Usually you let yourself get caught up in the quicker pace without realizing it. You're never quite set, there isn't time for composing yourself or analyzing what's going on in front of you. And those are two crucial elements of my game. I want constantly to be thinking about what's happening in the match. If you start playing faster than you normally do, you get mentally sloppy and physically careless.

So, what do you do? Simple. Know your speed limit. That means knowing the tempo you are comfortable playing at. *Don't let your opponent exceed it.* Be aware of when it happens. Don't be a good guy and just go along with it. Slow it down! When your opponent jumps up to the service line before you're set, hold up your hand and walk away. If he doesn't sit down for a break on the changeovers, be sure you do. Don't be afraid to towel off, adjust strings, or tie your shoes. The quick play artist will run you off the court if you let him.

In 1991 I played Andre in a semi-final match, and was fortunate enough to beat him in straight sets. Going into that match I was very intent on playing at *my* tempo: D.R.M. He wasn't. Lots of times he'd quickly skate back to the service line and want to get it going before I was ready. I made very sure I was set, made sure we didn't start rushing through points and games. I'd towel off, tie my shoe, check my strings. I checked my strings a lot that match. With Andre you've got to do that or he'll roll you right away. (In the finals of the '93 Volvo/San Francisco he got me back, winning in three sets and playing great tennis.)

You can do the same thing with the Rabbits you come up against.

Protect your tempo. Guard your rhythm. When you're on the other side of the net from a Rabbit, be very sure you don't let them dictate how fast the match moves along.

Playing Possum

There's another little situation or gambit that comes up occasionally that's worth mentioning as long as we're talking about gamesmanship. It's called "playing possum." It's when a player will fake or exaggerate an injury. It can have a very negative effect on the possum's victim.

You know how it works at the club level. The possum's opponent (you) are in a Catch-22 situation. The match really doesn't count if you win because your opponent is injured, right? If you lose, you've lost to somebody who's playing hurt. Very embarrassing. It's a no-win situation.

It almost always takes you out of your game. You don't try as hard. You don't concentrate as well. You play sloppy. And you can lose. That's when your opponent will say as you leave the court, "You know my leg didn't bother me as much as I thought it would. Good match and better luck next time." You've just been had by a possum.

Save Your Sympathy

Remember this: Whether an opponent's injury is real, exaggerated, or fake, *it gets no sympathy or attention from you until after the match.* If your opponent is healthy enough to walk out on the court and continue play, then he's healthy enough to deserve your best effort. Ignore anything he tells you about his aches and pains. Assume it's just for effect. Because whether the injury is real or not, it can have a negative impact on you. It can take you out of your concentration.

Case in point: I played Jimmy Connors in an A.T.P. semifinal match early in 1993. He actually came *limping* out on the court. I'm serious. He was noticeably favoring his right foot because of an ongoing problem with bone spurs. Now, Jimmy is a great manipulator and showman, so I'm trying to ignore what's going on—no sympathy for this devil.

But during the first set, it gets so bad he's actually pulling up on some shots because of the pain. This is no act. I cruise in the first set 6–1, and it only takes about ten minutes. I figure he'll default during the changeover. He doesn't.

I'm trying to figure out what's going on. There's no way he can finish the match—he probably can't even finish the set. This is awkward. The crowd can see he's struggling, and they're cheering his valiant efforts. Suddenly I'm a villain beating on a legend who's in pain. So what happens? Jimmy starts beating me. He goes up 4–1 and *then retires*. I know Connors was thinking, "Gotcha, Gilbert!" And he had.

Save the sympathy.

15

How to Handle Hooking

Occasionally in matches you'll run into the player who cheats on line calls (hooking). Also, you have to deal with the player who unintentionally makes a mistake on a call. Both situations are tough to deal with. I've seen both sides of the coin. I've given bad calls and I've gotten them.

As a junior player I had a terrible reputation for line calls. It was probably deserved. I wanted to win so much that I couldn't give the other player the benefit of the doubt. Then I corrected the problem and probably ended up getting as many bad calls as I gave. It was never anything to be proud of.

What do you do when it happens in your match, especially during a tournament? Here are some suggestions.

Don't argue about the marginal call. You may be wrong. But don't let a blatantly bad call go by without action. You don't have to be a jerk, but let your opponent know you aren't going to let them force you to hit to a smaller court than the ones marked by the white lines.

Start easy. Ask if they're sure of the call. Give it a longer look. Be controlled. Give your opponent a chance to be generous. If you start out accusing them of bad calls, they'll just get defensive and probably give you more of the same. An early notice that you expect fair calls will often sharpen up the opponent's eyes. In fact, after you've nudged someone on a bad call, you'll almost always see that for a while afterwards they'll call balls good that are out. Guilty conscience probably. So, initially, be diplomatic.

If diplomacy doesn't work, you know what most club players will do? They respond in kind, giving bad calls themselves. This isn't the way to go. Among other things, it takes you out of your concentration. You get caught up in the issue of good or bad line calls and forget about everything else. Believe me, it is rare when line calls make the difference in a match, so don't let them disrupt your mental management.

Hooking back doesn't work. Screaming doesn't work. (I've been screamed at and done my own share of screaming. It doesn't work.) But you can say that you thought the call was wrong. Hey, don't be afraid to smile when you say it. Give your opponent a chance to be nice.

If it continues, address the problem directly. Most tournaments have a person available to come in and assume responsibility for the line calls. Have them do it so you can concentrate on your game.

Ultimately, the best thing you can do with someone who is a chronic hooker is to cross them off your list of opponents. When you do find yourself in a situation where you can't choose your opponent (like a tournament), stand up for your rights. Try what I suggested. It usually helps.

The most exciting part of tennis is when you are fully engaged physically and mentally. Psych jobs are occasionally part of what goes on. It's important to recognize when you're being psyched and to know what you can do about it because what affects you mentally has an effect on you physically.

When I was coming up and playing junior tennis events, the psyching was brutal. It was good conditioning for what was ahead in the pro's.

You'll find a lot of satisfaction in being able to defend yourself when the other player (who just might be a friend) starts to reach into a bag of tricks to disrupt your game. Even if what they're doing is unintentional, you should be willing and able to deal with it effectively.

I knew a high school player who would measure the height of the net before every match. It was a great little routine he went through, and it put the opponent in a reactive or passive role. The guy measuring the net was taking control right away. He was saying that he was the more conscientious player, that he was the one who made the extra effort. He was the one determining if the net was okay. The opponent would stand around waiting for this guy to make his ruling. Great little bit of gamesmanship.

I played a match once when I was a kid and my opponent said

during a changeover, "Gilbert, you're too competitive." It threw me off back then because I thought I was doing something wrong. I backed off a little. It was a good ploy.

Remember this. Most of the matches you play are strictly for fun. The best thing to do when someone starts pulling objectionable stuff is to scratch them off your list of players. I mention "dirty tricks" so you get an idea of what it's like out there during a tournament. Maybe it'll help you when you run into a version of it in your own matches, especially in tournaments where you can't choose who your opponents are. Then you may want to fight fire with fire.

16

A Million-Dollar Match: War With Wheaton

> "Bradley was different. He wasn't a barn burner in high school. When he mentioned college we were shocked. We thought he'd eventually get a job, maybe $3.35 an hour, and work his way up."
> —Mrs. Elaine Gilbert, Brad's mother

The International Tennis Federation Grand Slam Cup in Munich is one of those events that shows how big tennis has gotten in terms of money. The winner gets $2 million. But here's the amazing part. The runner-up makes $1 million! That's a real heart-starter. It's about what John Newcombe made in his entire career.

I was invited to the 1990 Grand Slam Cup when Andre Agassi withdrew because of a torn rib cartilage. I worked my way up to the semifinals, where I was scheduled to face David Wheaton, a player I'd beaten earlier in a 15–13 fifth-set marathon that had moved me into the quarterfinals at Wimbledon. This confrontation had the added pressure of being worth more money than either of us had ever played for in our lives. The winner could retire; a victory was worth a million dollars and a chance at two million.

In many ways it was a culminating point in my career, as I was playing against some of the greatest players in the game for the biggest purse ever offered in a tournament. Kim and my two-year-old son Zach came along with me for moral support.

Pre-Match Mental Preparation

In mentally preparing for the match at the Munich Hilton I ran through a checklist on Wheaton's game: Huge first and second serve. Maybe the *best* second serve in the business. At Wimbledon he had aced me twenty-three times. Loves pace. Doesn't handle junk well. His speed is not spectacular and his footwork is occasionally off. Questionable forehand. Comes up late on his swing a lot. Makes a lot of mistakes on his forehand return of serve. (I've played him where he's missed twenty forehand service returns.) When he gets tight he tends to overhit his forehand returns—when he starts doing that, the rest of his game suffers a little.

I also knew Wheaton could take the choke. At Wimbledon he had a two-set lead and couldn't convert two match points when he had a chance.

The All-American Player?

That was the picture I had of his tennis, at least of his strokes and playing tendencies. But it was the other side of his game that I really thought about, the mental or emotional part. Wheaton's a very "in your face" kind of player, very emotional and confrontational. Plus, at that time in his career, he was wrapping himself in the flag (literally) by wearing a red, white, and blue headband or a shirt with stars and stripes on it.

That irritated me because he was obviously attempting to create an image for himself as being *the* American player, like he represented American tennis. I had played for the U.S.A. in the Olympics and earned a bronze metal. Several times I had been invited to be a member of the Davis Cup team and had been thrilled at representing my country. I didn't consider myself *the* American player and neither did great young guys like Chang, Sampras, Agassi, or Courier. This wearing the flag stuff by Wheaton seemed like a gimmick. It was baloney.

I also hadn't forgotten the tough match we played at Wimbledon. I knew Wheaton didn't roll over when he got behind. He fought to the finish. With that much money on the table I wanted to be ready for anything. As it turned out, the match called for everything I could muster physically, mentally, and emotionally.

John McEnroe and Jimmy Connors were willing and able to turn a tennis match into a tennis madhouse where they controlled the chaos. Lendl could strangle you in his own slow, powerful way. However, what I learned by going through those trials was going to serve me well in the most difficult and lucrative match of my life.

Over 14,000 fans had packed into Munich's Olympiahalle and they were obviously excited about the tennis ahead. I could hear their rumble from inside the locker room. They wanted to see some serious tennis. What they almost saw was some serious boxing. But that was still ahead.

An hour before the match I was trying to stay calm by playing with Zach in the player's lounge. They have a pinball machine set up there and we were fooling around with it just to keep busy. I'd pull the lever back and he'd laugh as the ball lit up the lights and rang the buzzers. At one point I looked down and he was trying to eat my shoelaces. He obviously wasn't nervous about anything. That helped me control my own emotions.

Our time together ended too soon. I headed to the locker room and Kim and Zach went to their seats in the Olympiahalle. Time to earn a living.

War With Wheaton

Grand Slam Cup matches are best of five sets (they want you to *work* for that money). When we headed out onto the court, I was as tight as I have ever been. The lights seemed brighter and the crowd noise seemed sharper. Everything seemed faster because of the tension and pressure. In the pre-match warm-up period I was talking to my feet and trying to breathe deeply, fighting off the nerves and establishing a little bit of rhythm. It wasn't easy. These were circumstances I had never played under before.

"Bitte Meine Herren, Spielen Sie Tennis" ("Gentlemen, Play Tennis")

Wheaton and I started out in typical style, scraping and digging hard for points and games. I won the first set. He got the second.

The third gets tough. His serve has clicked in and is huge. Twice it almost hits me it's coming in so fast. I haven't broken him since the first game of the second set and I don't break him in the third. He's holding easily and I'm struggling each time not to get broken. We head into a tiebreaker, which goes down to the wire—six points all. It's my serve, a Set-up Point. Win it and I'm looking at set point and a possible strangle-hold on the match. I'm two points away from a 2–1 lead in the match.

I decide to go at his forehand when I get a chance, remembering that it's vulnerable to pressure (and this is a million dollars' worth of pressure). I make a strong approach shot angled wide to his forehand. He moves to it and gives me a weak forehand crosscourt. I'm at the net and poke the volley to the ad court sideline, but I go for more than I have to.

I've got the whole side of the court open and I put the ball *out!* At least, the linesman calls it out. I slam my racket into the net. "Ahhhhhgh!" But before I can even protest the call, the chair umpire, Stephen Winyard from Briton, overrules: "Correction. Ball was good. Point Mr. Gilbert."

Now all hell breaks loose. Wheaton is screaming bloody murder at Winyard. And he had a right to be hysterical. It's bad to overrule calls when they're close. And especially at crucial moments. Was my shot in? I thought so, but it was a tough call either way. Very close calls aren't what overrules are intended to correct. It's the obvious mistake they're supposed to deal with. Was I glad he made the overrule? Very glad. However, I knew what Wheaton felt. I had been in his position with Connors in Chicago back in '85.

Family Feud

Wheaton can see that million-dollar check slipping away. He scrambles over to the chair and screams that the call can't be overruled, that it was out, that the linesman had a better look at it, that the umpire is destroying the match! He is vicious mad. He's jumping up and down like he's on a pogo stick. I don't blame him.

But that's not the end of it. Wheaton's brother now gets up behind the umpire and starts barking obscenities at the top of his lungs. He's screaming so loud you can hear him all over the arena as he runs from one side of the court to the other. Wheaton's completely lost it and is acting like an idiot. The brother is jumping back and forth. And the crowd is whistling and stomping and hollering. Another madhouse. But I'd been there before. Connors and McEnroe are world-class when it comes to creating this kind of situation. The overrule stood.

It's Wheaton's serve at 6–7. This is just a huge point—win it and I'm in great shape, up two sets to one. I am totally focused and ready. Wheaton makes his toss and serves. Ace! The ball is by me in a blur. Unbelievable. He's like McEnroe. The dispute seemed to give him energy and focus, to improve his game. Now it's 7–7 in the tiebreak. Another Set-up Point, this time for both of us. Big, big, big. Wheaton gets ready to serve again. He bounces the ball a couple of times and looks over at me. He makes his toss and swings. He faults. I like this.

Again he looks over at me and bounces the ball two or three times. Quickly he serves again. It's another fault. Double fault? Choke? Maybe he's not like McEnroe. I lead 8–7 and get ready to serve. I roll one in at about 80 miles an hour. Wheaton tries to crush it, over-swings, and nets it. "Set, Mr. Gilbert." I win 7–6 (9–7) and lead two sets to one. But the trouble isn't over.

On the changeover Wheaton's brother starts cursing at me from directly behind my back while I'm sitting down. He's yelling over and over, "I'm going to kick your ass, Gilbert!" This is the brother, now. He's not even playing the match, but I guess he's figuring some of that money could be his. I complain to Winyard that the brother is disrupting the match and should be told to shut up; that he's totally out of control. The umpire nods his head in agreement and cautions him to be quiet and stay off the court.

Nose-to-Nose With Wheaton

Now, as I pass Wheaton on the way back out onto the court, he has some choice words for me, all unprintable. He's incensed that I criticized his brother and he threatens me. I answer back with my own unprintables. It was like one of those schoolyard fights where everybody's calling everybody names. The crowd can see we're ragging on each other, so they start making even more noise, whistling and hooting. Wheaton bumps me as I bump into him. We are nose-to-nose and yelling in each other's face. It is a zoo.

In back I can hear the brother still honking at me. My wife is sitting near him. I'm hoping she doesn't go after him with her purse. It sounded like a boxing match after a knockdown. There was blood in the air. Bruno Rebeuh, another umpire, races toward us. He grabs Wheaton by the arm and pushes me back at the same time. He's chattering "Stop this! Stop this. Gentleman, please settle down!"

Wheaton said later, "I wouldn't have been disappointed if Gilbert had thrown the first punch." I may have been upset, but I wasn't about to get booted out of a million-dollar match just for that. Slowly order is restored and the crowd quiets down for the start of the fourth set, but not before Winyard gives us both warnings for unsportsmanlike conduct.

I felt good because I had learned my lesson well. I didn't let the confrontation or the obscenities from Wheaton or his brother rattle me going into the set. In fact, I was so calm I got careless, so relieved to get past that crisis and be ahead in the match that I came out of my game plan.

I'm up two sets to one, and instead of staying with my usual tactic of squeezing a lead (steady tennis, not risky tennis), I start getting a little ambitious—rushing some shots, going for winners too soon—just a little too aggressive. I felt like I had the match won. But it's dangerous to get comfortable with a lead, to start feeling as if the match is in hand. Remember, when I go ahead I want to become even more alert. I want to be even more concerned about the opponent's comeback power. I failed to do it here. I forgot my basic philosophy and became a happy camper. And just like that I lose the set 6–2. I haven't broken Wheaton's serve in nearly three sets.

We go to the fifth. One set for $1 million. If I stop to think about the money riding on it I doubt if I can breathe. But I'm so mad at myself for letting down in the fourth set my focus sharpens up a lot. Now our mind-sets are reversed. It was a classic case of the Wounded Bear (me) and the Happy Camper (Wheaton). I wanted to make something happen right away. He may have been relieved to have evened things up.

Before the start of the fifth set I take a long time to get ready. I want to stop his momentum. I don't want him to kick things off strong in this final set. There's no changeover so I walk back and pick up a towel. After I towel off I head over to a ball boy and hand it back. I go back over my game plan. What am I trying to do? What am I trying to keep him from doing?

I tell myself that I've let him hold serve too easily by missing too many returns. I want to get my service return *in play*, take a little off of it and make him hit some shots. I remind myself again to work on his forehand, try to break it down and hope he starts missing it. I decide to hit almost everything to that side. If he's solid there, I lose. But if he gets shaky, if he starts to overhit it, I'll win.

Wheaton serves to start the fifth. He's strong, but not as forceful as in the previous set. I stay in the game just scratching and clawing, nubbing a shot here, massaging one there. I'm staying in points just a little longer by trying to do less with my service return. Wheaton is having to hit an additional shot or two on each point. He's missing a volley occasionally.

That first game of the fifth set goes deuce ad several times. Finally I bust him for the break. I lead in the fifth 1–0. My serve. My strategy has been successful. He's having to work harder for points. I'm not giving him any donations. We make the changeover.

Again, I focus hard on my game plan. I've finally gotten a break. Now I want to squeeze him—no freebees, no donations—make him earn it the hard way. I stand up and head out to serve.

I immediately start hitting anything I can to his forehand. I keep massaging the ball with nothing on it, and he has trouble with it. I hold and so does Wheaton. I hold again and so does Wheaton. I lead 3–2. As we get deeper and deeper into the final set Wheaton knows that he has to make something happen. Otherwise I'll just grind it out to the finish.

And as he tries to make something happen he starts overhitting a few shots and making mistakes on his forehand side. And, true to form, he starts to make some errors on other shots as well. I don't break him again, but, more important, I don't *get* broken either. I keep holding serve until it's 5–4 *ad in* for the match and at least a million dollars in prize money.

I want to tell you that I was so focused on that match point that I felt no fear or nervousness. I *would* tell you that, except it would be a lie. I was nervous as hell. I looked across the net at Wheaton and saw a guy ready to fight for his life. He was bouncing up and down and shifting from foot to foot. It didn't look like he was going to retire because of fatigue.

I remembered my basic strategy. Just get the serve in and get it to his forehand. I bounced the ball twice. Took another look across the net and one deep breath. Then a beautiful toss and a great motion. Whap! My serve goes two feet into the net. Wheaton now is really getting excited. He's hopping up and down. Moving back and forth. He sensed I was in trouble.

Second serve. Win the point and I'm guaranteed a check for $1 million! Again I bounce the ball twice. Look over the net and toss the ball in the air. Not a great toss. Not a great serve. But it does crawl over the net and gravity does its job. And it goes to his forehand. Wheaton looks ready for it, but he misfires. Swings late and tries to overhit the ball. He plows it wide. I was never happier to see a ball sail out in my life. He had taken the collar. I had beaten him (and his brother) 6–4 in the fifth.

The match had started at 8:30 Saturday night, December 15. It was now 12:47 Sunday morning—over four hours of the most intense tennis I had ever played. I had just won a million bucks (minus a $5,000 fine both Wheaton and I had to pay for the altercation).

We shook hands. Barely. He was too tired to be mad. I just wanted to get out of there. I did some interviews, iced down, got a massage to loosen up my legs and took a shower. I finally got back to the hotel at 4:30 A.M. In less than ten hours I was scheduled to start the finals against my friend Pete Sampras. As it turned out, I had nothing left.

It was okay. I had played over four hours of unbelievably hard tennis against a very tough opponent. I got five hours of sleep and started getting ready for the finals. Even though I had beaten Pete in our two previous matches he cruised me in straight sets. I gave it everything I had. There just wasn't much left after the struggle with Wheaton. And Pete played super tennis.

I looked over at Kim during the award ceremonies. I could see tears in her eyes. The last twelve hours had been like nothing we'd ever been through before. The intensity had been almost overwhelming. I smiled at her and she waved back. Zach was sitting on her lap chewing on a tennis ball. Then I congratulated Pete and was handed a check for $1 million.

The Long and Winding Road

On the flight back to the United States following the tournament in Munich I thought of another flight and another tournament eight years earlier. That time I was on a plane heading back home after winning my first tournament as a pro. I'd been a professional for six months and all of a sudden I'd won this little event in Taipei. I beat a guy named Craig Wittus. It surprised everyone, including me. And to make it even sweeter they paid me in cash; no check, no money order, no wire transfer. Fifteen thousand dollars in cash!

I remembered flying back home from Taipei after that first win. My tennis rackets were in the overhead and $15,000 in cash was packed in the equipment bag on my lap. This may sound strange, but I actually got a bigger thrill out of that than the million bucks I earned in Munich. Nobody, but nobody, thought I had a chance out on the tour. I didn't have the strokes. I didn't have the natural ability. "Who you kidding, Brad? Get a real job." I knew my days were numbered if I didn't get results fairly soon.

So the flight back from Taipei was special. I'll never forget the feeling I had heading back to California holding that bag of money, sitting there in the darkness with a cold can of beer and looking down at the Pacific. I realized for the first time that maybe they were wrong. Maybe I could make it on the tour. Maybe this club player, this guy with the "ugly" strokes, had a life in front of him as a professional tennis player. Just before I fell asleep I remember thinking, "I hope this doesn't turn out to be a dream." It wasn't.

17

Tournament Tough
All the Time

How to Make It Part of Your Game

When I was a kid just getting into tennis I loved to play matches. If I couldn't play a match, Dad was always available to hit with me and help me work on my game. If he couldn't, then my sister Dana (who later played on the women's tour) or my brother Barry (who also played professionally) would hit with me. I loved it so much that if I couldn't find a partner I'd go hit against a wall and pretend I was playing a match. I spent thousands of hours in Piedmont, California, with a racket, a tennis ball, and a wall.

Gradually I developed my tennis skills and began to enter an occasional tournament around San Francisco. Every once in a while a local event in the Bay Area would loom on the horizon and I'd start practicing harder and paying more attention—making sure my equipment was all set and that I got a good night's sleep. My mother made sure I was eating right. For a tournament I paid a lot more attention to what I was doing before and during the match or matches. I'm sure you do the same thing.

In those early days I'd play thirty or forty "fun" matches (and hit against the wall for hours and hours) for every tournament that I entered. Over the years that ratio gradually changed. One day I woke up and realized (as a pro) that I didn't ever play a match just for "fun" anymore. Virtually every single match I played was a tournament match. I no longer had one set of rules that I used for "fun" or social matches and another set of rules for preparing for a tournament. I had to be tournament tough all the time. I had to pay attention all the time because a great deal of money was at stake.

My point is this. Many of the ideas and tips in this book require some effort to absorb and apply. But if you genuinely want to improve your game, proper integration of these ideas will give you dramatic results: you *will* win more often. And, you'll have a lot of fun bringing the mental part of tennis into your game.

Desire, Dedication, Diligence

Approach it as you would approach a tournament. Apply yourself to the task and make a conscientious effort to be a smarter and more aware player. Work at it. Most of what I discuss in *Winning Ugly* involves mental alertness: recognizing opportunity, analyzing options, capitalizing on the opportunity with the best option. Recognize. Analyze. Capitalize.

You might compare my approach to Tim Gallwey's in his book *The Inner Game of Tennis*. He focuses on the right brain, or intuitive process. I focus on the left brain process. The left side of your brain is the administrator, checking data and establishing priorities. In my approach to the game, that's crucial to winning.

Mental Management

In addition to the physical game of tennis there is a mental game going on that can have a profound impact on the outcome of the match. But you have to be able to recognize and take advantage of opportunities, to know what's going on before and during a match. You'll win if you play good left-brain tennis.

You must understand that playing tennis is not *just* either a right brain or left brain activity. It uses both sides in an incredible combination of spontaneous and creative mental and physical responses, plus a cold analytical approach that involves observation and calculation.

Acquiring these new mental habits and incorporating them into your game requires as much effort as developing new physical habits in tennis. You have to want to do it or it won't happen. You have to apply the same approach you would use before a tournament—diligence, desire, dedication.

The Early Edge

As you get ready for a match, make sure you are mentally and physically prepared. It's an opportunity waiting to be capitalized on, so give yourself the early advantage. Usually that opportunity is ignored, wasted. But for the smart player it is there, waiting to be used.

1. Pre-Match Mental Preparation: Think about your opponent and develop your game plan before you get to the court.
2. Tools of the Trade: Your *equipment* can save matches for you. It can also cost you matches. I can usually tell by looking at what a club player brings in their equipment bag how serious they are about winning.
3. Stretch for Success: Warm up the muscles and then stretch them for better performance and less risk of injury.
4. Get the Early Lead: Begin your match intelligently with the goal of grabbing a quick break and establishing early dominance.

Playing Smart

Always believe that most of the time there is a way for you to win. You just have to find it.

1. The Key to Victory: During a match accumulate information about how you're winning and losing points. Ask "Who's doing what to whom?"
2. Destroy Your Opponent's Game Plan: Know what to do when your opponent is winning points by attacking you in various ways.
3. The "Hidden" Ad Points: Recognize the overlooked dynamic

moments in the match and know what to do with them. But mainly, be aware of them when they occur.

4. The Player's Pit Stop: When the wheels come off a particular stroke, recognize it and make an effort to correct it before it's too late.

5. Learn From the Legends: Watch the top players and apply tactics that work for them to your own game.

Mind Games, Psyching, and Gamesmanship

Be aware of the *personal* dynamics of the match and recognize what the other player is doing to affect your game—gamesmanship, tempo, or anything else that can crack your concentration and take your mind off the goal. Protect yourself.

The two most common errors that recreational tennis players make are these:

1. They don't think about what they're doing.
2. They do it too fast.

Aerobic tennis is the result, players who rush around swatting the ball, oblivious to almost everything except keeping track of the score. There's nothing wrong with that—after all, it's good for your health—but if winning is important to you, then incorporating what's in this book will be worthwhile.

Gilbert's Golden Rules

1. Have a Plan

A player who has a plan is a thinking player. Even a bad plan is better than no plan at all. A bad plan will be recognized and changed by a thinking player. The result will be a better plan. Better plans win matches.

This applies to every aspect of your tennis. Have a plan for your mental preparation, stretching, warm-up, and the start of your match. Have a game plan during the match and a routine for assessing your effectiveness during the competition. Know what you're doing out on the court.

2. Don't Rush

Know what is the best pace or match tempo for you and stick with it. Don't let yourself get rushed into or through points. Be thoughtful, deliberate, observant, and analytical—incorporate left brain thinking into your tennis. You can't control your pace when you're playing aerobic tennis.

Follow these rules and the other ideas I've suggested and not only will you win more often, but you'll have a great time figuring out how to do it. Your opponents will start saying, "Hey, your strokes don't look any different. How come you're beating me more often?" Smile and say, "Just my day, I guess."

18

The Road to
Number One

Coauthor's Note: Much has happened since I first presented Brad Gilbert with an idea for a book called Winning Ugly: Mental Warfare in Tennis. *Among other things it has become one of the best-selling tennis books of the 1990s, receiving critical acclaim from the* Los Angeles Times, Tennis Week, *the* Indianapolis News, Inside Tennis, *the* Atlanta Journal, Los Angeles Daily News, Tennis, *the* San Francisco Examiner, *and other publications.*

Mary Carillo, John McEnroe, Barry MacKay, Fred Stolle, Cliff Drysdale, and other network tennis commentators began mentioning our new book in their television broadcasts: "Boy, that's a page right out of Winning Ugly!"

Coaches at high schools and colleges around the nation made Winning Ugly *required reading for many of their players. In fact, head coaches at Texas A and M, the University of Washington, Stanford, the University of California-Berkeley, the University of Florida, and elsewhere gave their entire teams copies of* Winning Ugly *to study. The N.C.A.A. Division I Coach of the Decade, Dick Gould, called* Winning Ugly *"superb!"*

Michael Chang was even spotted buying a copy of Winning Ugly. *It's being serialized in Japan by that country's leading tennis publication,* Tennis Classic, *and will be published soon in Europe. Hey, even Tony Bennett likes it.*

But, along the way something else happened that brought Winning Ugly *more attention than all of the above; namely, Andre Agassi asked Brad Gilbert to become his coach. Twelve and a half*

*months later Agassi had risen from number thirty-two in the world
to number one and had won two Grand Slam titles including the
U.S. Open.*

Suddenly such "un-tennis" publications as The New Yorker, Es-
quire, The New York Times, Men's Journal, *and* Newsweek *were
mentioning* Winning Ugly *in feature stories about Agassi's mete-
oric rise to the top and the role Brad Gilbert had played in it.
Recently, Brad was voted Coach of the Year by the United States
Tennis Registry.*

*In separate interviews I asked each of them to evaluate the other
and reflect and comment on what is one of the most extraordinary
tennis relationships in the history of the game.*

*What follows is the number one Coach and the number one
Player talking about losing, winning, and how they got to the top.*

"C'mon, Andre. Stop middle! Stop middle!" I'm watching Michael
Chang bounce the ball during this important semifinal match in the
'96 Sybase Open and know what's about to happen. Steve Jamison,
my coauthor, leans over and gives me a look. "Stop middle what?"
he asks.

Boom! Chang unloads an ace up the middle to take a 4–2 lead in
the third set of a match he should have lost in two. Jamison nods
his head as the crowd roars. Andre is steamed. "Middle! Middle!"
I'm thinking, "We've got a big problem. You don't let Chang back
into a match like this or you lose."

Coaching vs. Playing

One thing I've learned since Andre and I got together as player and
coach is that it's a lot tougher playing than coaching. Sitting on the
sidelines it's fairly easy to spot a match and see what's happening;
who's doing what to whom. It's totally something else to be in the
ring fighting for your life. It's easy to get distracted, and Andre
had gotten distracted; by the crowd, by mistakes caused maybe by
impatience, by Chang. Even his do-rag started bothering him.

Sitting in the comfort of the friend's box I could see Michael was
causing some major bleeding serving Andre up the center and he
was doing it on almost every important pressure point. Reason?
Chang is short, maybe 5'8", and it's tougher for him to hit the wide

serve because the net's higher at the sides. It's simple physics or geometry. Whatever it is, it's easier for him to do damage serving up the middle on both deuce and ad courts. A guy like Sampras doesn't have that problem because he's taller and has those long arms. Pete may stand 6 feet tall but he serves 7 feet tall and loves to swing you wide. *And* he can do it under pressure.

Even with Chang's new long racket he has more trouble going wide, especially under pressure. So he was picking up lots of points, big points, by pounding up the middle. At one stage he served middle nine straight times; five for clean winners or weak returns. Over and over. When he got ahead in a game he *might* try wide, but otherwise no. Middle.

World's Number One at Stake

This Saturday night match near San Francisco is important because if Andre wins he advances to the finals Sunday against Pete Sampras. The winner of *that* match then moves to number one in the world rankings. It would be the first time in the history of tennis two players, neither of whom are ranked number one, would fight for control of the top spot. (*ED. NOTE: Thomas Muster had been number one very briefly in February of '96, but by losing in the first round of a tournament elsewhere he was about to lose his top ranking. The winner of a Sunday night final-round Agassi/Sampras match would be elevated to a world ranking of number one.*)

A win here would start up '96 real good; a great return to form for Andre, who had ripped a chest muscle during Davis Cup play and had been out of action for three months until the '96 Australian Open. There Chang beat him in straights.

Off to a Quick Start

The night started out fine for Andre. He was hitting hard, very focused and methodical, and took the first set 6–2. No sweat. The second set got even better because Chang started making some very rare unforced errors as he tried to make something happen. Chang donating points is like snow in Las Vegas. Doesn't happen much. So, Andre is up a set and it's 4–2 in the second. Eight points from a ticket to the finals. But then it began.

I didn't notice at first, but very quietly a shift in the match takes place. Chang settles down and stops donating points, which I expected. But at the same time Andre begins to hurry it up just a little; rushing to finish the point off too quickly. Missing his first serve, giving Chang a look at the second. He may have been just a little eager to close out the match, but whatever it is he's changed his play pattern. Very subtle, but definitely a change.

Now Andre is serving at 4–2, up a set; a huge moment in the match. I call it the Super Set-Up Game because this game can really leverage Andre's position, putting him just 4 points away from victory. If he holds serve he's got Chang right in the cross-hairs. Losing gets Chang back on serve and could completely change the dynamics of the match. Chang gets a second suck of the gas. So I'm thinking, "Hold, Andre. Get that first serve in."

No such luck. Chang breaks back. Uh-oh. On serve at 3–4, second set. But, a break is never a break until you hold. Maybe breaking back will defocus Michael a little, make him a little overeager. Maybe not. Chang doesn't defocus twice in one match. Andre keeps trying for the quick kill; hasty, trying to finish it off maybe one or two shots early. Maybe three. And it continues that way, with Chang holding to go 4–4.

I think Andre's also a little agitated because the crowd is cheering Chang's comeback. They want a third set, and it doesn't matter who you are, the crowd will turn on you if it means they get more tennis. Andre throws off his do-rag when he looks up at the huge overhead monitor and notices that it's on crooked. That gets the crowd going again and over 10,000 fans start whooping it up. He doesn't look happy. I'm thinking he's got to get some patience.

The Perfect Point

What I mean by that is Andre ideally plays a point with Michael that goes between six and nine shots. In other words, against a retriever like Chang who gets to everything, Andre is best off if he hits the ball no fewer than six times and no more than nine times as he constructs the point trying to build an advantage or set up an opening.

More than nine shots and you're in a war of attrition and Michael looks good. Fewer than six hits and Andre is probably forced to go for the gigundo shot because the point hasn't really opened up right yet. I'm speaking generally now.

Obviously, there are exceptions, but over the course of a match this is what Andre's looking for against Chang: construct an opening with between six and nine shots.

Andre is letting Chang off the hook by trying to finish off points too soon. He's serving now at 5–6, second set; still missing that first serve and letting Chang look at too many seconds where he can take charge of the point. Chang breaks at love.

He's on cruise control. The match is even, but only in the score. Michael has all the momentum and he stays tough to go up 4–2 in the third. This one is slipping away and it's going to hurt. No way Andre should let Chang win this match.

Suddenly *Chang*'s just 8 points from the finals. But even though Michael's tenacious, let me tell you this about Andre Agassi: he is solid. I like his mental attitude these days. A few years ago he might have figured this wasn't his day and gone out quietly. Now Andre keeps looking for a way to dig it out right up until the end. He may not win it, but he'll fight you right down to the wire.

Chang has won six of the last nine games and is getting close to having a stranglehold on this thing. But Andre starts to settle down. I can see he's gotten back into his rhythm and is focused. He looks over in our direction and I can see his eyes look calm, focused. Actually *zoned* is a better description.

Andre wins 16 of the next 21 points and four straight games. He just really started racking the ball and dictating the points; waiting for the good opening. And he stops middle; makes the adjustment and starts anticipating middle for service returns that are huge. Just really sweet.

Sweeter than the next night when Pete shows up in his own zone. His first serve of the match is clocked at 126 mph. That's what you call coming out of the locker room ready to play. Pete said later it was the best he had ever played against Andre, and the win let him take over the number one spot at 12:01 A.M. February 19. But stay tuned, folks.

Rock and Roll Tennis

Andre was the wild child of tennis when he first came up ten years ago; almost like a rock star or something with the long hair, earrings, throwing his shirt into the crowd. A great showman.

None of that stuff mattered much to me. What got my attention was something that was *really* crazy as far as I was concerned. Namely, Andre wasn't using his talent right. Anybody could see he had awesome abilities, but what I saw was a guy who didn't capitalize on those abilities.

He sort of got away with it because he had so *much* talent that he was able to win matches in spite of himself. He also lost a lot of them he should have won.

Because he wasn't thinking out on the court he was never consistent long term. Players he should have beat would beat him. Matches he should have won he lost. Now and then he'd put it together and reach perfection, like when he beat Ivanisevic in the '92 Wimbledon finals to win his first Slam.

He got up to number three in the world at one point, but watching him play was almost painful for me at times because of this huge talent he was careless about. I'd see him make tremendous shots and then follow them up with a little drop shot from back of the baseline, almost like he was playing an exhibition and working to entertain the crowd.

So over the years I had kept track of his game just like I kept track of anybody else on the tour. I knew what he was doing and had a good idea of what he *should* be doing if he wanted to win more. But I never in a million years thought about coaching him or anybody else.

How I Became Andre's Coach

During the '94 Lipton Championships in Key Biscayne, Andre and I were having dinner at a little Italian restaurant on Fisher Island. Since winning Wimbledon Andre had dropped to number thirty-two in the world because of a variety of things including a wrist injury that required surgery and a layoff. But the wrist wasn't the real issue.

Somewhere between the spaghetti and the spumoni that night Andre asked me if I had any ideas that might improve his game. I thought he was just shooting the breeze, so I started telling him how he wasn't playing to his potential; how he could use more strategizing during matches; how he was playing *outside* the court, back on his heels behind the baseline. He used to be *inside* the baseline when he hit groundstrokes and I told him that. He is the greatest player in the history of tennis for taking the ball on the rise, so it made no sense whatsoever to be standing behind the baseline and letting the ball drop.

I also told him it seemed to me he was inconsistent from match to match; sometimes ready to go, but other times almost like he hadn't thought about the match or his opponent. I told him he'd play loose against a player until he got himself in trouble and then try to dig himself out by going for huge winners from the baseline.

But really, I don't think I told Andre anything he didn't already know or feel. He's smart, so what I was saying made sense with what he was thinking. It really happened that casually. He says, "Let's work together when we can. Keep it loose, hit at tournaments we're both playing and talk on the phone." I don't think the word "coach" was ever used and we didn't even have a contract.

At first I kept playing my own schedule of tournaments and just let things progress like we had discussed over dinner; hitting at tournaments, phone calls. I told Andre that I didn't expect to see any real results in tournaments for about five months because of his layoff. It turns out that was a good guess. Nothing happened at first and Andre's results at the Italian, French, Wimbledon, and elsewhere were generally not too good.

Then, almost exactly five months after we talked at Fisher Island over plates of pasta, he went to Toronto and won the '94 Canadian Open. Next stop: the U.S. Open, where Andre would go in unseeded because of his low ranking (number nineteen worldwide).

The Magic of Believing

I felt very strongly that Andre could win it all in New York because his game had really clicked in during the tournament in Canada. He was just thinking so well out on the court and I told him that he could go all the way in New York. He must have thought I was kidding because he said, "If I win you gotta shave off your body hair like I did at Wimbledon last year, OK?" I had a bad feeling I was going to be shaving my chest in about two weeks.

Nevertheless, Andre had a huge task in front of him as the tournament unfolded. He had to play Wayne Ferreira, Michael Chang, Thomas Muster, Todd Martin, and, in the finals, Michael Stich. Andre beat them all.

Nobody in the history of the U.S. Open had won the way he had done it: the hard way, beating five seeded players en route to the championship. Watching him gain momentum and confidence, seeing his performance and mental focus go higher and higher was stunning. His concentration just got white hot.

After that he started calling me "the Believer." More important than that, I saw that Andre was a believer.

Two days after he won his first U.S. Open title I made good on my promise and went on national television where my wife, Kim, got out the razor and shaved off my chest hair. I pay my bets.

Long-Term Thinking

But I wanted us both thinking beyond one tournament or title. I never felt the goal for Andre was to win another Grand Slam, but to win Grand Slam *titles*. That's why the only thing I said to him when he came over to the friend's box after beating Michael Stich in the '94 U.S. Open final was, "Australia's next." Nike gave a party for everybody later that night at Il Vagabondo restaurant in Manhattan and I repeated that message again. Six months later he beat Pete to win the '95 Australian Open.

On April 10, 1995, Andre hit number one and stayed there for thirty weeks. Pete grabbed it back, Thomas Muster had it for a few days, and then Pete reclaimed it that Sunday night at the Sybase tournament. I think Pete and Andre are going to be fighting for the top spot for a while.

19

Andre Agassi on "Winning Ugly"

"Winning Ugly" to me is being able to figure out how to win even when you're not at your best; when things aren't going your way and you've got to do more than just hit the ball hard. *That's* one of the big things I've learned from Brad—how to win ugly when it's necessary.

Brad Gilbert is a great talker. In fact, he's *always* talking. When I first met him on tour it really kind of bothered me because he talked so much; always saying something or trying to strike up a conversation with somebody. I'm wondering "Geez, how come this guy's in everybody's business? He's talking all the *time!*" But that's Beej. He's got an opinion on everybody and everything.

Then we played Davis Cup together in Germany back in '89 and I started to get to know him a little better. Plus, I met his wife, Kim, who's a great person, and I'm thinking, "If she thinks he's OK, maybe he is." We had dinner together a few times over the next couple of months and I learned that even though Beej may talk a lot, when it comes to sports he usually knows what he's talking about. Especially tennis.

So, that's how we got to know each other at first; hanging around before and after some Davis Cup matches and practice sessions, at other tournaments, a pizza once in a while. It was very casual, but gradually I got to know him better and we became friends. I'm glad we did.

Appreciating Brad's "Ugly" Game

What Beej has done for my game since we got together is unmistakable and nobody else could have done it because nobody knows the game better. There's no question in my mind about that. He has a tremendous understanding of the whole deal; strategy, tactics, match dynamics, and how to apply them to beat players like Pete, Michael Chang, Boris, Courier, and others.

He's very scientific when it comes to analyzing opponents. Brad puts them under a microscope and can just see really clearly where their flaws are and where they're strong; especially where the cracks in their game appear during big-point pressure, where it counts.

I first ran into that ability of his when I played him in tournaments. It was always a nerve-racking kind of experience, because he wouldn't let you play your game.

In preparation for him you could never feel as comfortable as you could with other guys, because you knew somehow Brad would take you out of your rhythm; that he would jerk you around out there. You ended up playing his game instead of making him play your game.

It was almost like taking a tennis lesson, because he was always coming up with surprises. You never knew when he was going to attack or when he wasn't. You never knew when he was going to pound the ball or when he was going to massage it. What you *did* know was that he would never let you settle into a groove and get comfortable hitting your good stuff.

Playing him was very frustrating because he had this tremendous ability to exploit a player's game; to just pick at a weakness until he would start to break you down. And in addition to having a great mind for tennis he also had heart. He just never gave up on a match.

And if you were a rookie, forget it. Rookies were breakfast for Brad. I know because the first time I ever played him as a rookie I went on the court thinking "easy match" and came off the court thinking I'd just had a bad dream. It was ugly. If you were a rookie, you weren't going to beat him.

By January of '94 I had fallen from a world ranking of number three to number thirty-two. My days with Nick Bolletieri were behind me. I had spent some time with Pancho Segura. I thought maybe Brad and I should have a little talk.

A Winning Formula

In Florida during the Lipton Championships in March of '94 I asked him if he had any ideas about my game; what I could do to pick it up. You can guess he wasn't at a loss for words. Right away he started telling me what I should be doing to win more. Everything he said was right. Mainly what he said was, "Think."

He told me, "If you play Sampras the same way you play Chang, you'll lose. If you play Becker like you play Courier, you'll lose. Each player is different. Your strategy should be different for each of them." He's right, and applying what he said has turned my game completely around.

"Work a Plan"

Brad believes that to win consistently at any level you've got to "work a plan." That means during a match you've got to have a clear strategy for what you want to do and then work hard to force it on your opponent. That sounds simple, but the key to its success is having the right strategy or plan. And in order to accomplish that you need to do three things correctly. Here's some basic Brad:

1. Know your strengths and weaknesses.
2. Understand your opponent's strengths and weaknesses.
3. Spend time thinking about "How can I put my strengths on my opponent's weaknesses?"

I wasn't doing it. Brad couldn't believe it when I told him that sometimes I'd decide where I was going to hit my serve during the ball toss. For Brad, that was unacceptable because he was the kind of player who would think about where he was going to hit his serve two weeks before the toss.

Strategizing

One of the first things he told me was I had to go in for the kill when I opened up the court. He felt I loved to pound the groundstrokes so much that even after I opened up the court by

swinging a guy out wide to get a weak return I'd stay back to hit
another hard one. Brad said, "When you get the chance to end a
point you've got to take it. Go in for the kill."

He also got me thinking about my serve. Instead of just spinning
it in, I started using it to help set up the point. In the '94 U.S. Open
final against Michael Stich, Brad and I discussed the need to mix
up my serves so he wouldn't be able to get comfortable, go on the
offensive, and take the net. It worked. Straight sets for a Grand
Slam title.

Turning Weakness into Strength

Now this may seem like fairly basic stuff, but it's amazing how
players limit their physical talents by not utilizing their mental
talents. I know this was true for me. In fact, there's no doubt that
my mind used to be my weakness because I didn't think I needed
to use it. I thought I could just go out there and hit harder than the
other guy.

Players knew that even when I was playing well, if they could
just hang in there long enough I would probably give the match
away. I really like the fact that I've proven to myself that you can
take a weakness and turn it into a strength.

I get the feeling now they know that even if I'm not playing great
I'll be on them so much that they may lose a little heart—like
maybe it's just not worth it.

I do feel that difference since Beej and I teamed up. Players give
me that kind of respect and I can sense it. They know that I'm out
there physically and mentally 100 percent until the last point.

Another big thing is that Brad has played and beaten the same
guys I'm facing out there. He knows from experience what they
can or can't do on the big points and he's good at working a plan to
match my game up against other guys.

Courier's Cannon

For example, with Jim Courier you know going in that his forehand
is a cannon. But a lot of players fear it so much that they'll try to get
the ball to his backhand early in the point. I don't do that now

because I've learned that while Jim's backhand is vulnerable, it's a lot more vulnerable if he has to hit it on the move.

So first I go to Jim's strength on the forehand side, which opens up the court and exposes that running backhand. That's when he'll have a lot more trouble than if he sets up for it. You've somehow got to open up the court so you can make him hit that backhand while he's moving. It's almost a sure point if I can do that.

Brad used to try the same thing as a player by swinging Jim wide off the deuce court with his serve. I do it on both the serve and with the groundstrokes early in the point.

The plan I work is only slightly different from what everyone else is trying to do against Jim, but it uses my strength (groundstrokes) to set up his weakness, which is not the backhand, but the *running* backhand. And the reason it's vulnerable is his grip. His hand is wrapped so far under the racket it looks almost like he's swinging a baseball bat. It's the kind of thing Brad likes to notice and exploit.

Becker Is Too Stubborn

My plan against Boris (Becker) is really almost no plan at all because of his stubbornness. Boris just plays me very straight up. He's a very stubborn person and because of it stays at the baseline too much and tries to pound me. This plays right into my strength, groundstrokes.

It's almost like Boris is so stubborn about what he believes he can do that it prevents him from accepting the fact that he can't win doing it against me. It prevents him from trying something else. It's very surprising. It's kind of like Boris attacks my strength with his weakness. Against other guys you'll see him mixing it up a lot. Against me he gets a little bit rattled. He waits a little too long for a short ball, and allows me to exploit his movement, which isn't as good as Courier's. His backhand becomes more of a weakness because of his lack of good foot speed.

The other advantage I work is off his serve. I return serve well, which takes away Boris's natural game.

Nevertheless, he is a very dangerous player. In the semis at Wimbledon in '95 I was up 6–2, 4–1 and playing absolutely perfect tennis. In fact, Boris said later my play in the first set was the absolute best tennis he had ever faced anywhere.

But at Wimbledon Boris is never dead, and he came back to life in the sixth game of the second set after a fantastic point that he managed to win. That single point convinced him that he could win the match. At the same time I had gone on cruise control and had mentally started thinking about the finals against Pete. Boris won in four sets, 2–6, 7–6, 6–4, 7–6. We met up again two months later at the U.S. Open with a better result for me.

Pete Is Nearly Perfect

Pete (Sampras) is the most talented player on tour. He does everything well and just doesn't have any really notable weaknesses. However, the one thing that maybe isn't as strong as everything else is Pete's return of serve. He likes to float that return back and then work himself into the point.

Brad emphasized that this is where you've got to hurt him quickly. I work on serving big into Pete to get the floater return or the shorter return and then try to hurt him right away. You can't wait for him to get back in the point. He can work that transition game, going from defense to offense, better than anybody in the world. You think you've got him on the defense and all of a sudden he explodes on one ball and he's on the offense.

So with Pete you've got to make him pay for every shorter ball that he gives you. In the past I wouldn't be that aggressive in capitalizing on the shorter ball opportunity. Brad made a living out of looking for the slightest opening. Now he's got me thinking more like that; looking to appreciate and exploit opportunities.

Of course, Pete's serve is something else. Even if you're leaning the right way he can beat you with it. You just have to hope you can guess right a lot or that he isn't on it. And if his first serve is missing, I've got to jump on his second serve. Brad also gets me to look for Pete to serve the wide slice to my forehand in the deuce court under pressure. He likes to hit it and then come in behind it with an approach shot. Same on the ad court; under pressure Pete likes to hit up the middle and come in behind it.

The other element of Pete's game that you've really got to respect is his running forehand both on the baseline and when he approaches behind it. It's a major weapon, but you can't respect it so much that you never go to it and just let him hit forehands from the backhand side. You'll see him camp about three feet to the left of the center of the baseline. Brad keeps telling me, "Get Pete off his pitcher's mound. Get him off that spot." So I try to work a point where he's not always hitting from his favorite spot on the court, which means going to his strength.

Brad and I talk a lot about that mixture of exposing a player's weakness or vulnerability by going at his strength. It's a delicate balance sometimes, but it's the key to cracking open a match. It works. I beat Pete in the finals of the Lipton Championships, Australian Open, and Canadian Open in '95. But it doesn't work all the time. He got me in the finals of the U.S. Open that same year. But as I've said before, when Pete's at 100 percent of his game and I'm at 90 percent of my game, it feels like I'm at about 60 percent.

Basically, when we play he's going to hold serve and I'm going to beat him from the ground. The question is, do I break him or does he beat me on the ground? The one who can do it usually wins.

Challenging Chang

Of all the top ten players, if I'm playing my game I prefer to play Michael Chang over anybody else. That's because I match up well against Chang. By that I mean I feel the only thing he does out on the court better than me is move. So, if I'm on top of my game he should have no say-so in the match. I just have more firepower than he does. It's like two heavyweight boxers going toe to toe and one of them weighs 25 pounds more than the other one. I should win.

What I do against Michael is attack his strength, which is speed. In fact, I look forward to his speed, because if he gets to one ball he'll have to run to another one. I want him to get to the ball. My mentality is, "I can hit these balls side to side a lot longer than Michael can run side to side." Basically, my strength is bigger than Michael's. What I have to be is patient. Brad's got me a lot better at being patient.

Overcoming My Own Mistakes

In the '95 Australian Open finals against Pete in the first set I was holding serve easily and had three chances to break him but didn't. Then I was serving at 4–5 and the game and set suddenly just sort of slipped away. Pete hits a good shot. I make one error. Suddenly it's love–30. Then 15–40. And then I double-fault to give away the set! A double fault to lose the first set of a Slam? It was unbelievable.

Believe me, I was upset; really angered because I should have won the set at least twice and instead lost it with a double fault. I was very angry.

But here's the difference. With Brad I've worked to turn that emotion, that anger, into a positive direction instead of negative. Instead of getting me down that anger can drive me to another level. I feel like I get a shot of adrenaline. Almost like I go into a full court press in basketball.

Against Pete in that second set in the Australian finals I just came out very intense; going after every rebound, the full court press, on him all over the court. I was fighting for everything and all of a sudden it's 6–1 and I'm back in the match. Not only back *in* the match. I won it in four.

Winning Ugly

One of the biggest things I've gotten from Brad is how to stay in a match when things aren't going my way. He believes that 5 percent of the time your opponent is in the zone and you won't win; 5 percent of the time you're in the zone and can't lose. But the other 90 percent of the time it's up for grabs; there is a way to win. You've just got to figure out what it is. And to do that you've got to stay positive. You've got to believe. I've been doing that a lot better these days, thanks to Brad.

About the Authors

Brad Gilbert is considered by most experts to be the world's foremost tennis strategist and tactician. He became Andre Agassi's coach in 1994, and twelve and a half months later Agassi had rocketed from number thirty-two to number one in the world and won two Grand Slam titles. Recently Gilbert was voted America's number one tennis coach. He lives in San Rafael, California, with his wife and two children.

Steve Jamison is a television producer and broadcaster, writer, and entrepreneur who produces the *Winning Ugly Sports Calendar™* and other *Winning Ugly™* products. His latest book, *In the Zone: How It Happens in Sports, How to Make It Happen in Business,* deals with the psychology of winning. Jamison is director of tennis at Los Flamingos Hotel in Acapulco, Mexico, and writes for *Tennis* and *Golf* magazines.

About the Cover Photographers

World-class sports photographer **Tony Di Zinno** is best known for his years of high-profile campaigns for Nike. His heroic images also appear in the illustrious pages of *Men's Journal, Outside, Road & Track, Rolling Stone, Spin, Sports Illustrated,* and *Vibe* magazines. When not on the road shooting on location, Tony makes his home in South Pasadena, California.

Photographer **Michael Baz** has traveled with the Men's Tennis Tour for twenty years. In his free time he fishes in South Florida with his son, Carlos. Carlos always catches more and bigger fish.